28-0987 RJ387.A25 89-4866 CIP

Children, adolescents, and AIDS, ed. by Jeffrey M. Seibert and Roberta A. Olson. Nebraska, 1990 (c1989). 243p index afp **ISBN 0-8032-4186-0, $19.95**

This volume provides a comprehensive review of current knowledge regarding AIDS in children and adolescents. The editors and contributors have expertise in research and clinical practice pertaining to AIDS in these age groups. One chapter addresses the needs of HIV-infected children, their families, and their communities as identified from findings in three model AIDS centers in Miami, Los Angeles, and New York City. Others offer an overview of the current medical aspects of AIDS, the special concerns associated with children with hemophilia, the needs and responses of school districts, strategies for providing AIDS information and education for children, prevention of pediatric AIDS, special concerns of pregnant women at risk for HIV infection, and research concerns specific to AIDS in children and adolescents. Extensive reference lists at chapter ends; several helpful tables and figures. The authors have minimized technical terminology and provide a glossary of terms in the first chapter. Recommended to academic and general readers interested in understanding AIDS in youth.—*M. Auterman, Augustana College (SD)*

CHILDREN, ADOLESCENTS, AND AIDS

CHILDREN AND THE LAW

General Editor

GARY B. MELTON
University of Nebraska – Lincoln

Editorial Board

THOMAS GRISSO
Univeristy of Massachusetts – Amherst

GERALD P. KOOCHER
Harvard University

ROBERT J. MNOOKIN
Stanford University

W. J. WADLINGTON
University of Virginia

LOIS A. WEITHORN
University of Virginia

Children,
Adolescents,
& AIDS

•

EDITED
BY
JEFFREY M. SEIBERT
&
ROBERTA A. OLSON

University of Nebraska Press

Lincoln & London

The paper in this book meets the minimum requirements of

American National Standard for Information Sciences –

Permanence of Paper for Printed Library Materials,

ANSI Z39.48-1984.

Library of Congress Cataloging-in-Publication Data

Children, adolescents, and AIDS /
edited by Jeffrey M. Seibert and Roberta A. Olson.
p.   cm. — (Children and the law)
Includes indexes.
ISBN 0-8032-4186-0 (alk. paper)
1. AIDS (Disease) in children—Social aspects.
2. AIDS (Disease)
in children—Psychological aspects.
I. Seibert, Jeffrey M., 1948–
. II. Olson, Roberta Ann.
RJ387.A25C45   1990
–362.1′989297′92—dc20
89–4866–CIP

Contents

ACKNOWLEDGMENTS

We wish to express our appreciation
to Division 37 for their support of this project
and especially to Gary Melton,
whose encouragement, support, and comments
were invaluable. We would like
to thank the parents, children, and health care
workers who shared their private fears,
hopes, and dreams with us. They have taught
us the importance of the struggle
to live each day with dignity
and hope.

•

CHAPTER ONE

Pediatric AIDS:
A Medical Overview

BRIAN E. NOVICK

INTRODUCTION

Pediatric human immunodeficiency virus (HIV) infection is a complex, nationwide problem encompassing medical, psychosocial, legal, and ethical issues. Despite the fact that as of March 1988 there were over 900 cases of pediatric HIV infection reported in the United States (1.5% of all reported cases), the rate of increase of new cases among children actually exceeds that among adults. The same is true in adolescents, among whom 250 cases have been reported. To date, 40 states have reported at least one case of acquired immunodeficiency syndrome (AIDS) in a child, and there is no doubt that, shortly, virtually every state will as well.

This chapter provides an overview of the epidemiology, the routes of transmission, and the distinct clinical features of AIDS in children. It includes discussions of ongoing research into the natural history of pediatric AIDS, current treatment modalities, and avenues for prospective treatments. The problem of HIV infection in adolescents is addressed in chapter 6.

BACKGROUND

In 1981, the first cases of a previously unrecognized immunodeficiency disorder in children were reported at the same time as a new immuno-logic disorder was being described in adults (Gupta, Sicklick, Bernstein, Rubinstein, & Rubinstein, 1982). The most striking aspect of the pediatric syndrome was that the patients' mothers were similarly affected. No other pediatric immunodeficiency had been so characterized. In 1982, the Centers for Disease Control (CDC) released its working definition for the diagnosis of this new disease of as yet undetermined etiology—"acquired immunodeficiency syndrome" (CDC, 1982).

The CDC functions as part of the Federal Public Health Service to monitor certain reportable illnesses nationwide (e.g., hepatitis, syphilis, toxic shock syndrome, rabies, etc.) and to investigate unusual outbreaks of disease (e.g., salmonella, Legionnaires' disease, etc.). In addition, when a new disease with unusual and widespread involvement of the entire population develops, such as AIDS, the CDC creates an epidemiologic definition of the disease that it can use to monitor trends in the illness. Such a definition was created when AIDS was recognized as a new entity. The initial definition emphasized several points: that a patient be definitively diagnosed with an opportunistic infection or unusual malignancy indicative of an underlying cellular immunodeficiency; that a patient having any congenital immunodeficiency or viral infection be excluded; that a patient have no prior illnesses predisposing to an immunodeficiency; and that a patient not be taking immunosuppressive drugs.

This initial definition did not, however, embrace the full spectrum of features of AIDS in children (CDC 1982). In fact, many experts continued to deny the existence of AIDS in children until 1983, when the first extensive case studies were published (Oleske et al., 1983; Rubinstein et al., 1983). These reports highlighted the key clinical features of AIDS-related infections in children without a documented opportunistic infection: recurrent bacterial infections and sepsis; failure to thrive; chronic diarrhea; and recalcitrant thrush.

That same year, a retrovirus was isolated from a patient with AIDS (Barre-Sinoussi et al., 1983). This virus, initially called human T cell lymphotropic virus-III (HTLV-III), then lymphadenopathy associated virus (LAV), and now human immunodeficiency virus-I (HIV-I), is the etiologic agent of AIDS. The discovery of HIV broadened the description of this disorder and opened new avenues for research toward understanding this complex disease. Subsequently, various testing modalities were developed that now compose an essential part of the diagnosis of HIV infection.

DIAGNOSIS

The most widely used screening test available, as of April 1988, is the enzyme linked immunoabsorbent assay (ELISA), which detects circulating antibodies when patients' serum is reacted with viral lysate (broken-down viral particles). Confirmatory testing is done with the Western blot technique, which measures antibodies that have developed in reaction to specific viral proteins. There is a good correlation between positive results on these two tests and isolation of the virus itself from a patient's blood. Antigen detection techniques (demonstrating the presence of viral protein in the blood) are also being utilized, but further refinement is necessary to make them more useful than the antibody ELISA tests. Culturing a virus from blood or tissue is the most definitive diagnostic tool, but it is performed in only a few laboratories and is time consuming, complicated, and expensive.

One problem confounding the diagnosis of HIV infection in a very young child is the presence of maternal antibodies in the fetal circulation. If a mother is infected with HIV, then her HIV antibodies will usually cross the placenta and be detected in umbilical cord blood at birth. These antibodies usually persist for several months in the infant's circulation, whether or not the child is infected. On occasion, they can be detected as late as 18 months of age. Therefore, in the absence of other supportive data (i.e., clinical signs and symptoms), a child cannot be

3

considered definitively seropositive until after 15 or 18 months of age. Another, minor problem involves false negative tests. Children may not produce their own HIV antibodies until 12 or 15 months of age or, rarely, even later because of associated defects in the humoral immune system. Therefore, a child may occasionally have several clinical and laboratory parameters highly suggestive of an HIV infection and yet remain negative on HIV antibody testing until 12 or 15 months. In such a case, one can either attempt to obtain viral culture evidence of an HIV infection or consider the child "possibly" infected and seek the assistance of an experienced immunologist. This will be a difficult problem to solve because both maternal antibodies and some small viral proteins can cross the placenta and enter the fetus. Ongoing research is attempting to solve these diagnostic dilemmas.

In June 1985 (CDC, 1985b), the revised case definition of AIDS included additional clinical criteria for diagnosis in children. The key difference revolved around a type of pulmonary disease not usually seen in adults and now considered diagnostic of pediatric AIDS—pulmonary lymphoid hyperplasia (PLH), previously referred to as lymphocytic interstitial pneumonitis (LIP). This unusual form of pneumonia often produces significant hypoxemia and subsequent morbidity (Rubinstein et al., 1986). In contrast to pneumocystis carinii pneumonia (PCP), PLH is associated with the insidious onset of dyspnea (difficulty breathing), generalized lymphadenopathy, parotitis, and a characteristic nodular pattern on chest x-ray with a mild elevation of a common serum enzyme, lactate dehydrogenase (LDH). Of additional interest is the detection of Epstein-Barr virus—specific DNA in lung tissue—in several of these patients, suggesting a concurrent Epstein-Barr virus infection. The significance of this association is undergoing further study.

In August 1987, the CDC further revised its surveillance case definition for AIDS (CDC, 1987b) in order to facilitate reporting, improve recognition of various HIV-related complications, and improve the definition by using additional laboratory parameters that are more predictive of infection. Certain changes are significant with respect to pediatric AIDS in that they recognize immune defects seen only in children, not adults. Children are now diagnosed with AIDS if they are

4

seropositive and have had at least two serious bacterial infections, HIV-related encephalopathy, HIV wasting syndrome, (severe weight loss with chronic diarrhea or weakness and unexplained fever), or other specified conditions. In addition, the criteria for diagnosing AIDS in children younger than 15 months were made more stringent to address the issue of the persistence of maternal antibodies in a child's circulation up to 12 or 15 months after birth.

Early in 1987, a new pediatric HIV classification was published (CDC, 1987a). This classification, which is distinct from the CDC definition, is not used to report or recognize new cases. Rather, it facilitates the clinical description of the disease. Categories are broader so that the various types of morbidity resulting from HIV infection can be taken into account. The new classification also recognizes that physicians are often unable or unwilling to perform procedures that would provide definitive pathological specimens and that therefore many genuine cases cannot be reported.

The new classification categories include: *Class P-0*, children younger than 15 months who cannot be definitively determined to be infected but who have circulating HIV antibodies; *Class P-1*, older children infected with HIV who may not have immunologic abnormalities but who do not have clinical symptoms; and *Class P-2*, children with known HIV infection who display the characteristic signs and symptoms and who can be further subdivided according to the organ systems involved. These expanded criteria will provide a more realistic picture of the extent of the problem of HIV infection in children and a means to predict future morbidity and mortality. Presently, it is estimated that, for every case of CDC-defined AIDS reported, there are four more children with other forms of HIV infection. The CDC case definition for pediatric AIDS and other HIV infections in children undergoes constant evaluation and probably will be revised periodically.

DEMOGRAPHICS

The earliest reports of AIDS in children were of infants born to intravenous drug abusers or women with multiple sexual partners in New York and New Jersey (Oleske et al., 1983; Rubinstein et al., 1983); one transfusion-related case was reported in California, however (Ammann et al., 1983). By December 1988, 1,346 (1.5%) of the more than 82,000 cases of AIDS reported to the CDC were children younger than 13 years of age. Perinatally acquired cases are found predominantly in the metropolitan areas of New York, Newark, and Miami and account for 61% of the total. Transfusion-related cases account for only 30%.

The overall racial distribution of cases is 54% Black, 25% Hispanic, and 21% White (CDC, 1988). However, the proportions differ if one examines the etiologic categories. Of the 702 perinatally acquired cases, 599 (87%) are found in Black or Hispanic children, while 104 (59%) of the 175 transfusion- or hemophilia-related cases are found in White children. Interestingly, while boys account for 54% of all pediatric AIDS cases, they compose 50% of the perinatally acquired cases and 63% of the transfusion-related cases (not including hemophiliacs). Finally, with respect to age, more than 75% of children are diagnosed in the first 3 years of life and 88% by age 5. These trends have not changed significantly since 1981.

The geographic and ethnic distribution of cases today reflects the means of transmission. Initially, reported cases of pediatric AIDS were confined to major metropolitan areas because of the concentration there of adult intravenous drug abusers and large Haitian communities with many recent immigrants. The women themselves were mostly infected through drug use. Estimates in the metropolitan New York area alone are that 75% or more of intravenous drug users are seropositive. Now, the incidence of heterosexual transmission of HIV is rising in both urban and suburban areas. Women living in and around these large cities are being infected by sexual partners whose past history of drug abuse or multiple sexual partners is unknown. Increasing numbers of children are being born to these women. Two-thirds of the states have reported at least one case of pediatric AIDS. With time, there is no doubt that the phenomenon will be seen nationwide.

In November 1987, the New York State Department of Health performed a statewide seroprevalence study of all infants born during that 1-month period. In all, 19,157 infants were anonymously tested. In

New York City, 148 of the 9,047 infants born (1.6%) were HIV sero-positive. Hence, all these babies' mothers were infected, and studies estimate that 30%–40% of seropositive infants will be truly infected. This study underscores the potentially explosive problem of HIV infection in women and children and the need for health officials to address this complex problem immediately.

Prospective studies are underway that follow high-risk women who are of child-bearing age to determine the effect of pregnancy on the women themselves and the incidence of transmission of HIV to the newborn. It is estimated that, in 1988, more than 3,000 intravenous drug abusers will carry a pregnancy to term. Clearly, the potential increase in the number of infected infants is staggering. If one assumes that 50% of these babies will be seropositive for HIV, one may expect to see almost twice the number of HIV-infected children by the end of 1988. The CDC projects that by 1991 there will be over 3,000 children with AIDS and over 10,000 HIV-infected children (Morgan & Curran, 1986).

CLINICAL SIGNS AND SYMPTOMS

The symptomatology and natural history of transplacental HIV infection in children are distinct from those in adults. Unlike adult cases, children often develop recognizable signs and symptoms within the first year of life, usually at six or seven months. Typically, a child presents with failure to thrive, delayed development, recurrent bacterial infections, lymphadenopathy, and persistent thrush. Serologic testing for HIV will be positive, and the mother, if available, will also test seropositive. The mother will usually be identified as a member of a group at risk or perhaps will be the sexual partner of a male at risk (see Table 1). A very small number of children infected in this fashion will remain asymptomatic beyond 3 years of age. Cases that present at a later age (in the absence of a transfusion-related history) must lead one to consider unusual modes of transmission.

At least two such examples have been identified. A previously well boy presented at 5 years of age with a typical picture of HIV infection. Careful questioning revealed that his father had recently died of AIDS

7

Table 1: Pediatric HIV Disease—Risk Factors

I. Maternal HIV infection.
   A. Intravenous drug use.
   B. Sexual partner of an infected male (drug user or bisexual).
   C. Artificially inseminated or organ recipient from infected donor.
   D. Recipient of infected blood or blood products.

II. Pediatric HIV infection.
   A. Recipient of infected blood or blood products (hemophiliac).
   B. Breast fed by HIV-infected mother.
   C. Sexual abuse.
   D. Injection with HIV-infected needles.

---

and that the boy had been sexually abused by his father. This case is more characteristic of typical "adult" sexual transmission because it initially showed a long symptom-free interval (as is often observed in adults). Another case is that of a previously well 7-year-old girl who presented with PLH and a severe kidney infection. In time, it was learned that her HIV-positive mother probably shared needles with the girl while injecting her with drugs. Again, the mode of transmission dictated an atypical clinical course.

Children who have been infected by means of the transfusion of infected blood or blood products often have the longer incubation period seen in adults. Cases have been reported in which children have developed symptoms 5 years after a transfusion. Prognostic statements are therefore difficult to make; however, some generalizations are seen. A child who has not had an opportunistic infection by age 3 has a better outlook than one who has had such an infection prior to age 3. The latter frequently dies within 12 or 18 months. Large prospective studies are under way to define these parameters more precisely.

The risk of contracting an HIV infection through blood transfusion now is virtually nil. Before the spring of 1985, blood banks nationwide used a predonation questionnaire that discouraged at-risk individuals

Table 2: Prominent Clinical Findings in Pediatric HIV Infection

---

   I. Failure to thrive.

  II. Recurrent bacterial infections.

 III. Chronic or recurrent diarrhea.

 IV. Lymphadenopathy.

  V. Chronic pneumonitis (PLH, LIP)

 VI. Recalcitrant thrush.

VII. Developmental delay.

---

from donating blood for any but research purposes. After the spring of 1985, blood banks began using ELISA and Western blot techniques to screen all donated blood products for HIV antibody and discarded any repeatedly positive units. The estimated risk of receiving an infected unit now approaches 1 in 100,000 (J. Ward, personal communication, August 21, 1987). Newly diagnosed and treated hemophiliacs will no longer be at risk for HIV infection because the heat treatment of the blood products they now receive inactivates the virus.

A significant cause of morbidity in children with HIV infection (see Table 2) is secondary bacterial infections (Bernstein, Krieger, Novick, Sicklick, and Rubinstein, 1985). Such manifestations of B cell abnormalities appear to occur more frequently in children than in adult patients. These are often pyogenic infections caused by common bacteria: sepsis, urinary tract infections, pneumonia, and meningitis. The organisms isolated from the blood of these patients include *Pneumococcus, Salmonella, H. influenza,* and *Staphylococcus.* If diagnosed promptly, the patients usually respond well to antibiotics. Some immunologists have treated children who have had repeated serious bacterial infections and immunologic evidence of B cell dysfunction with intravenous gammaglobulin. This practice has significantly decreased the number of subsequent infections in these patients (Calvelli & Rubinstein, 1986). Studies are currently being performed in a double-blind, placebo-controlled fashion to confirm these initial findings.

Several of the opportunistic infections related to HIV infection are

9

diagnosed both in children and in adults. Most common in all age groups is PCP. In contrast to a child with PLH, one with PCP usually develops acute respiratory distress, bilateral interstitial infiltrates, and a sudden isomorphic rise in serum LDH levels (Silverman & Rubinstein, 1985). Mycobacterium avium-intracellulare infection is another frequent opportunistic infection being found in specimens of liver and bone marrow and in peripheral blood cultures taken from children. Candida esophagitis and disseminated cytomegalovirus are also frequently diagnosed. Two other rare but reported complications in children are primary B cell lymphoma of the brain and Kaposi's sarcoma (Buck, Scott, Valdes-Dapena, & Parks, 1983).

Another significant type of morbidity in HIV-infected children is neurodevelopmental abnormality. Reports have described a 40%–50% incidence of neurological defects in HIV-infected adults, including an Alzheimer's-type syndrome with progressive encephalopathy (Snider et al., 1983). Neurological involvement in infected children may be as high as 60%–70% (Belman et al., 1985; Epstein et al., 1985; Ultmann et al., 1985). Initially, there was speculation that such involvement represented another secondary infectious complication. However, several studies have been performed that clearly demonstrate the role of HIV in directly producing central nervous system (CNS) involvement. The virus has been isolated from cerebrospinal fluid and brain tissue (Epstein et al., 1987; Ho et al., 1985; Shaw et al., 1985), confirming its primary role. It has the ability to cause significant anatomic cerebral damage and consequent neurodevelopmental abnormalities. In fact, neurodevelopmental dysfunction may be the presenting sign of pediatric HIV infection.

Extensive clinical studies have revealed a pattern of key neurological findings: acquired microcephaly, encephalopathy, and pyramidal tract signs. In addition, radiological and laboratory evaluations demonstrate cerebral atrophy, calcifications in the basal ganglia, electroencephalogram (EEG) abnormalities, and cognitive deficits with developmental delays (Belman et al., 1985; Epstein et al., 1985; Ultmann et al., 1985).

Several institutions have been involved in long-term, prospective neurodevelopmental studies of HIV-infected children; their studies are detailed below. Neurological evaluations include serial neurological exams, including head circumference; CAT (computerized axial tomography) scans with and without contrast; EEG; brain stem auditory evoked response (BAER); visual evoked response (VER); spinal fluid analysis; and viral serologic titers. Developmental evaluation consists of birth history; developmental milestones; Bayley scales (< 30 months); Stanford-Binet (> 30 months); and serial Denver testing.

Belman et al. (1985) initially reported on six children with AIDS who were followed for up to 14 months. Three had dementia, and three had cognitive deficits and developmental delays. The dementia group demonstrated progressive neurological impairment, while the latter group had a more static course. The study was expanded, and, as of June 1987, 68 children aged 4 months to 9 years had been followed up to 48 months. Several patterns emerged while evaluating these patients, 90% of whom showed evidence of CNS abnormalities (Belman et al., 1988): (1) 43% demonstrated subacute encephalopathy with plateau periods in which the patient was neurologically stable; (2) 18% showed subacute encephalopathy with a relentlessly downhill course; (3) 10% had a static encephalopathy; (4) 7% had evidence of developmental delays without any neurological abnormalities; (5) 7% had a fulminant encephalopathy; and (6) 7% tested within normal limits. Other neurological defects included focal motor deficits, ataxia, spastic diparesis, and spastic quadriparesis with rigidity.

Ultmann et al. (1987) recently published a follow-up study of the developmental problems in symptomatic HIV-infected children. The initial study of 16 children aged 10–74 months showed that most had delayed acquisition of milestones; in fact, one child was diagnosed during a developmental assessment session. The patients with AIDS-related complex (ARC) had more variable abnormalities than those with AIDS. Cognitive dysfunction was also more prominent in those with AIDS. At the end of the 2-year follow-up period, a variable course continued. Five patients with developmental progression showed a static neurological picture, while another five showed neurological deterioration. Finally, of interest are four patients who showed a deteriorating neurological exam with progression through developmental milestones.

Epstein et al. (1985, 1986) have also performed extensive, prospective neurodevelopemental studies of HIV-infected children. Their most recent report discusses results in 36 children. Several patterns similar to Belman's and Ultmann's findings were found: progressive encephalopathy with interspersed plateaus in 20; static encephalopathy in eight; and minimal neurological deficits in eight. Epstein specifically remarks on the poor prognosis in those with a rapidly progressive neurological deterioration. In developmental exams, he also found a variety of abnormalities, including receptive and expressive language deficits and low IQ scores. Such prospective, comprehensive studies will help delineate the neurodevelopmental course in HIV-infected children. These findings, taken in conjunction with the growing numbers of HIV-infected children reaching school age, portends a growing problem that will require intervention from mental health specialists, school authorities, and public health officials.

TRANSMISSION

Seventy-seven percent of children with HIV infection are born to women who are themselves in a high-risk group (CDC, 1988). Most of these women are intravenous drug users, but a significant number were infected through heterosexual contacts. In some cases, the child's father was the index case, and the mother was an asymptomatic carrier. The proportion of women infected in such a manner is steadily increasing. In utero infection with HIV prevents the normal development of the immature fetal immune system, establishing the bases for the short incubation period and the severity of signs and symptoms seen in children. Virological evidence exists to support such early infection—the virus has been cultured from the thymus and brain of a 13-week abortus and from the liver, spleen, and brain of a 15-week abortus (A. Rubinstein, personal communication, February 1987).

Further evidence for in utero transmission of HIV lies in the recent description of a new embryopathy—the AIDS fetopathy (Marion, Wiznia, Hutcheon, & Rubinstein, 1986). As in fetal alcohol syndrome, but clearly different from this syndrome, distinct facial features exist in some HIV-infected infants indicating an in utero insult, probably in the first trimester. The features include hypertelorism (widespread eyes), blue sclerae, microcephaly (small head circumference), and frontal bossing (protruding forehead). Finally, transplacental transmission is supported by cases in which infants have been born by Cesarean section, been separated from the mother (e.g., placed in foster care), and later developed typical symptomatology (Lapointe, Michaud, Pekovic, Chausseau, & Dupuy, 1985; Scott, Fischl, Klimas, Fletcher, et al., 1985).

Human immunodeficiency virus has been isolated from breast milk (Thiry et al., 1985), and three purported cases of transmission through breast milk have been described. Two of the cases occurred in Africa and the third (reported by Ziegler, Cooper, Johnson, Gold, and the Sydney AIDS Study Group 1985) in Australia. In the latter case, the mother received two units of infected blood postpartum and breast-fed the infant for 6 weeks. Subsequently, both mother and child seroconverted. Until definitive studies are completed, HIV-positive women in developed countries should be advised not to breast-feed (CDC, 1985a), both because of the possibility of infecting an uninfected child and because ongoing exposure of an already infected infant may hasten the transition to overt symptomatology.

Approximately 14% of reported cases in children have been linked to the transfusion of blood or blood products. Children with hemophilia compose approximately 5% of the total number of cases. New patients from both of these groups will diminish over time since screening of all blood donors was instituted nationwide in the spring of 1985 and heat treatment of clotting-factor concentrate began. Studies show that heat-treated factor does not transmit HIV. However, patients who are already infected may not manifest symptoms for several years.

In New York City, the chance of receiving contaminated blood was 1 in 5,000 in 1978 and 1 in 50,000 in April 1985. Mandatory screening of donated blood begun in April 1985 made that risk virtually nil (Altman, 1987). The CDC estimates that, nationwide, 12,000 people were infected prior to April 1985 while millions of transfusions were administered. The remaining 5% of cases in children represent instances in which parents were not available to be interviewed or refused to be interviewed or in which risk-factor determination was in progress.

A frequently posed but as yet unanswered question is the risk that an infected woman has of giving birth to an HIV-infected child. The few limited studies reported to date show a wide range of figures. In one study of 92 pregnant intravenous-drug-using women, 56% tested seropositive, and 35% of the seropositive group gave birth to an infected infant. Other studies with smaller numbers have reported rates as low as 0%. The reason for this discrepancy is not clear. Transmission for subsequent pregnancies may be as high as 65% (Scott, Fischl, Klimas, & Parks, 1985). Large, prospective studies are under way to define the risk of transplacental transmission more clearly and perhaps identify factors predictive of fetal infection.

Horizontal transmission (i.e., through the casual contact of day-to-day living) has not been linked to any reported cases of HIV infection. Kaplan et al. (1985) reported such findings after studying a small cohort in New Jersey, and Berthier et al. (1986) demonstrated no cases of seroconversion in a group of nonhemophiliac children living in a boarding school along with hemophiliacs, 50% of whom were seropositive. In another recent study (Biberfeld et al., 1986), 56 nonsexual household contacts of HIV-infected hemophiliacs were tested with ELISA and Western blot techniques, including 30 parents, 13 siblings, and 13 children. All nonsexual contacts tested negative, while 10% of regular heterosexual partners tested positive. Fischl, Dickinson, et al. (1987) studied 45 adult patients with AIDS, and the patients' spouses, children, and household contacts. They also demonstrated no horizontal spread. Finally, my institution has followed almost 200 close household contacts who lived with at least one HIV-infected child, some for as long as 6 years. The contact in these homes included sharing beds, toothbrushes, and bottles and living in crowded conditions. To date, not one of these individuals shows seropositive results on ELISA or

Western blot tests (Novick, Sicklick, & Rubinstein, 1987). These ports and others give further support to the premise that HIV is spread by casual contact.

TREATMENT

As of July 1987, no effective, specific treatment existed for children with HIV infections. When dealing with children, practitioners must first emphasize diagnosis and treatment of associated bacterial infections. As mentioned previously, the secondary infections are an important cause of morbidity but respond well to appropriate therapy when instituted early. A major reason for these recurrent infections is the underlying deficiency in the humoral immune system caused by the HIV infection. Several years ago, we began to treat these children with intravenous gammaglobulin (IVGG), as is done for children with congenital immune B cell defects. In one study (Calvelli & Rubinstein, 1986), 41 patients were followed, and 14 treated were with IVGG. There was a significant decrease in the number of infections in the group that received treatment but not in the untreated group. Further, the IVGG slowed immunologic deterioration. Subsequent studies with IVGG also showed some improvement in other immune functions (Gupta, Novick, & Rubinstein, 1986). Controlled trials are in progress on a large scale to corroborate and further elucidate the role of IVGG in the treatment of HIV infection in children.

Developing an antiviral therapy with which to treat HIV infections is an important current research goal (Yarchoan & Broder, 1987). If such a goal is to be met, first the replicative cycle of HIV must be understood and then techniques devised to arrest that cycle, thereby inhibiting viral replication (Ho, Pomerantz, & Kaplan, 1987). One such drug—azidothymidine (AZT)—acts by preventing formation of some of the proteins that the virus needs to reproduce. It has been used in preliminary treatment trials of adult patients with AIDS/ARC, with promising results (Fischl, Richman, et al., 1987). Some patients improved both clinically and immunologically, even patients with neurological abnormalities. That AZT can penetrate the brain is of particular significance in view of the high incidence of neurological complications associated with HIV infection. In March 1987, the Food and Drug Administration approved AZT for use with adult patients with AIDS. Early trials of AZT with children began in the spring of 1987. Preliminary studies, as of 1989, are very promising. Two other drugs being tested are DDI and CD4. They may be more potent than AZT with fewer side effects.

Several other drugs tested inhibit the functions of reverse transcriptase (RT), an enzyme required for viral replication. One drug that had been used in early research in HIV-infected adults was suramin, which had previously been used to treat African sleeping sickness. Unfortunately, early results showed no significant clinical improvement, and the drug was not tested extensively in children because of secondary toxicities. Studies conducted with HPA-23 also produced no clinical improvement, and the drug is no longer used extensively to treat AIDS. Ribavirin, however, has shown promise in early trials in the United States. Finally, although phosphonoformate, an antiviral drug, is used against the herpes virus, insufficient data are presently available to evaluate its usefulness in treating HIV infections.

Other than IVGG, no agents that can boost the immune system have proved worthwhile. Trials with interleukin-2, thymic hormones, and thymic transplants have, in fact, often contributed to the progression of the immune defects. Perhaps such treatments will be more successful if used in conjunction with specific antiviral therapy, when the latter is developed.

General supportive measures are the only recommendations that can currently be made for the care and treatment of HIV-infected children. Maintenance of good nutritional status is important, for the immune system functions poorly in states of malnutrition. At times, intravenous nutritional measures are required and may continue for months at a time. Additionally, if at all possible, an infected child should avoid exposure to potentially serious infections (e.g., chicken pox, measles). Any child with an immunodeficiency could develop a serious, even fatal outcome in such a situation. Specific treatments do exist, however, for an HIV-infected child so exposed.

Much progress has been made since 1979, when the first cases of pediatric AIDS were described. The etiologic agent, HIV, has been identified, and a great deal is known about its genetic behavior, protein composition, and transmission. The natural history of this disease in various age groups is in the process of being elucidated, as improved medical care allows patients to be supported for many years. Research is ongoing in all areas, including transmission, latency, disease progression, organ system involvement, and treatment. At the same time, there are complex psychological and behavioral problems intertwined with the medical ones. An increasing amount of research is being devoted to these crucial issues, and one cannot address them without a sound foundation of medical knowledge. Such a comprehensive approach will lead to the successful development of preventive interventions for the patients, their families, and their communities.

GLOSSARY

Antibodies. Collections of protein molecules produced by B lymphocytes in response to the presence of an antigen (i.e., any foreign substance). Antibodies bind to the specific antigen whose presence triggered their production and help destroy it.

Antigens. Any foreign substance that induces the development of an immune response.

B Lymphocytes. See Lymphocytes.

Cellular immune system. That part of the immune system predominantly containing T lymphocytes (T cells).

HIV. The human immunodeficiency virus, the virus that causes AIDS. It was previously referred to first as human T cell lymphotropic virus-III (HTLV-III) and then as lymphadenopathy associated virus (LAV).

HTLV-III. See HIV.

Humoral immune system. That part of the immune system predominantly containing B lymphocytes.

Hypoxemia. Inadequate oxygen in body tissues, a condition that can lead to tissue damage.

Immune system. The system that equips an individual to defend against infection. A contemporary definition of the term "immunity" emphasizes the ability to recognize materials or agents as foreign and to neutralize, eliminate, or metabolize them with or without injury to the host's tissues.

Incubation period. The time between infection by a disease-causing organism and the onset of overt symptoms of the disease. This time period is at present unknown in AIDS and has been estimated to be between 6 months and 7 years or, perhaps, more.

Kaposi's sarcoma. A previously rare form of cancer characterized by dark blue or purple-brown nodules that usually affects the skin of the extremities. Classic Kaposi's sarcoma generally follows a slow, indolent course, but in AIDS patients it is highly aggressive, spreading rapidly and involves many organs.

LAV. See HIV.

LIP. See PLH.

Lymphadenopathy. An abnormal enlargement of the lymph glands (nodes). This is often a sign of an infection.

Lymphocyte. One of the white blood cells that plays a key role in the functioning of the immune system. There are two main types, B lymphocytes and T lymphocytes. B lymphocytes produce antibodies, and T lymphocytes are involved in the overall control of the immune system, including the regulation of B cell action and the destruction of cells infected with virus.

Opportunistic infections. Various infectious organisms, mostly viruses, fungi, and parasites, take the "opportunity" to infect a host whose immune system is deficient and thus cannot fend off the diseases caused by the agent. Hence, the term "opportunistic infections." These infections are frequently the immediate cause of death in AIDS patients, though the underlying "cause" is the immune deficiency.

Parotitis. Abnormal swelling of the salivary glands in the cheeks.

PLH. Pulmonary lymphoid hyperplasia, a condition in which lymphocytes invade the lungs and cause a "noninfectious" type of pneumonia. It was previously referred to as lymphocytic interstitial pneumonitis (LIP).

PCP. Pneumocystis carinii pneumonia, a form of pneumonia caused by a parasite. It usually does not cause an infection in a host with an intact immune system. This organism is the most common one isolated in AIDS patients and is associated with a high death rate.

Retroviruses. Viruses known to cause cancer in animals. Recently, genes from these viruses have been found to be very similar to oncogenes or so-called cancer genes found in human and other cells. The virus that causes AIDS, HIV, is a retrovirus.

Sepsis. A serious infection of the blood stream.

T helper cells. These are one of the subpopulations of T lymphocytes that aid in the cytotoxic or killing function of T lymphocytes. In AIDS patients, there is a lowering in the number of T helper cells. T helper cells also help regulate T suppressor cells and B cells.

Thymus. The gland responsible for the development of lymphocytes. The name "T lymphocytes" shows that these lymphocytes are thymus derived. Studies show that the thymus also makes several hormones to aid in its function.

T lymphocytes. See Lymphocytes.

T suppressor cells. Suppressor T cells regulate the activity of B cells and also that of other T cells.

REFERENCES

Altman, L. (1987, March 20). U.S. seeking to allay fears over a call for AIDS tests. *New York Times,* p. A.14.

Ammann, A. J., Wara, D. W., Dritz, S., Cowan, M. J., Weintrub, P., Goldman, H., & Perkins, H. A. (1983). Acquired immunodeficiency in an infant: Possible transmission by means of blood products. *Lancet, 1,* 956–958.

Barre-Sinoussi, F., Chermann, J. C., Rey, F., Nugeyre, M. T., Chamaret, S., Gruest, J., Dauguet, C., & Axler-Blin, C. (1983). Isolation of a T lymphotropic retrovirus from a patient at risk for acquired immune deficiency syndrome (AIDS). *Science, 220,* 868–871.

Belman, A. L., Diamond, G., Dickson, D., Llena, J., Lantos, G., and Rubinstein, A. (1988). Pediatric acquired immunodeficiency syndrome—neurologic syndromes. *American Journal of Diseases in Children, 142,* 29–35.

Belman, A. L., Ultmann, M. H., Horoupian, D., Novick, B., Spiro, A. J., Rubinstein, A., Kurtzberg, D., & Cone-Wesson, B. (1985). Neurological complications in infants and children with acquired immune deficiency syndrome. *Annals of Neurology, 18,* 560–566.

Bernstein, L., Krieger, B., Novick, B., Sicklick, M., & Rubinstein, A. (1985). Bacterial infection in the acquired immunodeficiency syndrome. *Pediatric Infectious Diseases, 4,* 472–475.

Berthier, A., Fauchet, R., Genetet, N., Pommereuil, M., Chamaret, S., Fonlupt, J., Gueguen, M., Ruffault, A., & Montagnier, L. (1986). Transmissibility of human immunodeficiency virus in hemophilic and non-hemophilic children living in a private school in France. *Lancet, 2,* 598–601.

Biberfeld, G., Bottiger, B., Berntorp, E., Schulman, S., Egberg, N., Stigendal, L., Blomback, M., & Nilsson, I. M. (1986). Transmission of HIV infection to heterosexual partners but not to household contacts of seropositive hemophiliacs. *Scandinavian Journal of Infectious Diseases, 18,* 497–500.

Buck, B. E., Scott, G. B., Valdes-Dapena, M., & Parks, W. P. (1983). Kaposi's sarcoma in two infants with acquired immune deficiency syndrome. *Journal of Pediatrics, 103,* 911–914.

Calvelli, T. A., & Rubinstein, A. (1986). Intravenous gammaglobulin in infant acquired immunodeficiency syndrome. *Pediatric Infectious Diseases, 5,* S207–S210.

Centers for Disease Control. (1982). Update on acquired immune deficiency syndrome (AIDS)—U.S. *Morbidity and Mortality Weekly Report, 31,* 507–514.

Centers for Disease Control. (1985a). Recommendations for assisting in the prevention of human T-lymphotropic virus III/lymphadenopathy-associated virus and acquired immunodeficiency syndrome. *Morbidity and Mortality Weekly Report, 34,* 721–732.

Centers for Disease Control.(1985b). Revision of the case definition of acquired immunodeficiency syndrome for national reporting—U.S. *Morbidity and Mortality Weekly Report, 34,* 373–375.

Centers for Disease Control. (1987a). Classification system for human immunodeficiency virus (HIV) infection in children under 13 years of age. *Morbidity and Mortality Weekly Report, 36,* 225–236.

Centers for Disease Control. (1987b). Revision of the CDC surveillance case definition for acquired immunodeficiency syndrome. *Morbidity and Mortality Weekly Report, 36* (Suppl.), 3S–15S.

Centers for Disease Control. (1988, March 14). *AIDS weekly surveillance report— United States* (DHHS Publication No. 396). Atlanta, GA: Centers for Disease Control.

Epstein, L. G., Goudsmit, J., Paul, D. A., Morrison, S. H., Connor, E. M., Koenigsberger, M. R., & Oleske, J. (1987). Expression of human immunodeficiency virus in cerebrospinal fluid of children with progressive encephalopathy. *Annals of Neurology, 21,* 397–401.

Epstein, L. G., Sharer, L. R., Joshi, V. V., Fojas, M. M., Koenigsberger, M. R., &

Oleske, J. (1985). Progressive encephalopathy in children with acquired immune deficiency syndrome. *Annals of Neurology, 17*, 488–496.

Epstein, L. G., Sharer, L. R., Oleske, J. M., Connor, E. M., Goudsmit, J., Bagdon, L., Robert-Guroff, M., & Koenigsberger, M. R. (1986). Neurologic manifestations of HIV infection in children. *Pediatrics, 78*, 678–687.

Fischl, M. A., Dickinson, G. M., Scott, G. B., Klimas, N., Fletcher, M. A., & Parks, W. (1987). Evaluation of heterosexual partners, children and household contacts of adults with AIDS. *Journal of the American Medical Association, 257*, 640–644.

Fischl, M. A., Richman, D. D., Grieco, M. H., Gottlieb, M. D., Volberding, P. A., Laskin, O. L., Leedom, J. M., Groopman, J. E., Mildvan, D., Schooley, R. T., Jackson, G. G., Durack, D. T., King, D., & the AZT Collaborative Working Group. (1987). The efficacy of azidothymidine (AZT) in the treatment of patients with AIDS and AIDS related complex. *New England Journal of Medicine, 317*, 185–191.

Gupta, A., Novick, B. E., & Rubinstein, A. (1986). Restoration of suppressor T-cell function in children with AIDS following intravenous gammaglobulin treatment. *American Journal of Diseases of Children, 140*, 143–146.

Gupta, A., Sicklick, M., Bernstein, L., Rubinstein, E., & Rubinstein, A. (1982, May 15). Recurrent infections, interstitial pneumonia, hypergammaglobulinemia and reversed T-4/T-8 ratio in children with high antibody levels to Epstein Barr virus. Paper presented at the meeting of the American Academy of Pediatrics, New York.

Ho, D. D., Pomerantz, R. J., & Kaplan, J. C. (1987). Pathogenesis of infection with human immunodeficiency virus. *New England Journal of Medicine, 317*, 278–286.

Ho, D. D., Rota, T. R., Schooley, R. T., Kaplan, J. C., Allan, J. D., Groopman, J. E., Resnick, L., Felsenstein, D., Andrews, C. A., & Hirsch, M. S. (1985). Isolation of HTLV-III from cerebrospinal fluid and neural tissues of patients with neurologic syndromes related to the acquired immunodeficiency syndrome. *New England Journal of Medicine, 313*, 1493–1497.

Kaplan, J. E., Oleske, J. M., Getchell, J. P., Kalyanaraman, V. S., Minnefor, A. B., Zabala-Ablan, M., Joshi, V., Denny, T., Cabradilla, C. D., Rogers, M. F., Sarngadharan, M. G., Sliski, A., Gallo, R. C., & Francis, D. P. (1985). Evidence against transmission of human T-lymphotropic virus/lymphadenopathy associated virus (HILV-III/LAV) in families of children with the acquired immunodeficiency syndrome. *Pediatric Infectious Diseases, 4*, 468–471.

Lapointe, N., Michaud, J., Pekovic, D., Chausseau, J. P., & Dupuy, J. M. (1985). Transplacental transmission of HTLV-III virus. *New England Journal of Medicine, 312*, 1325.

Marion, R. W., Wiznia, A. A., Hutcheon, R. G., & Rubinstein, A. (1986). Human T-cell lymphotropic virus type III (HTLV-III) embryopathy. *American Journal of Diseases of Children, 140*, 638–640.

Morgan, W. M., & Curran, J. W. (1986). Acquired immunodeficiency syndrome: Current and future trends. *Public Health Reports, 101*, 459–465.

Novick, B. E., Sicklick, M. J., & Rubinstein, A. (1987). [Lack of horizontal transmission of HIV]. Unpublished data.

Oleske, J., Minnefor, A., Cooper, R., Jr., Thomas, K., DelaCruz, A., Ahdieh, H., Guerro, I., Joshe, V. V., & Desposito, F. (1983). Immune deficiency in children. *Journal of the American Medical Association, 249*, 2345–2349.

Rubinstein, A., Morecki, R., Silverman, B., Charytan, M., Krieger, B. Z., Andiman, W., Ziprkowski, M., & Goldman, H. (1986). Pulmonary disease in children with acquired immune deficiency syndrome and AIDS-related complex. *Journal of Pediatrics, 108*, 498–503.

Rubinstein, A., Sicklick, M., Gupta, A., Bernstein, L., Klein, N., Rubinstein, E., Spigland, I., Fruchter, L., Litman, N., Lee, H., & Hollander, M. (1983). Acquired immunodeficiency with reversed T4/T8 ratios in infants born to promiscuous and drug addicted mothers. *Journal of the American Medical Association, 249*, 2350–2356.

Scott, G. B., Fischl, M. A., Klimas, N., Fletcher, M. A., Dickinson, G. M., Levine, R. S., & Parks, W. P. (1985). Mothers of infants with the acquired immunodeficiency syndrome—evidence for both symptomatic and asymptomatic carriers. *Journal of the American Medical Association, 253*, 363–366.

Scott, G. B., Fischl, M. A., Klimas, N., & Parks, W. P. (1985, April 14). *Mothers of infants with acquired immunodeficiency syndrome: Outcome of subsequent pregnancies.* Paper presented at the International Conference on Acquired Immunodeficiency Syndrome, Atlanta.

Shaw, G. M., Harper, M. E., Hahn, B. H., Epstein, L. G., Gajtbusch, D. C., Price, R. W., Navia, B. A., Petito, C. K., O'Hara, C. J., Groopman, J. E., Cho, E., Oleske, J., Wongstahl, F., & Gallo, R. C. (1985). HTLV-III infection in brains of children and adults with AIDS encephalopathy. *Science, 227*, 177–181.

Silverman, B., & Rubinstein, A. (1985). Serum lactate dehydrogenase levels in adults and children with acquired immunodeficiency syndrome and AIDS related complex. *American Journal of Medicine, 78*, 728–736.

Snider, W. D., Simpson, D. M., Nielson, S., Gold, J. W. M., Metroka, C. E., & Posner, J. B. (1983). Neurological complications of acquired immune deficiency syndrome: Analysis of 50 patients. *Annals of Neurology, 14*, 403–418.

Thiry, L., Sprecher-Goldberger, S., Jonckheer, T., Levy, J., Van de Perre, P., Henrivaux, P., Cogniauz-LeClere, J., & Clumeck, N. (1985). Isolation of AIDS virus from cell-free breast milk of three healthy virus carriers. *Lancet, 2*, 891–892.

Ultmann, M. H., Belman, A. L., Ruff, H. A., Novick, B. E., Cone-Wesson, B., Cohen, H. J., & Rubinstein, A. (1985). Developmental abnormalities in infants and children with acquired immune deficiency syndrome (AIDS) and AIDS-related complex. *Developmental Medicine and Child Neurology, 27*, 563–571.

Ultmann, M. H., Diamond, G. W., Ruff, H. A., Belman, A. L., Novick, B. E., Rubinstein, A., & Cohen, H. J. (1987). Developmental abnormalities in children with AIDS: A follow-up study. *Journal Of Neuroscience, 32*, 661–667.

Yarchoan, R., & Broder, S. (1987). Development of antiretroviral therapy for the acquired immune deficiency syndrome and related disorders: A progress report. *New England Journal of Medicine, 317*, 557–564.

Ziegler, J. B., Cooper, D. A., Johnson, R. D., Gold, J., & the Sydney AIDS Study Group. (1985). Postnatal transmission of AIDS-associated retrovirus from mother to infant. *Lancet, 1*, 896–898.

•

CHAPTER TWO

Three Model Pediatric AIDS Programs: Meeting the Needs of Children, Families, and Communities

JEFFREY M. SEIBERT

ANA GARCIA

MARCY KAPLAN

ANITA SEPTIMUS

INTRODUCTION

Pediatric acquired immunodeficiency syndrome (AIDS) has been a major problem in a few regions of the country for the past several years. Three metropolitan areas—New York, Miami, and Los Angeles—have been among the most severely affected. In each of these cities, programs

The order of authorship among the three social workers is alphabetical and does not reflect their relative roles in the preparation of this chapter since each contributed equally. The idea for this chapter emerged from a symposium presentation involving three of the four authors at a national conference entitled "The Challenge of AIDS," held in Miami, Florida, in November 1986. The writing of this chapter was supported in part by a grant from the State of Florida Department of Health and Human Services, Office of Developmental Disabilities, and the Florida Developmental Disabilities Planning Council.

have been providing services to families of children infected with human immunodeficiency virus (HIV). The programs deliver psychosocial support and educational services to the families in addition to ongoing medical treatment. In this chapter, we describe the results of a survey of three of these programs, highlighting similarities and differences among the programs and the families served, including identified needs and services provided. We conclude by considering psychosocial and educational issues and strategies that are in need of research.

A number of dimensions of pediatric AIDS/HIV can be related to existing medical/social problems. The following brief review of the relevant literature is not intended to be exhaustive. Rather, it suggests a way of assembling the pieces of the AIDS puzzle that may help provide a clearer picture of the unique combination of psychosocial and educational problems posed by pediatric AIDS/HIV and ways in which these problems can be addressed.

1. Pediatric AIDS is a chronic, terminal illness. There is an expanding literature on social, psychological, and educational issues with chronic childhood illnesses, such as cancer (e.g., Koocher, Sourkes, & Keane, 1979), diabetes (e.g., Newbrough, Simpkins, & Maurer, 1985), and cystic fibrosis (e.g., Walker, Ford, & Donald, 1987). For families with chronically ill children, problems caused by lack of money, community isolation, prejudice, misunderstanding in school, depression, and loneliness are common (Brantley, Stabler, & Whitt, 1981). The psychological effects of chronic illness on a child can be expected to vary as a function of age of onset of the illness (Lapham & Shevlin, 1986), interacting with the child's developmental level. Models have been described for determining how to assess and meet the needs of chronically ill children and their families and how to develop programs with multidisciplinary input (e.g., Hobbs & Perrin, 1985). Strategies for dealing with school-related problems, including days lost because of illness or repeated hospitalizations and subsequent school reentry, have also been addressed (e.g., Hennings & Fritz, 1983; Morrow, 1985). Other

research has looked at the reactions of mental health workers providing services to children with what are commonly terminal illnesses, such as cancer, and what preventative actions can be taken to reduce emotional burnout (e.g., Koocher, 1980). In most pediatric AIDS/HIV cases, the mother and other family members are also infected, further complicating the family dynamics of dealing with a chronic childhood illness.

2. The most common mode of transmission of pediatric HIV infection is perinatal, from mother to child. In a small number of past cases, the virus was transmitted through contaminated blood products. Little research has been conducted on psychological reactions to the transmission of infectious diseases through blood products or from mother to child, as occurs, for example, with syphilis or cytomegalovirus. However, issues explored with parents who have given birth to a child with a genetically based disorder such as sickle-cell anemia (e.g., Headings, 1979), cystic fibrosis (e.g., Fischman, 1979), or Down's syndrome (e.g., Antley, 1979) may be relevant. Feelings of victimization, fault finding, and anger directed at the partner, fear of stigmatization, shame and helplessness, rage, survivor guilt, and sadness over loss, both real and symbolic, have all been identified as responses of parents of children with a genetically transmitted disease or disorder (e.g., Headings, 1979; Kessler, 1979). Genetic counseling strategies for helping families move through feelings of guilt or shame have been suggested (Kessler, Kessler, & Ward, n.d.).

3. Pediatric AIDS/HIV is most commonly linked to intravenous drug use by the mother or her sexual partner. There is a growing literature on the problems of intravenous drug use, its causes, the limited successes of various treatment and rehabilitation programs, and the relation to AIDS and AIDS prevention (e.g., Des Jarlais, Friedman, & Strug, 1986; see also chapter 6).

4. Pediatric AIDS/HIV infection is associated with neurological impairments and developmental delays. There is an extensive literature on psychological and educational issues with families of developmentally

27

disabled children. Investigators have looked at parents' grief at the birth of a developmentally disabled child (e.g., Emde & Brown, 1978; Pueschel, 1983) and other psychological problems confronted by parents of disabled children (e.g., Breslau, Staruch, & Mortimer, 1982). Various models have been described for providing educational and psychosocial support services to handicapped children and their families (e.g., Allen, Holm, & Schiefelbusch, 1978; Bricker, Seibert, & Casuso, 1980; Guralnick & Bennett, 1987; Schlesinger & Meadow, 1976).

5. Pediatric AIDS/HIV is affecting disproportionate numbers of economically disadvantaged families from cultural and ethnic minorities. Models for working with children from disadvantaged families have been described extensively (e.g., Bryant & Ramey, 1987; Gray & Klaus, 1976; Lambie, Bond, & Weikart, 1974). Just as many programs for developmentally disabled children (who are also disproportionately represented among economically disadvantaged families), these models often include coordination of social service support for families' basic needs, counseling and emotional support for the parents, education for parents that addresses their children's special educational and therapeutic problems, and interdisciplinary interventions with the children.

Despite the similarities, no other childhood disease, condition, or social problem rivals pediatric AIDS/HIV for the range of difficult issues raised. Models for other pediatric medical/social problem are relevant, but none is comprehensive enough to address all the complex issues. Pediatric AIDS/HIV, at the intersection of many individual, interpersonal, and societal issues, poses a unique challenge to our educational, psychological, and social service delivery systems. The extreme social stigma associated with pediatric AIDS/HIV and the potentially serious consequences of disclosure of the diagnosis to others represent additional dimensions of the disease that much be addressed by any comprehensive model.

The remainder of this chapter will report the findings of the survey of the psychosocial and educational needs of families with HIV-infected

children in New York, Miami, and Los Angeles and present a description of three programs' responses to the identified needs.

THE SURVEY

Three programs participated in a survey designed to gather basic demographic information on project families and children, to identify issues commonly focused on when counseling the infected child's
primary care giver, and to obtain descriptions of the psychosocial and
educational services offered by each project. The psychological data,
based on the social workers' observations of families at each project,
represent the first empirically based effort to characterize major social-
emotional issues for this population. Although no data on reliability
and validity of the reports were gathered, the findings provide a preliminary overview from which future, more structured research can be
developed.

The project social worker completed the survey, with assistance on
the medical data from a physician on the project. Each social worker had
from 2 to 4 years' experience working with pediatric AIDS families at the
time of the survey. A case study was provided by each project to illustrate some of the problems families served by that project characterist-
ically face. Names, dates, and other identifying information have been
changed to protect the confidentiality of the persons involved.

The three projects are representative both of the major geographic
regions where pediatric AIDS is a significant problem and of the differ-
ent causes of child and maternal HIV infection. The programs are the
Weiler Hospital of the Albert Einstein College of Medicine (WHAE-
COM-NYC) of Yeshiva University, the Bronx, New York, under the direction of Dr. Ayre Rubinstein; the University of Miami/Jackson
Memorial Medical Center, Miami, Florida, under the direction of Dr.
Gwendolyn B. Scott; and the Childrens Hospital of Los Angeles (Childrens-LA) program, Los Angeles, California, under the direction of
Drs. Joseph A. Church and Edward D. Gomperts. Each program has
made significant contributions to the understanding of pediatric AIDS

(e.g., Church, Allen, & Stiehm, 1986; Rubinstein et al., 1983; Scott, Buck, Leterman, Bloom, & Parks, 1984).

SURVEY FINDINGS
Demographics

Nearly all the data are reported for current caseload (i.e., as of the date given in Table 1) rather than for total caseload. The first case of pediatric AIDS was reported by WHAECOM-NYC in 1979, although that case was not indentified as AIDS until several years later. Miami saw its first case in 1982, and the first case at Childrens-LA was identified in 1983. The largest total caseload is reported by WHAECOM-NYC; however, these figures do not represent all the cases in New York, and the reported findings should not be generalized to the city as a whole (e.g., there are many more black families in other sections of the city). Miami and WHAECOM-NYC have similar distributions of cases by level of symptomatology, for both total and current caseload. Childrens-LA reports a larger percentage of children in the asymptomatic category. The mortality rates range from 25% at WHAECOM-NYC to 40% at Miami.

Nearly all WHAECOM-NYC's and Miami's cases involve perinatal transmission. Childrens-LA, however, records a larger number as well as percentage of transfusion-related cases, many of which were identified by the American Red Cross Look-Back Study of blood transfusions. The reason for the greater incidence of transfusion-related cases at Childrens-LA is not known. Other differences emerge when mother's mode of infection is considered. Nearly all the WHAECOM-NYC cases (consistent with other reports—e.g., Rubinstein & Bernstein, 1986), about half the Childrens-LA cases, and only one-fourth of the Miami cases are related to intravenous drug use. Heterosexual transmission among recent Caribbean Island immigrants, apparently not related to drug use, is the most common mode of maternal infection reported at Miami. Childrens-LA reports the greatest diversity of mode of maternal infection, including cases associated with a bisexual partner and artificial insemination.

Miami and WHAECOM-NYC report approximately equal ratios of infected males to females. Childrens-LA has treated nearly twice as many males as females, a trend that is consistent with national figures showing males to be over represented in transfusion-associated cases (Centers for Disease Control [CDC], 1988). The current age distribution for infected children is relatively similar across all three projects. About one-fourth of the current caseload at each site is school aged, that is, above 5 years of age. This figure is perhaps unexpected since most cases of pediatric HIV infection have occurred within the past 5 years.

The ethnic distributions of patients at the projects show significant differences. The caseload at WHAECOM-NYC is predominantly Hispanic, that at Miami is predominantly Black, and that at Childrens-LA is relatively equally divided among Blacks, Hispanics, and non-Hispanic Whites. These distributions also reflect the mother's first language: predominantly Spanish at WHAECOM-NYC, other (Haitian Creole) in Miami, and English with a substantial minority of Spanish at Childrens-LA.

Although all three programs report a significant percentage of children living with someone other than their natural parents, at WHAECOM-NYC less than one-fifth of the children live with their natural parents. Sixty percent of the children at WHAECOM-NYC, a little more than one-fourth of the children at Miami, and less than 10% of those at Childrens-LA are in foster care. Few mothers at WHAECOM-NYC or Miami are married; at Childrens-LA, however, the majority of mothers are married. About half or more of the mothers at each site are living with a partner. Nearly all WHAECOM-NYC's families have a standard of living below poverty level. In Miami, almost all the families live either below or just above the poverty level. Childrens-LA has a more nearly equal distribution of families across income levels, with more than one-third reported to be middle income or better. Nearly all the WHAECOM-NYC parents are unemployed (data not reported in Table 1); a little fewer than half the parents at Miami have either part-time or full-time employment. Most fathers in the Childrens-LA sample are employed full time, and most mothers have no employment.

Table 1: Demographic Characteristics of Pediatric Populations by Project

	WHAECOM-NYC	Miami	Childrens-LA
Date survey completed	4/30/87	9/1/87	8/1/87
Year of first case	1979	1982	1983
Total cases, N (%):	250	172	47
AIDS	75(30)	67(39)	25(53)
ARC	173(69)	105(61)	13(28)
HIV positive only	2(1)	0(0)	9(19)
Deaths	50(25)	69(40)	14(30)

Following Data Based on Current Caseload Only

	WHAECOM-NYC	Miami	Childrens-LA
Current caseload (%):	120	83	32
AIDS	30	19	31
ARC	68	81	41
HIV positive only	2	0	28
Mode of transmission to child (%):			
Hemophilia/coagulation disorders	1	. . .	9
Transfusion	3	4	50
Mother infected	96	96	41
Mode of transmission to infected mother (%):			
Blood transfusion	2	1	8
IV drug use	75	20	23
IV drug partner	23	4	38[a]
Other heterosexual	. . .	71	. . .
Bisexual partner	. . .	33	15
Artificial insemination	. . .	. . .	8
Unknown	. . .	1	8

Table 1, continued

	WHAECOM-NYC	Miami	Childrens-LA
Sex of child (%):			
Males	55	42	66
Females	45	58	34
Current Age (%):			
less than 1 year	15	8	16
1–4 years	60	70	56
5–10 years	25	22	16
11–13 years	. . .	. . .	. . .
14–20 years	. . .	. . .	12
Ethnic distribution (%):			
Black, not Hispanic	22	84	19
Hispanic	70	12	38
White, not Hispanic	8	4	34
Other	. . .	. . .	9
Mother's first language (%):			
English	30	32	53
Spanish	70	13	38
Other	. . .	55	9
Child's primary care giver (%):			
Mother	16	66	74[b]
Father	2	6	10
Grandparent or other relative	22	18	. . .
Foster, adoptive, or residential	60	10	16

Table 1, continued

	WHAECOM-NYC	Miami	Childrens-LA
Partner status of mother (%):			
Married, living			
together	7	27	61
Single, with partner	52	20	10
Divorced/separated	20	1	10
Single/never	1	29	6
married			
Partner deceased	. . .	8	3
Mother deceased	20	15	10
Family income level (%):			
Below poverty	90	38	26
Between poverty			
and middle			
income	9	54	39
Middle income or	1	8	35
better			

Note. Figures do not represent all cases in these cities, but only those cases seen by clinic completing the survey. Those for Miami are based on 79 families because several children are siblings. Those for Los Angeles are based on 31 families because the oldest child in the sample (a 20-year-old) is living independently.

[a] Includes two bisexual men not isolated in bisexual category.

[b] Includes one joint custody.

The Case Studies

Because family demographics and the most common mode of maternal and infant infection differ among the three programs, many of the issues commonly addressed at each project differ. The following case reports highlight some of these regional differences.

A Case Report from New York: Rosa, a 9-month-old Hispanic female, was found to be HIV antibody positive and diagnosed with AIDS-related complex (ARC) at WHAECOM-NYC in the summer of 1986. Her 26-year-old mother, Lea, also tested positive for HIV antibodies but showed no symptoms. Lea had been diagnosed several years earlier with a borderline personality disorder with addictive features. About 4 years ago, Lea had become depressed at the death of her husband and began drinking and using drugs. She became involved with a man named Rick who was heavily addicted, who physically assaulted her, and who stole money from Lea and her family. She had two children by Rick, including Rosa, both of whom he abused.

When Lea learned of Rosa's and her conditions, she became very agitated and would not listen to any medical information on AIDS. She reported feeling anger toward her boyfriend, whom she blamed for infecting her. In counseling with the social worker, she expressed obsessive thoughts of smothering Rosa with a pillow and putting a gun to her own head. Lea was admitted for psychiatric hospitalization but left because she reported feeling like a "leper" as a result of the staff knowing of her infection status. The social welfare office reportedly requested that she deal with them only over the phone.

Lea came to weekly group and individual sessions at WHAECOM-NYC. With the exception of her grandmother, Lea's family blamed her for bringing the condition on herself and offered her little support. Two of her aunts, however, did take Rosa and Lea's older uninfected son into foster care. Lea responded well in therapy and began job hunting. On several occasions, she lost her housing when landlords learned of her HIV infection. But Lea persisted. She participated in a seminar for health care professionals at WHAECOM-NYC and reported feeling elated at the supportive response she received from the audience when she shared her story. She also appeared in court against her ex-boyfriend Rick, who had been charged with assault against her and abuse of her children.

Relapses did occur. Lea disappeared for about 6 weeks when she returned to Rick, still heavily involved with drugs. He set her hair on fire when she refused to turn her welfare check over to him. She ran away and hid on a roof for 2 days, sleeping at night in 20-degree weather, before finally returning to the WHAECOM-NYC staff. She was pregnant again. Lea accepted psychiatric inpatient care to give her time to assess her situation, decide what to do about her pregnancy, and arrange housing. During all this time, Rosa remained in the good care of Lea's aunt. Rosa developed no new infections associated with HIV but began to show some mild neurological signs and mild developmental delay.

This is a typical profile of an HIV-infected family in New York in crisis, involving substance abuse, domestic violence, child abuse, poverty, and obstructed opportunities for employment, housing, and education. It is not, however, one of New York's worst scenarios, such as those cases exacerbated by the deterioration and death of the child and/or one or both parents. The case was chosen because it illuminates the extent of psychosocial problems experienced by an HIV-infected family, regardless of the level of the diagnosis.

A Case Report from Miami: Ginette was the firstborn child of two Caribbean Islanders who had immigrated to Miami a number of years ago. She began showing respiratory symptoms and "failure to thrive" when she was about 6 months old. She was diagnosed with AIDS at the Miami program in the fall of 1984. Ginette died at 11 months of age. The social worker assisted her parents, Jean and Claire, in the bereavement process. Jean, a U.S. citizen, was fluent in English, but Claire needed an interpreter. Claire was pregnant and near term. Because they were asymptomatic, neither of them seemed to understand the meaning of their positive HIV antibody test results. The idea of a latent virus was foreign to their way of thinking about health and illness.

Friends inadvertently learned the cause of Ginette's death at her funeral, and the word spread. As a result, Jean lost his job, he and Claire were evicted from their apartment, and their friends and even some relatives began to avoid them. Jean told the social worker that he believed that the hospital was somehow responsible for his daughter's death and his family's subsequent misfortune.

Jeanine, their second daughter, was born 2 weeks after Ginette's death, her health stable and her infection status unknown. Because Jean had difficulty keeping steady employment, money became a problem. Claire was eligible for Aid to Families with Dependent Children (AFDC) because she and Jean were not legally married. Despite Jean's opposition to any form of welfare, a cultural value he shared with many immigrants from his homeland, Claire enrolled in AFDC.

The social worker counseled Jean and Claire about the risks of additional pregnancies and about birth control options. Since neither of them were showing symptoms, they saw no reason to follow the suggestions. With infant mortality a common phenomenon in their homeland and large families valued, the expectation was that a woman would become pregnant again after the death of a young child. Over the next year, Claire gave birth to their first son, Junior, and became pregnant for a fourth time. During this pregnancy, both Claire and Jeanine began showing symptoms of HIV infection, including chronic diarrhea and weight loss. In counseling with the social worker, Claire expressed a willingness to consider pregnancy termination. Jean, however, objected strongly and encouraged Claire to have the baby. Their fourth child, Pierre, was born premature, failed to gain weight, and showed respiratory problems symptomatic of HIV infection. He was placed in the neonatal intensive care unit. At the same time, Jeanine was diagnosed with ARC and hospitalized for a respiratory infection. Jeanine recovered and returned home to Jean and Junior. Pierre died in the intensive care unit at about 2 months of age. Claire's condition worsened as she continued to lose weight and began to show signs of dementia. She died a few weeks after Pierre's death.

Jean expressed intense grief and guilt over Claire's death in counseling with the social worker. Although Jean brought Jeanine regularly to the clinic for intravenous gammaglobulin treatments, he would not acknowledge that any of his family had died of AIDS or that he or his surviving children could be infected with the virus.

When Jeanine was hospitalized several months later for a respiratory infection, Jean and Junior disappeared. Jeanine was referred for foster care, but no placement could be found, and she remained in the hospital. Jean reappeared 5 months later, explaining that he had gone back to his native country to be with his dying mother and had taken Junior with him. Jeanine was returned to him, and the family disappeared from the service delivery system until 6 months later, when an alleged uncle brought the two children to the hospital. Nothing was known of Jean's whereabouts. Junior was now old enough to provide unequivocal antibody test results and was found to be virus free. He and Jeanine were placed in separate foster care homes. Jean was not seen again.

This case study illustrates some of the kinds of issues that the Miami project has had to address when providing psychosocial and educational services to families from culturally different backgrounds. Language differences, differences in basic understanding about health and disease processes, and different cultural values and beliefs about families and family dynamics must all be recognized and dealt with if interventions are to be effective. When cultural differences are not considered, the result can be painful, frustrating clashes between families and direct service staff.

A Case Report from Los Angeles: Louise, a Caucasian female, was diagnosed with ARC at Childrens-LA when she was 4 years old. She had exhibited symptoms of the disease for 2 years prior to the diagnosis, including failure to thrive, otitis media, and pneumonia. The parents, both employed and middle class, reported feeling shocked at the diagnosis but relieved to have an answer after 2 years of not knowing what was wrong with Louise. Louise had received a blood transfusion, apparently HIV contaminated, when she had been in a neonatal intensive care unit shortly after birth. The parents reported feeling a great deal of anger about their daughter's condition, anger directed in particular toward members of the identified AIDS risk groups who may have donated the infected blood.

Two weeks after the initial consultation with the family, Louise was hospitalized for 3 weeks with bacterial pneumonia. Her activity level became depressed, but she responded well to a child life specialist and an art therapist before returning home.

Louise's parents had little concern about problems with handling Louise's bodily fluids at home because she was toilet trained, but they had to be reassured that there was no risk in Louise kissing her healthy, uninfected 9-month-old brother. They discussed at length with the social worker the implications of sharing Louise's diagnosis with family members and friends before deciding whom to tell. Both sets of grandparents were informed and provided a great deal of support, offering occasional respite by baby-sitting Louise and her younger brother. When at one point the parents became concerned that the maternal grandfather was becoming too involved by insisting that he participate in all decision making about Louise, the social worker helped them set limits.

In counseling with the social worker, the parents' relationship with each other appeared strong and mutually supportive. They realized that they had developed a tendency to withdraw from contact with friends and to restrict their social life to the immediate family. They discussed the advantages and disadvantages of their decision to isolate themselves from their social network. They seemed to have generally realistic perceptions of Louise's situation even though they occasionally speculated on Louise's life as an adult, whether she would marry and have children. The social worker helped them focus on some of the more immediate issues, such as Louise's relationship with peers and potential problems with school attendance in the near future. Confidentiality and who would need to be informed at school became special concerns, as the parents became aware of stories in the media of discrimination and isolation against other school-aged HIV-infected children around the country. As Louise began to experience a series of illnesses, the parents began to consider home teaching to reduce the likelihood of exposure to additional infections. They also expressed fears about Louise's becoming developmentally disabled as a result of the HIV infection. They found their concerns increasing as she began to display some hearing deficits and speech difficulties, including stuttering and below-age-level grammatical sentence structure.

The parents discovered that Louise's condition was significantly affecting decisions in other areas of their lives. The father considered taking a new position with a different company, but this raised concerns about medical coverage for Louise's preexisting condition under any new insurance plan. Participation in a group at the hospital with parents of other children with AIDS or ARC became one of their major sources of emotional support. They reported that Louise's illness and her uncertain future caused them to take life one day at a time.

This case study was selected to show some of the issues confronted by middle-class families with an HIV-infected child, a group well represented in the Childrens-LA sample. When a family is relatively secure financially and well integrated into the cultural mainstream, the project staff may find themselves dealing with subtler issues of family adjustment and the expression of more hypothetical concerns about the future.

Descriptions of the Psychosocial and Educational Programs

In this section, we summarize survey findings of the kinds of services being provided across projects. The projects are expanding services as additional funding becomes available, and our description is therefore accurate only for the dates and caseload figures noted for the survey.

Staffing Patterns: All three projects include a full-time master's-level social worker, and WHAECOM-NYC also has a bachelor's-level social worker. At least one nurse (registered nurse or nurse practitioner) works full time at the New York and Miama projects and half time at the Los Angeles project, involved in medical counseling and health-related education with families as well as in inpatient and outpatient clinic activities.

The projects differ in what other disciplines are included. A clinical psychologist is available to the New York project 1 day a week and on a consulting basis for administering psychological tests. A developmental psychologist is assigned half time to the Miami project to carry out program model development and evaluation and to coordinate staff activities for developmental testing and intervention.

Consultations for physical therapy, occupational therapy, speech therapy, and neurology are available through the hospitals where the projects are located. New York also has access to a dentist, New York and Miami to a psychiatrist and a dietitian, and Miami and Los Angeles to a child life specialist, all on a consulting basis. Referrals for consultations are made by either the social worker or the nurse, usually on the basis of their clinical judgment of what kinds of services and information the child and the family need.

A variety of problems may lead to referrals. As noted in chapter 1 and corroborated by results from the project surveys, developmental disabilities are common in children with HIV infection. Estimates of the percentage of children who are developmentally delayed range from about 50% of the caseloads in Miami and at Childrens-LA to 80% at WHAECOM-NYC. Further research is needed, however, to determine how much of the problem is directly attributable to HIV infection of the central nervous system and how much is the result of other factors, such as secondary infections and environmental circumstances. Among the other problems that may lead to referrels are failure to thrive, noted in the Miami case study, and allergies. Both conditions require input from a dietitian, and special diets may need to be coordinated with medications for secondary infections. The parents, if infected with HIV, may also manifest neurological and psychiatric problems requiring psychiatric referrals.

The scope of the problem presented by children with AIDS is clearly multidisciplinary. A comprehensive team approach is therefore evolving at each site to address the many needs of each family. Such an approach is, however, difficult to develop and maintain when funding constraints (to be discussed later) limit the core staff on each team to the physician, social worker, and nurse and when all other services are provided primarily on a consulting basis.

Social Services and Counseling: The social worker's responsibilities at each project include assessing the family's basic needs for medical, financial, and social service support, making referrals to the appropriate agencies, and educating families about how to obtain needed services. At WHAECOM-NYC, over 90% of the families served receive AFDC and food stamps, and Miami reports that 28% and 31% receive AFDC and food stamps, respectively. At Childrens-LA, however, 71% of the families are on AFDC and none on food stamps. Over half the WHAECOM-NYC families but few families at the other projects receive Supplemental Security Income. Forty percent of the WHAECOM-NYC, 19% of the Miami, and 10% of the Childrens-LA families are enrolled in Women, Infants, and Children.

At all three projects, most families lack private medical insurance for their children: 74% are uncovered at Childrens-LA, 87% at Miami, and 97% at WHAECOM-NYC. There are some backup systems for medical coverage, such as Medicaid or Medical, and these are used by 97% of the WHAECOM-NYC, 71% of the Childrens-LA, and 35% of the Miami families. At Los Angeles, California Children's Services covers all medication costs not covered by Medical as well as up-front costs of medication that are reimbursed only later. Visiting nurse services have been utilized on a limited basis by all three projects, for 10% of the families at Miami, 16% at Childrens-LA, and 25% at WHAECOM-NYC. Childrens-LA is the only project to report using Hospice, for 10% of its families.

The social worker helps coordinate alternative placements for a child when foster or residential care is required, usually because of death or abandonment by the parents. As noted earlier, WHAECOM-NYC has by far the greatest number of children in alternative placements. Various incentive reimbursements have been implemented or are being considered by the social service systems in each city to attract more potential foster parents. A program in Miami is being developed to recruit and train potential foster parents for HIV-infected children. However, the numbers of children expected to need alternative placements in the future are so great that additional options, including small group homes, are being explored.

The social worker also provides counseling and emotional support to the families, beginning at the initial diagnosis. At least 90% of the families at all three projects receive some individual counseling, and family therapy is provided to 30% of the families at WHAECOM-NYC, 52% at Childrens-LA, and 61% at Miami. A mothers' group in New York and a parent group in Los Angeles serve 20% and 39% of the families at each project, respectively. Psychiatric referrals have been made for 20% of the current caseload at WHAECOM-NYC, 10% at Childrens-LA, and 3% at Miami. The range of social-emotional issues addressed in counseling with the primary care giver will be discussed in a later section.

Educational Services: The project nurse is responsible for providing important medical, health, and family planning/birth control information and education to the families as a follow-up to the physician's efforts. The nurse coordinates educational efforts with the counseling support provided by the social worker.

The nurse provides families with information and education about AIDS, its cause, the levels of symptoms, modes of transmission and prevention, and infection control. These issues are important to all families, but they are especially critical for families where the mother herself is infected. The infected woman is at risk of bearing additional infected children and of transmitting the virus to sexual partners. Consequently, the nurse and social worker emphasize family planning and birth control as an important part of family counseling and education efforts. The nurse also provides information to the families on nutrition, well child care, and child development. The Miami project presents information to the families on sexually transmitted diseases and preventive health practices.

Each of the projects has also been involved in adopting or adapting available educational materials or, when relevant materials are not available, developing their own materials to augment educational efforts with the families. These materials include pamphlets and brochures that describe the disease, procedures for its management, and precautions to be taken. The projects also have various plans for the develop-

43

ment of audiovisual materials, including slides and videotapes, which will be especially valuable for families who cannot use written materials.

Cultural/Linguistic and Literacy Issues: Both counseling and educational efforts with the families are complicated by several factors. For many families, English is not an appropriate language for education and counseling. This is the case for over half the families at Miami, about one-fourth of the families at Childrens-LA, and 5% of the families at WHAECOM-NYC. Miami's population is the least literate, with written materials, regardless of the language, reported to be effective with less than half the families. A substantial minority of the families at Los Angeles—one-fourth—and 10% at WHAECOM-NYC have similar literacy problems. Pamphlets, brochures, and written instructions, therefore, will be of minimal value to many families unless they contain graphic symbols to communicate ideas and information. Audiotapes and videotapes in the family's native language, currently being developed at Miami, can be valuable supplemental educational tools. The Miami project, where the language problem is most serious, has on staff a bilingual social worker (English and Spanish) and a multilingual nurse (fluent in Haitian Creole, French, Spanish, and English). When necessary, staff on each of the projects rely on the services of a hospital interpreter. An interpreter can be used most effectively if the focus is on communicating ideas rather than on merely translating words. This can be difficult when medical terminology must be communicated (Nachman, 1984).

All three projects serve a substantial number of families for whom cultural differences produce obstacles to understanding medical information, ranging from over half at Miami to 40% at WHAECOM-NYC and 26% at Childrens-LA. Some of the problems include lack of understanding about infectious diseases, germ transmission, and potential illness in the absence of any perceived symptoms. Some families have little or no familiarity with the American medical system and its degree of specialization. Instructions may need to be very specific and physically demonstrated to assure proper use of medications (e.g., in appropriate amounts, delivered to the appropriate part of the body, and at appro-

44

priate intervals). There may be other barriers to effective communication. For example, some families may misunderstand the physician and think that, because a disease is incurable, nothing is to be gained by monitoring and treating it. Consequently, obtaining a family's compliance with administration of medications and clinic visits can be difficult. The counselor/educator must be a good listener who takes the time to allow the families to share their feelings about what is happening in their lives and what is being asked of them. The effective educator also encourages families to repeat what they have heard and to demonstrate their understanding of procedures. To do this in a way that does not appear condescending to the family is difficult but important.

Developmental and Educational Services for the Children: Day-care placements are not generally available to preschool children who are known to be H IV infected or ill. Some parents seek placements without telling the programs of their child's infection status. Others keep their child at home rather than risk any problems or confrontations. If there is any risk to the child, or if the child should pose any risk of infection to others in day care (e.g., oozing sores), the projects advise parents to keep their child at home.

A daycare program operated by the hospital is available at W HAE-COM-NYC, and there are plans to move it out into the community. The program serves an average of 15 children 6 hours a day, 5 days a week. A nurse monitors the children daily for infectious diseases and attempts to separate the infected children from the healthy. Miami is exploring options for integrated day-care intervention; Childrens-LA has decided that a day-care program is not feasible at this time.

Providing these children the opportunity for peer interaction instead of creating a program in isolation has benefits that are believed to outweigh concerns about placing children in a setting where their exposure to infectious diseases is increased. At what ages and in what ways H IV-infected children should be allowed to be mainstreamed into regular day care, nursery school, and other educational settings will continue to be debated for some time (see chapter 4). Staff from the Miami project have participated in a task force at the University of Miami's

45

Mailman Center for Child Development in an effort to develop written guidelines for the center's educational and nursery school programs for infants, toddlers, and young children. The guidelines are intended to help in making decisions about appropriate and least restrictive placements for HIV-infected children.

Many HIV-infected children qualify for some type of special education services because of developmental disability. Seventy percent of the WHAECOM-NYC and 35% of the Childrens-LA children so identified are currently receiving special educational services. To monitor each child's developmental progress, the projects in New York and Miami are administering several developmental and psychological tests, including the Denver Developmental Screening Test (Frankenburg & Dodds, 1969), the Bayley Scales of Infant Development, both Mental and Motor (Bayley, 1969), and the latest revision of the Stanford-Binet (Thorndike, Hagen, & Sattler, 1986). New York also uses the Kaufman-ABC (Kaufman & Kaufman, 1983). All three sites also test neurological functioning. The results of these various tests help determine which children will be referred for special educational services in the community (see chapter 1 for a summary of published developmental and neurological research findings). The nurses at New York and Miami also provide training in developmental and educational activities that parents can carry out at home in an attempt to facilitate their child's development.

Links to Community AIDS Organizations and Educational Outreach Efforts: The programs recognize that they do not exist in isolation and that other AIDS-related support services are available in the community. All three projects report links with community AIDS organizations (e.g., Gay Men's Health Crisis in New York, Health Crisis Network in Miami, and AIDS Project of Los Angeles) for such activities as sharing information, networking volunteers, making or receiving referrals, obtaining direct client services such as counseling, participating jointly in community education efforts, and serving on the organizations' governing boards.

All three programs report varying degrees of community education efforts to reach beyond their clinic population. Their audiences range from health care providers in hospitals and clinics, to day-care and school personnel, to general community groups such as schools, churches, and civic groups. Childrens-LA and WHAECOM-NYC report roughly four community presentations and Miami about one or two per month. The scope of these education efforts is also national, through participation in conferences, task forces, and review panels as well as the related media exposure.

Funding: Funding sources for the psychosocial and educational support services come from the state (the New York State AIDS Institute) and private foundations in New York, from the state (the Department of Health and Human Services, Office of Developmental Disabilities, and the Florida Developmental Disabilities Planning Council) and the National March of Dimes Birth Defects Foundation in Miami, and from the county (the County of Los Angeles Department of Health Services) in Los Angeles. The long-term stability of funding from these sources is, however, uncertain, especially in Miami and Los Angeles. Alternative sources—for example, state and federal governments and private foundations—are being sought to support current as well as expanded services in all three cities. Increased funding will be needed to develop a comprehensive interdisciplinary team approach to the problem of pediatric AIDS and to address the demands for expanded outreach activities at the local, state, and national levels.

Social-Emotional Issues of the Families

The case reports illustrate how a diagnosis of AIDS, ARC, or asymptomatic HIV infection in a child can affect a family, placing stresses on a system that in many cases is already fragile. In this section, we report results from that part of the survey designed to identify common social-emotional issues across families and across projects. The social-emotional data may apply to either the natural mother or father or a foster or adoptive parent, depending on who is the primary care giver for the index child in the family. We consider the primary care giver in relation to himself or herself, in relation to a partner if one is present, in relation

47

to the index child, in relation to other family members, and in relation to friends. In interpreting the data, we focus mainly on identifying issues that recur across projects and on interpreting those similarities, but we also discuss significant differences among projects. Our results are presented in Table 2. There are a number of similarities to issues noted earlier in the literature review.

Intrapersonal Issues: All three projects report that anxiety, depression, and grief/mourning are the major concerns with which the care giver must deal. Both WHAECOM-NYC and Childrens-LA also report significant preoccupation with the issues of health/illness, death and dying, loneliness, guilt/shame, and independence/control. Denial is a problem for the majority of families in Los Angeles and is also reported for a substantial minority of the families in New York and Miami as well.

Partner Issues: All three projects report that most care givers with partners have problems related to emotional support, communication, trust, and anger/blame. Although these problems may have existed prior to the diagnosis, the diagnosis and disease process are likely to exacerbate the situation. The programs in New York and Miami, where maternal and partner infection is more common, also report disagreement about family planning/birth control. In Miami, this issue includes concern for potential as well as current partners. Another major partner issue at WHAECOM-NYC and Childrens-LA is health/illness.

Index Child Issues: Attachment/nurturance issues are reported to be significant concerns of care givers in Miami and Childrens-LA. Apparently, this reflects, at least in part, an ambivalence about establishing relationships with children who may soon die. Overprotectiveness with the index child is a frequent problem reported by all three projects, a common finding in dealing with chronically and terminally ill children. Concern about developmental disabilities is especially high at WHAECOM-NYC and Childrens-LA, where high percentages of children with developmental problems have been reported. Only Childrens-LA reports the health/illness of the index child as a major counseling concern. In general, the lower level of concern about health/illness issues re-

48

Table 2: Percentage of Primary Care Givers Having Social-Emotional Issues Requiring Counseling, as Reported by Project Social Workers

	WHAECOM-NYC	Miami	Childrens-LA
Intrapersonal issues of the primary care giver:			
Body image	. . .	16	61
Health/illness[a]	80	22	71
Self-esteem	80	43	42
Assertiveness	. . .	32	61
Independence/ control[a]	80	38	52
Depression[b]	100	78	100
Anxiety[b]	100	78	100
Guilt/shame[a]	100	13	65
Loneliness[a]	100	27	81
Death and dying[a]	100	11	90
Grief/mourning[b]	100	51	90
Family planning	30	82	42
Drug use	40	5	26
Denial around diagnosis	30	27	71
Suicide:			
Ideation	40	6	3
Attempt	0	0	0
Issues with partner:			
Emotional support[b]	100	59	100
Sexual satisfaction	20	14	29
Communication[a]	75	49	71
Trust[b]	75	54	81
Compatibility	75	14	42
Anger/blame[b]	100	55	61

Table 2, continued

	WHAECOM-NYC	Miami	Childrens-LA
Abuse	50	2	3
Dependability	70	9	10
Health/illness[a]	90	4	90
Family planning[a]	60	85	19
Drug use	20	1	0
Issues of primary care giver with index child:			
Attachment/ nurturance[a]	30	89	90
Communication	. . .	76	3
Stigma/shame/ embarrassment	. . .	19	3
Discipline/limit setting	. . .	13	10
Abuse/neglect/ rejection	30	3	16
Over protectiveness[b]	90	97	84
Developmental delays/handicap[a]	70	20	90
Health/illness	. . .	38	100
Issues of primary care giver with other family members:			
Emotional support[b]	90	60	71
Confidentiality[b]	80	82	94
Cohesiveness[b]	70	51	84
Dependability[a]	75	40	52
Communication[b]	75	70	81
Inclusion/isolation[a]	80	22	71

Table 2, continued

	WHAECOM-NYC	Miami	Childrens-LA
Respect	60	4	. . .
Fear[a]	95	12	74
Health/illness	90	24	42
Issues of primary care giver with friends:			
Emotional support	90	41	29
Confidentiality[b]	70	100	94
Dependability	70	40	42
Inclusion/isolation/			
discrimination[a]	90	38	90
Respect	50	25	29
Fear[a]	90	36	90

[a]An issue for at least 50% of the care givers at two sites.

[b]An issue for at least 50% of the care givers at all three sites.

ported by WHAECOM-NYC and Miami may reflect a greater resignation to the diagnosis among disadvantaged families, for whom sickness and disease are more common experiences.

Issues with Other Family Members: The area of relationships with other family members, including the care giver's and the partner's parents and siblings, produced the greatest number of reported concerns for most care givers across all three projects. Emotional support, confidentiality, cohesiveness, and communication were all major issues at each project. Concerns related to dependability, inclusion/isolation/ discrimination and fear were also identified as important at WHAECOM-NYC and Childrens-LA. These findings suggest that the extended family may be a great source of either support or stress and that efforts to address the entire system may be of value.

Issues with Friends: Across projects, the one major issue with friends was confidentiality—who and who not to tell and what the consequences might be. The related issues of fear and inclusion/isolation/ discrimination were also important to most care givers from WHAE-COM-NYC and Childrens-LA.

Although the diagnosis of pediatric AIDS itself is a stressful event, the responses of those around the child and the care giver to that information may play a critical role in how well or poorly the care giver is able to cope with the situation. Identifying the potential support network and providing appropriate counseling and information to key individuals in that network may be important to success in nearly all other aspects of the psychosocial and educational interventions with the families.

GENERAL STRATEGIES FOR WORKING WITH FAMILIES
The survey did not specifically assess the strategies that social workers, nurses, and other staff employ in addressing the identified concerns, but, from many discussions, some general observations can be made. Project staff in most cases encourage the parent to share the diagnosis with the partner, particularly in cases of perinatal transmission, because of the possible risk to both partners of repeated exposure to the virus and additional pregnancies through unprotected sexual activity. Staff, experienced with the range of reactions that project families have encountered from others in the past, generally advise caution in sharing the diagnosis with those outside the immediate family until the potential consequences have been thought through and discussed. The care giver's use of denial has been reported for a significant minority of the families across projects. It may serve a valuable adaptive function for the care giver, but its implications for counseling and education efforts need to be evaluated.

In dealing with other systems, the social worker and other project staff have often developed special procedures for making referrals and obtaining needed support services without disclosing the nature of the family's medical problem to the social service agency. On occasion, other agencies recognize the name of the referring physician or social worker and assume that the referred family has a child with AIDS. In some cases, where disclosure may be necessary for obtaining available services (e.g., Social Security Disability), efforts are made to identify key contact persons within the referral agency who are sensitive to the special needs of project families and who are careful to maintain confidentiality. In many situations, project staff provide informal education and counseling to staff in other agencies to make them aware of the facts about AIDS and to help them address their own feelings and fears.

Maintaining confidentiality about the presence of AIDS in a family remains one of the major concerns of the project staff, not only in dealing with other systems, but sometimes in dealing with curious staff from other programs within the hospital. For, once confidentiality is violated, the family has little legal recourse or protection from discrimination (e.g., see the discussion of unwanted disclosure of diagnosis in chapter 4). Staff have become aware of the need to avoid discussions of families in the halls and general access areas of the hospital.

For many families, the social worker, nurse, and other project staff to whom they can comfortably relate become important sources of emotional support. To establish such rapport, staff need to make it clear that they do not judge the family for the illness or how it may have been contracted, especially in cases of perinatal transmission. The staff may need to support the family in resolving their own judgment and guilt and in dealing with the judgment of others. To forgive themselves and others may be a very important step for families in healing themselves at an emotional and spiritual level, when physical healing is very unlikely (Jampolsky, 1983).

FUTURE DIRECTIONS AND ANTICIPATED NEEDS
Expanded Prevention Efforts

To increase women's understanding of risks both to themselves and to their as yet unborn children, there needs to be education aimed at prevention (see chapter 5) (CDC, 1985; Koop, 1986). Higher-risk groups in particular should be targeted, including women who use intravenous drugs or who have partners who use intravenous drugs, female partners of HIV-infected hemophiliacs, and women with multiple male sexual partners, especially those living in areas of the country where the incidence of AIDS and HIV infection is especially high.

The need is greater than ever for expanded drug prevention and treatment programs (Drucker, 1986) and for the exploration of controversial programs aimed at encouraging the cleaning of intravenous needles and avoiding sharing needles (National Academy of Sciences, 1986). Other controversial but potentially discriminatory approaches include mandatory premarital screening and mandatory screening for pregnant women in higher-risk groups. However, because of the potentially discriminatory consequences of positive test results, such approaches may actually keep women away from the prenatal care that they need. The emphasis instead should be on education, voluntary screening, and pretest and follow-up counseling.

Birth control will be central to any educational and counseling efforts with at-risk and infected women and their partners. Such efforts will have to be approached with sensitivity to individuals' religious and cultural beliefs about birth control and family planning.

Program Evaluation and Research

In the midst of the crisis, when the human need is so great, it is easy to overlook the importance of program evaluation. Initially, before a problem is fully defined and understood, many different intervention alternatives will be tried and modified or discarded without any formal evaluation. However, accountability eventually becomes an issue, especially when systems are confronted with limited resources. Evaluation of the effect of the psychosocial and educational programs developed to address the needs of families with HIV-infected children must become a priority. As models are further defined and refined, the literatures noted earlier may become increasingly relevant as sources of hypotheses about how best to proceed.

The project at Miami has included an evaluation component in its program development during the past year, supported by the state funding noted earlier. The evaluation design involves random assignment of 40 families to either an individualized intervention condition or a comparison condition. All families receive a minimum level of intervention to address their needs for basic support services, counseling and emotional support, and education. The intervention families, in addition, receive individualized attention and follow-up, initiated by project staff rather than simply provided in response to family requests. Individual plans are developed for each intervention family to address needs identified through a needs-assessment process. A survey of knowledge about health-related issues, including AIDS, has been developed to assess parents' baseline levels of knowledge and understanding at entry into the program and the changes that occur over time as a result of the different level of intervention. The program evaluation will also examine effects on number of infections in the index child, clinic visits and hospitalizations, number of repeat pregnancies, and the child's developmental progress. It is recognized that the small number of families in this study may make conclusions difficult to draw for some of these issues.

Any prevention and health promotion program will need to be evaluated in terms of effectiveness in facilitating behavioral change that leads to a reduced rate of transmission of the virus. Previous education campaigns targeting other health issues, such as smoking (e.g., Graham, 1968; Warner & Murt, 1983), suggest that the factors to be considered are complex. There is good reason to maintain a healthy skepticism about the probable success of such efforts, especially in the communities where the risk of pediatric HIV infection is greatest. Educational programs that involve only dissemination of information are not likely to be effective.

Research is needed on the long-term developmental and neurological consequences of perinatal HIV infection, especially in children who remain otherwise healthy. What are the short-and long-term psychological effects on family dynamics, especially as they relate to mode of transmission? The issues identified in the social-emotional section of the survey need further investigation. What can be learned from studies of other chronically ill children? Answers to these and a number of related questions will be important in assuring that the far-reaching consequences of HIV infection in the young child are recognized and responded to in a way that is appropriate and sensitive to the special needs of the individuals affected.

Long-Range Planning

Realistically, the problem of pediatric AIDS will be here for a long time. With the increases projected for the next several years in heterosexually transmitted cases of HIV infection, including many women of childbearing age (National Academy of Sciences, 1986), the number of cases of perinatal transmission of HIV will continue to rise. Most will be related to intravenous drug use (De Jarlais et al., 1986). *Confronting AIDS*, a report from the National Academy of Sciences (1986), cites Public Health Service projections of 3,000 cumulative cases of pediatric AIDS by the end of 1991. It is estimated that there may be an additional 10,000–12,000 cases of HIV infection by that time.

Long-range planning to anticipate what service needs may be in 5, 10, or more years should begin now. Many more children will be infected with the virus as it continues to spread to more women and their as yet unborn children in other regions of the country. The needs of these families will be extensive and complex, as this chapter has illustrated. The service programs evolving at the different sites we have considered are all interdisciplinary in nature, yet even more comprehensive, integrated models of service delivery need to be developed. What began as the concern primarily of the pediatric infectious disease specialist is becoming the concern of professionals in social work, nursing, psychology, psychiatry, neurology, education, nutrition, and speech, physical, and occupational therapies.

The programs described here are committed to helping families with HIV-infected children find some meaning and dignity in their lives in the face of intense grief and loss. The pain and suffering of the children and their families have made the human side of this major public health problem even more visible. Many individuals who have shown little concern for the infected and ill adults have opened their hearts to the children. Perhaps it is in a recognition of our common humanity that the meaning of this epidemic is to be found.

REFERENCES

Allen, K. E., Holm, V. A., & Schiefelbusch, R. A. (1978). *Early intervention: A team approach*. Baltimore: University Park Press.

Antley, R. M. (1979). Genetic counseling for parents of a baby with Down's syndrome. In S. Kessler (Ed.), *Genetic counseling: Psychological dimensions* (pp. 115–134). New York: Academic Press.

Bayley, N. (1969). *The Bayley Scales of Infant Development*. New York: Psychological Corp.

Brantley, H. T., Stabler, B., & Whitt, J. K. (1981). Program considerations in comprehensive care of chronically ill children. *Journal of Pediatric Psychology, 6* (3), 229–237.

Breslau, N., Staruch, K. S., & Mortimer, E. A. (1982). Psychological distress in mothers of disabled children. *American Journal of Diseases of Childhood, 136*, 682–686.

Bricker, D., Seibert, J., & Casusuo, V. (1980). A program of early intervention. In J. Hogg & P. Mittler (Eds.), *Advances in mental handicap research* (Vol. 1, pp. 225–266). New York: Wiley.

Bryant, D. M., & Ramey, C. T. (1987). The analysis of the effectiveness of early intervention programs for environmentally at-risk children. In M. J. Guralnick & F. C. Bennett (Eds.), *The effectiveness of early intervention for at-risk and handicapped children* (pp. 33–78). Orlando, FL: Academic Press.

Centers for Disease Control. (1985). Recommendations for assisting in the prevention of perinatal transmission of human T-lymphotropic virus type III/lymphadenopathy-associated virus and acquired immunodeficiency syndrome. *Morbidity and Mortality Weekly Report, 34*, 721–732.

Centers for Disease Control. (1988, January 25). AIDS *weekly surveillance report*. Atlanta.

Church, J. A., Allen, J. R., & Stiehm, E. R. (1986). New scarlet letter(s): Pediatric AIDS. *Pediatrics, 77*, 423–427.

Des Jarlais, D. C., Friedman, S. R., & Strug, D. (1986). AIDS and needle sharing within the IV-drug use subculture. In D. A. Feldman & T. J. Johnson (Eds.), *The social dimensions of* AIDS (pp. 111–126). New York: Praeger.

Drucker, E. (1986). AIDS and drug addiction in New York City. *American Journal of Drug and Alcohol Abuse, 12,* 165–181.

Emde, R., & Brown, C. (1978). Adaptation to the birth of a Down's syndrome infant. *Journal of the American Academy of Child Psychiatry, 17,* 299–323.

Fischman, S. E. (1979). Psychological issues in the genetic counseling of cystic fibrosis. In S. Kessler (Ed.), *Genetic counseling: Psychological dimensions* (pp. 153–166). New York: Academic Press.

Frankenburg, W. K., & Dodds, J. B. (1969). *The Denver Developmental Screening Test.* Denver: University of Colorado Medical Center.

Graham, S. (1968). Cancer of lung related to smoking behavior. *Cancer, 21,* 523–530.

Gray, S. W., & Klaus, R. A. (1976). The Early Training Project: A seventh-year report. In A. M. Clarke and A. D. B. Clarke (Eds.), *Early experience: Myth and evidence* (pp. 229–246). New York: Free Press.

Guralnick, M. J., & Bennett, F. C. (1987). A framework for early intervention. In M. J. Guralnick & F. C. Bennett (Eds.), *The effectiveness of early intervention for at-risk and handicapped children* (pp. 3–32). Orlando, FL: Academic Press.

Headings, V. E. (1979). Psychological issues is sickle cell counseling. In S. Kessler (Ed.), *Genetic counseling: Psychological dimensions* (pp. 185–197). New York: Academic Press.

Hennings, J., & Fritz, G. K. (1983). School reentry in childhood cancer. *Psychosomatics, 24,* 261–269.

Hobbs, N., & Perrin, J. M. (Eds.). (1985). *Issues in the care of children with chronic illness.* San Francisco: Jossey-Bass.

Jampolsky, G. (1983). *Teach only love.* New York: Bantam.

Kaufman, A. S., & Kaufman, N. L. (1983). *Kaufman Assessment Battery for Children (K-ABC).* Circle Pines, MN: American Guidance Service.

Kessler, S. (1979). The processes of communication, decision-making and coping in genetic counseling. In S. Kessler (Ed.), *Genetic counseling: Psychological dimensions* (pp. 35–52). New York: Academic Press.

Kessler, S., Kessler, H., & Ward, P. (n. d.). *Psychological aspects of genetic counseling: Management of guilt and shame.* Unpublished manuscript, University of California.

Koocher, G. P. (1980). Pediatric cancer: Psychosocial problems and the high costs of helping. *Journal of Clinical Child Psychology, 9*(1), 2–5.

Koocher, G. P., Sourkes, B. M., & Keane, W. M. (1979). Pediatric oncology consultations: A generalizable model for medical settings. *Professional Psychology,* *10*(4), 467–474.

Koop, C. E. (1986). *Surgeon general's report on acquired immune deficiency syndrome.* Washington, DC: U.S. Department of Health and Human Services.

Lambie, D. Z., Bond, J. T., & Weikart, D. P. (1974). *Home teaching with mothers and infants.* Ypsilanti, MI: High/Scope.

Lapham, E. V., & Shevlin, K. M. (1986). *The impact of chronic illness on psychosocial stages of human development.* Washington, DC: Georgetown University and Medical Center.

Morrow, G. (1985). *Helping chronically ill children in school: A practical guide for teachers, counselors and administrators.* West Nyack, NY: Parker.

Nachman, S. (1984). *Recommendations based on Creole-English Communication Study (Pediatric Walk-In Clinic).* Unpublished manuscript, University of Miami.

National Academy of Sciences. (1986). *Confronting* AIDS*: Directions for public health, health care, and research.* Washington, DC: National Academy Press.

Newbrough, J. R., Simpkins, C. G., & Maurer, H. (1985). A family development approach to studying factors in the management and control of childhood diabetes. *Diabetes Care, 8,* 83–92.

Pueschel, S. M. (1983). Parental reactions and professional counseling at the birth of a handicapped child. In J. A. Mulick & S. M. Pueschel (Eds.), *Parent-professional partnerships in developmental disability services* (pp. 35–42). Cambridge, MA: Ware.

Rubinstein, A., & Bernstein, L. (1986). The epidemiology of pediatric acquired immunodeficiency syndrome. *Clinical Immunology and Immunopathology, 40,* 115–121.

Rubinstein, A., Sicklick, M., Gupta, A., Bernstein, L., Klein, N., Rubinstein, E., Spigland, I., Fruchter, L., Litman, N., Lee, H., & Hollander, M. (1983). Acquired immunodeficiency with reversed T4/T8 ratios in infants born to promiscuous and drug-addicted mothers. *Journal of the American Medical Association, 249,* 2350–2356.

Schlesinger, H. S., & Meadow, K. P. (1976). Emotional support for parents. In D. L. Lillie & P. L. Trohanis (Eds.), *Teaching parents to teach: A guide for working with the special child* (pp. 35–48). New York: Walker.

Scott, G. B., Buck, B. E., Leterman, J. G., Bloom, F. L., & Parks, W. P. (1984). Acquired immunodeficiency syndrome in infants. *New England Journal of Medicine, 310,* 76–81.

Thorndike, R. L., Hagen, E. P., & Sattler, J. M. (1986). *The Stanford-Binet Intelligence Scale: Fourth edition.* Chicago: Riverside.

Walker, L., Ford, M., & Donald, W. (1987). Cystic fibrosis and family stress: Effects of age and severity of illness. *Pediatrics, 79,* 239–246.

Warner, K. E., & Murt, H. A. (1983). Premature deaths avoided by the anti-smoking campaign. *American Journal of Public Health, 73,* 672–677.

•

CHAPTER THREE

Psychosocial Aspects of AIDS and HIV Infection in Pediatric Hemophilia Patients

PATRICK J. MASON

ROBERTA A. OLSON

INTRODUCTION

July 16, 1982:

> CDC [Centers for Disease Control] recently received reports of three cases of *Pneumocystis carinii* pneumonia among patients with hemophilia A and without other underlying disease. Two have died; one remains critically ill. All three were heterosexual males; none had a history of intravenous drug abuse. . . . Although the cause of the severe immune dysfuction is unknown, the occurrence among three hemophiliac cases suggests the possible transmission of an agent through blood products. . . . CDC has notified directors of hemophilia centers about these cases and, with the National Hemophilia Foundation, has initiated collaborative surveillance. A Public Health Service advisory committee is being formed to consider the implication of these findings. Physicians diagnosing opportunistic

Both authors contributed equally to this manuscript and share first authorship.

infections in hemophilia patients who have not received antecedent immunosuppressive therapy are encouraged to report them to CDC through local and state health departments. [Centers for Disease Control (CDC), 1982, p. 365]

This single statement marked the beginning of a new era in the treatment of hemophilia. In order to understand how acquired immunodeficiency syndrome (AIDS) has affected the pediatric hemophilia population, this chapter will take a historical perspective on the psychosocial and medical treatment of hemophilia. It will also examine the psychological implications of human immunodeficiency virus (HIV) infection for the pediatric hemophilia population as well as what is presently known about children who have been infected with HIV through blood transfusions. Finally, ways in which mental health professionals can work within the structure of comprehensive hemophilia centers to provide psychosocial services will be suggested.

DEFINITION OF HEMOPHILIA

Hemophilia is a sex-linked inherited disease in which an abnormal gene results in a deficiency in blood coagulation factors—either factor VIII (hemophilia A) or factor IX (hemophilia B). This deficiency causes internal hemorraging, usually in large muscle groups and joints. In general, individuals with hemophilia A experience more frequent bleeding episodes and require more aggressive treatment than individuals with hemophilia B. The related Von Willabrand's disease is a deficiency in both platelet functioning and factor VIII. The National Hemophilia Foundation (NHF) estimates that there are approximately 20,000 hemophiliacs in the United States (13,000 hemophilia A, 4,000 Von Willabrand's disease, and 3,000 hemophilia B).

Hemophilia occurs almost exclusively in males. All daughters of fathers with hemophilia are carriers of the abnormal gene, and they will have a one in two chance of bearing a hemophiliac son. Because of the advances in medical treatment, hemophilia is now considered a very manageable disease. Many carriers no longer consider it to be lethal, and, thus, the incidence of hemophilia is increasing.

HISTORICAL PERSPECTIVE
Before HIV-Contaminated Blood Supply

Medical: Prior to 1965, the treatment of choice for hemophiliacs was the infusion of fresh or fresh frozen plasma (FFP). Because its concentration of factor VIII is low, however, FFP is limited in its ability to stop bleeding episodes. Increasing the quantity of FFP to levels sufficient to force clotting ran the risk of heart failure. Typically, patients were treated with palliative measures, including the application of ice packs, immobilization of affected joints, and medication for pain.

The primary complication of bleeding episodes was progressive deterioration of large joints. By 12 years of age, most children experienced crippling arthritis. Surviving adults were typically wheelchair bound. The median age at death for hemophiliacs in 1968 was 19.6 years (Hilgartner, Aledrot, & Giardina, 1985). Because it had to be stored in a deep freeze, FFP was a very restrictive form of therapy. Family and personal life-styles were curtailed by the need to maintain immediate access to a supply of FFP. Hence, vacations with the family, camping trips, and other pleasurable activities were often impossible for hemophiliacs.

When slowly thawing FFP, a cloudy substance forms and settles to the bottom of the plasma bag. In 1965, Judith Graham Pool (Pool & Shannon, 1965) discovered that this precipitate was rich in factor VIII. This substance was termed *cryoprecipitate* (*cryo* = *cold*). The advantage of using cryoprecipitate instead of FFP is that cryoprecipitate has more concentrated factor VIII and has fewer factors that are not necessary for the treatment of a bleeding episode (e.g., plasma proteins). Each unit of cryoprecipitate is derived from a single blood donor.

Another factor-rich blood product that was developed in the 1960s is called *factor concentrates*. Factor concentrates of a specific clotting factor are manufactured from batches of plasma that are pooled from thousands of donors per batch (Jones, 1984). The final product consists of a powdery substance that is quite rich in a specific clotting factor. This lyophilized or freeze-dried substance is stored at room temperature and must have water added to it just prior to infusion. Concentrates have been available to most hemophiliacs since the late 1960s.

The use of cryoprecipitate and factor concentrates has had a profound effect on the lives of hemophiliacs. The median age at death for hemophiliacs had risen by 1974 to 30.7 years (Hilgartner et al., 1985). Most of the hemophilia population was expected to enjoy a normal life span. More aggressive treatments, with factor concentrate, at earlier ages allowed individuals with hemophilia to lead more active and productive lives. Furthermore, the factor concentrate was made available in a powder form and was a much less fragile product. It could be taken on trips without remaining frozen. Parents could feel more comfortable allowing their hemophiliac child to engage in physical activity. Some hematologists began advocating the prophylactic use of factor concentrate. In short, life was good for the hemophiliac and his family and rewarding for the health care provider.

Psychosocial: Psychological research before 1965 focused on personality variables of children with hemophilia and their parents as well as on the relation between psychological or "emotional" variables and spontaneous bleeding episodes. Most studies from this time period employed projective testing and/or in-depth interviews. Children were typically described as passive and restricted (Browne, Mally, & Kane, 1960), fearful of injury, or risk takers in response to parental overprotection (Agle, 1964).

One of the most ambitious studies undertaken during this period assessed the psychosocial functioning of 1,100 adolescents and adults with hemophilia (Goldy & Katz, 1963; Katz, 1963). An initial questionnaire examined educational level, occupational status, and level of physical disability. The authors conducted in-depth interviews with 40 of the respondents, 20 classed as "well functioning" and 20 as "poorly functioning" (e.g., unemployed and still living with parents). The authors did not state exactly what criteria were used to make these classi-

64

fications or what the distribution for the entire sample was for the criteria. The interviews focused on the relation between subjects' previous childhood experiences and psychosocial functioning. Interview data suggested that the primary predictive variable for level of autonomy in adulthood was parental child-rearing practices. Well-adjusted individuals described their fathers as being either indifferent or permissive. Poorly adjusted hemophiliacs described their fathers as being overly protective. Both groups described their mothers as being overly protective. In general, the description of mothers as being overly protective and experiencing feelings of guilt is a consistant theme throughout the research of this time (e.g., Browne et al., 1960).

During the early 1960s, bleeding episodes were treated through immobilization of joints, ice packs, and FFP. Because medical treatments were not very effective and required long hospital stays, psychologists and physicians began to focus on the association between spontaneous bleeding episodes and emotional distress (Agle, 1964; Browne et al., 1960; Mattsson & Gross, 1966). Studies during this time provided self-report data that suggested that spontaneous bleeding episodes were associated with "highly anticipated events" (Mattsson & Gross, 1966, p. 1350; see also Agle, 1964), reactions to stressful events (Agle, 1964), and psychic conflict between the child's desire to be active and the mother's overly protective stance (Browne et al., 1960).

In summary, the psychological literature on hemophilia during this period of time consisted primarily of descriptive studies of personality factors of children and their parents. Intervention focused on general advice: mothers should feel less guilty and not be overprotective, and fathers should be more involved with and supportive of the child with hemophilia. In addition, since medical treatment at that time was only moderately effective, a number of studies began to suggest there were psychophysiological variables influencing spontaneous bleeding episodes. This intriguing notion has, unfortunately, not received the necessary attention.

Psychological research conducted after the advent of cryoprecititate and factor concentrates began to shift away from the relation between emotional factors and bleeding episodes and toward issues of compliance with treatment regimens, pain control, and improved personal health strategies (Varni, 1981; Varni, Gilbert, & Dietrich, 1981). Advances in medical management also had a significant effect on child-rearing practices. A study of child-rearing practices indicated that the healthy adjustment of children was related to mutually supportive parents, consistent discipline, and an emphasis on teaching self-care skills (Markova, McDonald, & Forbes, 1980). Advice to parents focused on maintaining a realistic view of the disease, decreasing protectiveness of the child, and facing hemophilia as a challenge (Agle & Mattsson, 1968). More effective treatments allowed parents to be less protective and children to live more active lives. A recent study of parents indicated high levels of acceptance of their child's disease and low levels of overprotection (Handford, Mayes, Bagnato, & Bixler, 1986). (The Handford articles—see also Handford, Mayes, Bixler, & Mattison, 1986—make no mention of AIDS and hemophilia. It is assumed that his studies were conducted prior to the subjects' knowledge of their risk of HIV exposure and are therefore reported in this section.)

Research on children with hemophilia began to identify healthy behaviors and a decrease in maladjustment. By the time they had reached 7 or 8 years of age, children were encouraged to assume greater responsibility in the management of their treatment (Agle & Mattsson, 1968). A study of personality characteristics conducted in the early 1970s failed to demonstrate a single hemophiliac personality type (Olch, 1971). Researchers began to focus on children's styles of coping with a chronic illness instead of trying to find separate personality traits that matched the various childhood chronic illnesses. A study of 50 hemophiliac children between 5 and 19 years of age, using standardized personality instruments, found the sample to be more stable, secure, and intelligent than healthy males (Handford, Mayes, Bixler, & Mattison, 1986). The adolescents with hemophilia were described as independent in health care behaviors and able to use intellectualization as a defense mechanism. The authors suggested that this style helped adolescents cope effectively with a chronic and potentially debilitating disease.

While children with severe hemophilia were found to be more self-controlled, serious, and passive that those with mild or moderate hemophilia, all three groups of subjects fell within the normal range.

Comprehensive Treatment Centers For Hemophilia: Regional centers serving hemophiliacs and their families have made possible improved medical, psychological, and occupational care. The development and maintenance of the comprehensive care centers has been supported by the federal government, through Title XI funds. There are now 32 regional centers and 60 affiliated centers receiving federal funds in the United States, and it is estimated that approximately 70% of all hemophiliacs receive medical treatment through these centers (Goldsmith, 1986). A landmark evaluation of the effectiveness and efficiency of comprehensive treatment centers indicated significant decreases in the number of hospital admissions, days in the hospital, and days absent from school or work, a decrease in the number of unemployed patients, and a reduction in health care costs (Smith & Levine, 1984).

After HIV Exposure

A retrospective evaluation of frozen blood samples suggests that the first occurrence of HIV infection associated with a blood coagulation disorder occurred in 1978 (Ragni et al., 1986). The recognition of HIV infection of blood products began to be reported in the literature in early 1983 (Davis, Horsburgh, Hasiba, Schocket, & Kirkpatrick, 1983; Elliott et al., 1983; Goldsmith, Moseley, Monick, Brady, & Hunninghake, 1983; Luban, Kelleher, & Reaman, 1983; Meyer et al., 1983; Poon, Landay, Prasthofer, & Stagro, 1983). Serological tests to identify HIV-infected blood products were not commercially available until 1985.

The enormity of the problem was demonstrated in a study of one batch of HIV-infected factor VIII concentrate given to 33 hemophiliac patients (Ludlam et al., 1985). It was found that 15 patients became HIV positive as a result of this infected factor concentrate while 18 patients had not seroconverted. The probability of seroconversion from HIV negative to HIV positive was associated with the number of trans-

67

fusions from the infected concentrate batch and the total amount of factor VIII used. A single batch of factor concentrate, which is made from thousands of blood donors, needed to be infected by only a single blood donor to cause the spread of HIV to almost half those treated.

HIV antibodies have now been detected in 92% of persons with hemophilia A and 52% of individuals with hemophilia B who have been tested ("Surveillance," 1986). The difference in conversion rates is associated with the more frequent use of blood products by individuals with hemophilia A. As of January 4, 1988, a total of 534 hemophiliacs or individuals with coagulation disorders have been reported to the CDC as having developed AIDS (CDC, 1988a). Children with hemophilia between 1 and 13 years of age account for 40 of the 534 reported cases.

The CDC have suggested that both screening donated blood for HIV antibodies and using a heat-treatment process on concentrate to kill HIV and other viruses may be necessary to assure an additional margin of safety in blood products. This recommendation followed a finding that three pediatric hemophilia patients were seronegative at 8, 12, and 16 months after first receiving heat-treated factor concentrate. The plasma used in the factor concentrate was collected prior to the availability of serologic screening tests ("Survey," 1987).

All the concentrate sold in the United States is now heat treated and presumed to be free of HIV. Many comprehensive hemophilia centers routinely test their patients for the presence of antibodies to HIV and perform other tests of immunologic functioning (e.g., T helper/suppressor ratios, absolute T 4 [helper] counts). Unfortunately, a small number of cases continue to be reported of patients testing positive to HIV antibodies who had been using heat-treated concentrate for as long as 18 months prior to seroconverting (CDC, 1988b). The seroconversion of persons with hemophilia may demonstrate a longer latency period than that observed in other risk groups. There have been six reported cases, worldwide, of seroconversion among individuals with hemophilia who have received only donor-screened *and* heat-treated blood products (CDC, 1988b).

PSYCHOSOCIAL EFFECT OF HIV INFECTION
Research Findings

Families' Needs: Recognition that HIV could be transmitted through blood products has had a profoundly negative effect on hemophiliacs and their families. Since contaminated blood supplies and transfusion-related transmission of AIDS were first reported, many hemophilia treatment centers have experienced a dramatic increase in phone contacts and clinic visits. Research has therefore begun systematically to assess the knowledge and the changing psychosocial needs of hemophiliacs and their families (Agle, Gluck, & Pierce, 1986; Brondolo, Clemow, & Saidi, 1986; Mason, Olson, Myers, Huszti, & Kenning, in press).

One multicenter study (Agle et al., 1986) found that hemophiliacs were distressed about the possibility of HIV transmission and were at risk for developing psychological and social problems. Three questionnaires were developed by Agle and administered to hemophiliacs over 16 years of age, their spouses or mates, and parents of hemophiliacs. The questionnaires were administered by mail and during clinic visits throughout the United States. Agle reported a favorable response rate that resulted in 116 completed questionnaires from hemophiliacs, 40 from spouses, and 94 from parents of hemophiliacs.

The questionnaires were designed to assess emotional and behavioral responses to the threat of AIDS. Agle found that parents reported significantly greater levels of concern, anger, and unhappiness than did the hemophiliacs and their spouses. A small percentage of parents (approximately 7%) reported fear of getting AIDS and being reluctant to be physically close to their son. Agle also found that parents were more likely to take precautions to avoid bleeding episodes than were the hemophiliacs. He noted that parents and hemophiliacs reported treating fewer bleeding episodes per month after they learned about the relation between AIDS and hemophilia than they had before.

The questionnaires were designed to have the respondents first report retrospectively how they felt and behaved at the time they first learned about AIDS and then respond to the same questions in the present tense. Agle found a significant decrease in distress over time and concluded that, in general, the sample appeared to be coping well. He cautioned, however, that there "is a troubled minority who are symptomatic and may be at risk for significant psychological dysfunction" (Agle et al., 1986, p. 15). Another report (Brondolo et al., 1986) also found low to moderate levels of emotional distress among hemophilia patients and their relatives.

The NHF, in cooperation with the CDC, conducted a national study of a sample of 107 hemophiliacs to examine their knowledge of HIV testing and AIDS (Hargraves et al., 1986). The respondents, as a group, were aware that homosexuals and intravenous drug users were at high risk for contracting AIDS. They also understood the meaning of seropositive test results. However, a significant percentage of respondents did not know that spouses of AIDS patients (29%), children with hemophilia (32%), and sexual partners of hemophiliacs (47%) were at risk for contracting AIDS. The results of the study indicated a need for further education about the risk faced by hemophiliacs and their sexual partners.

The initial studies of hemophiliacs focused on knowledge about HIV testing, risk factors associated with the spread of HIV infection, and AIDS. A study evaluating both the knowledge and the perceived needs of hemophiliacs was conducted 10 months later through the Oklahoma Comprehensive Hemophilia Diagnostic and Treatment Center (Mason et al., in press). One hundred thirty-two adolescent and adult patients, parents, and spouses completed the AIDS Knowledge and Assessment Inventory (Hargraves et al., 1986) and the HIV Needs Assessment of Hemophiliacs, which was developed for this assessment. Approximately one-third of the respondents were patients, 57% were parents of a child or an adolescent with hemophilia, and 11% were spouses. Analyses of responses to questions assessing knowledge, sources of information, or needs for additional information/support did not differ among adolescent patients, adult patients, parents, and spouses.

The respondents in the Oklahoma survey demonstrated higher levels of knowledge about AIDS and HIV infection than were demonstrated by participants in the earlier national survey (Hargraves et al., 1986). For example, only 14% (vs. 32% in the Hargraves study) did not know that children with hemophilia were at risk for AIDS, and only 9% (vs. 29%) did not realize that spouses of hemophiliacs were at risk. Although knowledge of risk factors associated with the transmission of AIDS appeared to be more accurate, important gaps remained. A large percentage of the respondents either did not know whether or were incorrect in their belief that AIDS could be spread through saliva (71%), kissing (50%), and sharing eating utensils (38%). Many respondents did not know that a person with a seropositive HIV antibody test could transmit the virus (60%), has the AIDS agent in his or her blood (31%), is not protected from AIDS (34%), and does not necessarily have AIDS (45%).

The HIV Needs Assessment of Hemophiliacs examined the sources of information about ten AIDS topics, the sources that provided the most information, and sources for additional information. The perceived usefulness of the information was also assessed. The media (television, newspapers, magazines) were the most frequently endorsed source for all topics except the relation between AIDS and hemophilia. Respondents indicated that they preferred to receive further information on all AIDS topics from the hemophilia center.

Responses obtained about the amount of useful information received on each of ten AIDS topics were used as an indication of perceived need for more information. The greatest need was in the area of AIDS and coping with stress (86%), while the least need was in the area of AIDS and sexual transmission (56%). Relatively few (less than 10%) of the HIV-positive hemophiliacs in the United States have been diagnosed with AIDS. Nonetheless, 79% of the respondents indicated a need for additional information about AIDS and the treatment of AIDS.

One interpretation of these findings is that patients and their families were more interested in receiving information to help them better "cope and hope with the fears and social stigma associated with AIDS" (Mason et al., in press). Information related to necessary changes in sexual practices may be difficult for adolescents and young adults to re-

71

quest. Relatively lower desire for more information about preventing the spread of the virus may indicate discomfort with the subject, denial of dangerous behavior, or resistance to change established practices.

Clinical Observations

The risk of HIV transmission through blood products has been virtually eliminated by the use of donor-screened, heat-treated products (Levine, 1985). Knowledge that blood products have in the past been contaminated with HIV and HIV-positive test results have created high levels of anxiety and stress among individuals with hemophilia and their families. For example, Goldman (1985) reported a 20%–30% reduction in the use of heat-treated clotting factor, despite the fact that failure to treat joint bleeds may lead to serious life-long disabilities. Parents and health care workers also expressed concern about HIV infection through contact with seropositive children during the administration of factor concentrate. Parents of 27 seropositive pediatric hemophiliacs were followed and tested during a 3-year span (Lawrence et al., 1985). None of the parents experienced seroconversion during this period.

Children: Clinical observations by providers of mental health care to children, adolescents, and adults with hemophilia and their families attending comprehensive treatment centers throughout the United States have revealed several recurring themes. The experience of parents of young hemophiliacs has been especially difficult. Some parents, already coping with the diagnosis of a chronic disease, home factor replacement therapy, and issues related to discipline and overprotection, now have to deal with the fact that their child is HIV positive. The initial reaction of many parents with an HIV-positive son was anger and panic, commonly followed by an expressed need for information about HIV infection and AIDS. Many parents held to be a sign of hope the fact that relatively few of the HIV-infected hemophiliacs had developed AIDS. Yet each minor cold or illness was feared to signal AIDS.

Parents of HIV-positive children must endure a stressful period of waiting. The latency period between exposure to the AIDS virus and development of AIDS was initially thought to have ranged from 5 months to 5 years, with a mean of 2 years (Curran et al., 1984; Eyster et al., 1985). More recent information, however, indicates that the latency period may be 10 years or longer (Piot, 1987; Redfield & Burk, 1988). Parents of an HIV-positive child must also decide whether to inform extended family, neighbors, or schools of their child's HIV status as well as what information to share with the child. Coloring that decision is an awareness of the ostracism the child and his family might face in the school and community once the child's positive HIV antibody status becomes known.

Parents who learned that their hemophiliac child tested HIV negative were initially relieved. However, as the public becomes increasingly aware of the association between hemophilia and AIDS, the family with an HIV-negative hemophiliac child is at greater risk of experiencing discrimination and ostracism.

Adolescents: Parents of adolescents face an even greater dilemma. They may want to protect their children from the knowledge that they are HIV positive. There is no consensus, at present, concerning the rights of an adolescent to know his HIV status, and there is no consistant policy among the comprehensive hemophilia care centers regarding the age at which children are informed of their HIV status. Many parents believe that the knowledge of a positive HIV test result may only increase an adolescent's anxiety and place him at further risk for feelings of alienation. Other parents feel that such information may lead their teenage boys to act out in an irresponsible manner.

Failure to inform adolescents of their HIV status and provide a detailed explanation of safe sexual practices may result in both legal and ethical problems for the families of hemophiliacs and health care workers. If a sexually active adolescent is HIV positive and his parents chose not to inform him of his HIV status, then transmission to others may occur. It is unclear who would be considered at fault for this transmission of HIV. Could the parents of the adolescent be held responsible? The responsibilities of the physician, nurse, psychologist, social worker, and the treatment center are also unclear. In one case, a 13-year-old hemophiliac was informed that he had tested positive for HIV antibodies. The mother reported that her child later experienced feelings of anxiety and fear. She responded to her son's concerns by telling him that the test results were in error and that he did not have the AIDS virus. This example illustrates the two factors related to HIV testing: the need to counsel both parents and children about HIV-positive results and the need for a national policy on testing procedures for hemophiliacs.

The decision to protect children and adolescents from knowledge of their HIV status may actually do more harm than good. In the past, a "protective stance" was advocated for children with cancer. Despite attempts to protect children from a frightening illness, clinicians discovered that many children were aware that they had a potentially fatal disease (Mulher, Crisco, & Cumitta, 1981). Since parents and physicians did not discuss a diagnosis of cancer, the child often maintained misperceptions of the causes and prognosis of his or her illness. Children were not able to ask questions openly or to express fears. Because the mass media have repeatedly reported the possibility of hemophiliacs contracting AIDS, a fatal disease, through the use of blood products, parents and health care workers cannot protect children from the knowledge that they are in a group at high risk for contracting AIDS. Lack of accurate information about HIV status and how to prevent the spread of AIDS may only create increased feelings of anxiety and fear of death for the child. Attempts at hiding a seropositive HIV finding from a child or an adolescent prevent opportunities for the expression of feelings and for learning how to cope with an uncertain future.

Adolescent AIDS Education: The majority of adolescent hemophiliacs are HIV positive and are capable of infecting others through sexual contact. Positive HIV findings in adolescents are of special concern. It is estimated that 50% of all adolescents will have had at least one sexual experience by the age of 19 (Allgeier & Allgeier, 1984). Data on other sexually transmitted diseases indicate high transmission rates among adolescents and minimal use of condoms to prevent the spread of infection (National Institute of Allergies and Infectious Disease Study Group, 1980). A study conducted in San Francisco of 1,326 adolescents' knowledge of AIDS found significant misperceptions and lack of adequate information about how AIDS is spread (DiClemente, Zorn, & Temoshok, 1986). An evaluation of adolescent and adult hemophiliacs' and family members' knowledge of AIDS (Mason et al., in press) found that 50% of the respondents did not know or did not believe that sexual partners were at risk for HIV infection. In addition, many of the respondents did not know what a positive HIV finding meant.

The surgeon general has strongly recommended teaching children and adolescents about AIDS and safer sexual practices. (See also chapter 5.) This recommendation, under the best of circumstances, is a major undertaking requiring the support of school administrators, teachers, health care workers, and parents. A recent evaluation of teachers and health care workers (Liebling, Wertz, Sorenson, Kessler, & Heeren, 1986) has indicated an inadequate knowledge of AIDS and the means of transmitting the virus. Results from a recent survey of school nurses attending a seminar on AIDS education revealed that, as a group, they had less accurate knowledge than a hemophilia sample from the same region (Huszti, Olson, & Mason, 1987). It will be necessary to provide a means of teaching large groups of educators and health care workers about AIDS before any national school program can be implemented. In the rapidly changing field of AIDS research, new information is being published each month. For example, a different but related immuno-deficiency virus, variously called HIV-2 and HTLV-IV, has been found (Gallo, 1987). At the time of this writing, little was known about the natural history, or incubation period of HIV-2. Therefore, educational programs must present both what is known and what is not known.

Adults: The increased survival rates for hemophiliacs in the past 2 decades has allowed a large number of young men with hemophilia who would not have lived long enough in the past to enter the work force, marry, and father children. Adults with hemophilia who are HIV-positive must now consider the risks to themselves as well as their partners of not engaging in safer sexual practices and of having children. A survey of hemophilia treatment centers by the NHF and the CDC found that 10% of the wives of HIV-positive hemophiliacs also had HIV antibodies (CDC, 1987). A more recent study of heterosexual contact between adults where one partner had contracted AIDS through intravenous drug use, blood products, or homosexual activities indicated that 58% of the spouses had HIV antibodies at the time of enrollment in the study or demonstrated seroconversion during the 18-month study (Fischl et al., 1987). Failure to use barrier contraception and engaging in oral-genital sex were associated with seroconversion. Although sexual transmission of AIDS in the United States has primarily been through homosexual contact, data from Africa suggest that there is a one to one ratio of males to females contracting the disease, presumably through heterosexual contact. The data strongly suggest that spouses of hemophiliacs are at risk for contracting HIV unless they choose to engage in safer sexual practices. Obviously, one consequence of safer sexual practices is indefinately postponing conception. Should the female partner become pregnant, the parents must decide between terminating the pregnancy or risking the birth of an HIV-infected child.

Summary of Clinical Observations: The primary mandate with respect to AIDS from federal funding sources for the comprehensive hemophilia centers is to prevent the spread of the HIV virus and minimize the negative psychosocial effect associated with the threat of AIDS. It has been suggested that models of coping with seropositive HIV test results may be analogous to coping styles used by newly diagnosed oncology patients. Furthermore, Faulstich (1987) has suggested that the same pattern of responses and coping styles (i.e., denial, anger, bargaining, and acceptance) are seen in individuals diagnosed with cancer and those diagnosed with AIDS. Nevertheless, receiving a diagnosis of AIDS, a diagnosis of cancer, or an HIV-positive test result is each a uniquely different situation, none of which lends itself to a common pattern of coping. The diagnosis of cancer presents the individual with a serious illness and an uncertain outcome. The diagnosis of AIDS presents the individual with what is now considered a fatal disease—most individuals have survived only 24–36 months (Volberding, 1985). The

76

HIV-positive test result presents the individual with very ambiguious information about a fatal disease.

Certain reactions to the three diagnoses do differ. Susan Tross (1986) evaluated gay men who had been informed of a positive HIV seroconversion and found that many of them suffered from extreme anxiety and suicidal ideation. Depression, panic attacks, and suicidal thoughts have also been found in gay men receiving a diagnosis of AIDS (Dilley, Ochitill, Perl, & Volberding, 1985). However, among cancer patients, denial is the more common reaction at diagnosis, and suicidal ideation is not commonly observed among hemophiliacs receiving an HIV-positive test result or a diagnosis of AIDS.

A model that explains the different reactions to the finding of a HIV antibody screening test must take into account the premorbid functioning of the individual, the manner in which the individual has handled stress and illness in the past, the meaning of this illness for any individual, and the changing reactions of the public toward individuals in various high-risk groups. For example, an intravenous drug user may have used drugs as a means of coping with stress and avoiding painful situations, may have had a premorbid personality that included significant personality dysfunction, and may have had little social support form family and friends. Again, a positive HIV finding may force some homosexuals to inform friends and family members of their sexual orientation. The social stigma of AIDS contracted through homosexual contacts may cause increased social isolation and stress. Feelings of guilt and punishment concerning homosexual activity may surface at this time.

Hemophiliacs, however, have had to deal with the effects of a chronic illness all their lives. Issues of control, altered life-style, and medical treatment are not new to them, and blood products have always carried the potential risk of hepatitis infection. The initial response of hemophiliacs and their families to this new crisis seems to have been that of feelings of anxiety and the need for accurate information from a trusted source. Long-term adjustment suggests a return to daily living, coping with life events, and maintaining a low level of anxiety. Hemophiliacs appear to have maintained social contacts and family support and continue to use the psychological support available through hemophilia centers. It therefore appears that the psychological reactions of hemophiliacs to HIV-positive test results are significantly different from the reactions of other groups to AIDS and of cancer patients (Agle et al., 1986; Tross, 1986).

Effect on Comprehensive Care Centers

Organizational Structure: In order to understand the profound effect that HIV infection has had on comprehensive hemophilia care centers, it is necessary first to describe the typical organizational structure, staff composition, and responsibilities of a comprehensive care team. A basic understanding of such centers and how patients and families have utilized them will enable the incoming mental health professional to integrate his or her expertise more effectively within the overall goals of the team. The vast majority of pediatric hemophilia patients in the United States are receiving services through comprehensive care centers. It is therefore unlikely that a mental health researcher/practicioner will experience any success in providing services to the pediatric hemophilia population without the cooperation of the centers.

Comprehensive hemophilia diagnostic and treatment centers usually have a core team that consists of a hematologist (medical director), a nurse coordinator, a social worker, and possibly a secretary or an office manager. In addition, consultants to the core team include an orthopedic surgeon, a dentist, a physical therapist, and a psychologist or psychiatrist. Only 7% of the comprehensive centers enjoyed the full-time services of a mental health professional in 1986. Evaluation and crisis intervention are usually handled by a social worker. Until very recently, it has been uncommon for a psychologist to be actively involved in the comprehensive care of the child with hemophilia and his family.

According to the *Directory of Hemophilia Treatment Facilities* (1986), there are 131 comprehensive hemophilia clinics in the United States. Of these, 64 (49%) have a full-time nurse coordinator, nine (7%) have a full-time mental health professional, and one has a physician devoting full time to hemophilia-related activities. There are not enough hemophilia patients enrolled at each center to employ all members of the team fully. Most patient management is accomplished over the phone by the nurse coordinator, the physician's assistant, or (less frequently) the hematologist. The medical director may have a personal interest in hemophilia; however, the director's caseload of cancer patients typically prohibits his or her active involvement in the administration concerns and daily care of the pediatric hemophiliac and his family.

Typically, only the nurse coordinator's position is fully funded in hemophilia treatment centers (*Directory of Hemophilia Treatment Facilities,* 1986). As a result, counseling parents about medical, financial, social, family, and occupational concerns falls to the nurse coordinator. In addition, the nurse coordinator may be placed in the position of carrying out the administrative functions of the center. Thus, the nurse coordinator, or some other designated individual, is left in the difficult position of having the majority of responsibilities but only limited training and authority. The nurse coordinator is typically the hemophilia families' pipeline to the hospital and to the specialists on the comprehensive team.

Prior to the discovery of an HIV-contaminated blood supply, the primary tasks of the core comprehensive team (especially the nurse coordinator, social worker, and physician's assistant) were education about hemophilia, encouragement of compliance with home treatment, record keeping, and counseling parents concerning child rearing. Decreased hospitalizations and increased employment of individuals with hemophilia demonstrated the centers' excellent record (Goldsmith, 1986).

During the development of regional comprehensive centers, many health care workers were drawn to hemophilia care because it provided them with the opportunity to treat patients with a chronic but not terminal illness. In fact, it was not uncommon for health care providers in oncology settings to transfer to hemophilia clinics in an effort to avoid the stresses associated with caring for many terminally ill patients.

Hemophilia clinics offered health care workers the opportunity to form long-term personal relationships with the patients and their families and to become a part of the hemophiliac's family system. The treatment centers have earned the trust of the hemophilia patient and his family because they have provided excellent health care. They have also been effective in that they have allowed parents to share concerns about and responsibility for child-rearing decisions. As a result, parents and health care workers have established a mutually supportive and satisfying relationship. The parents and patients have developed a healthy dependency on the treatment centers. Now this relationship is threatened on several fronts.

Effect of AIDS: Contamination of the blood supply with HIV has presented the hemophilia staff with the task of treating the terminally ill patient and his family. They have had to accept the fact that many of their pediatric patients, whom they have followed since infancy, are at risk for developing AIDS.

At NHF conferences during 1985–86, providers openly expressed their feelings of sadness as well as overwhelming guilt for advocating a treatment regimen that has eventually led to their patients' contamination. Physicians and nurses must now focus their energy on helping families cope with the stress of a child's or spouse's exposure to a deadly virus and the inability of the medical community to predict who will develop AIDS. Education about AIDS and the prevention of the spread of the virus has become a primary focus. Mental health professionals are being enlisted to join the medical staff to meet these new challenges.

An initial response from the NHF to the HIV-infected blood supply was to attempt to prevent panic among patients and families and encourage them *not* to avoid treating bleeds. In 1985, there was concern that individuals with hemophilia would be associated with illegal intravenous drug use and/or homosexual activity. It was feared that such an association would present such problems for hemophiliacs as expulsion from school, loss of jobs for family members, or quarantining of all hemophiliacs. These concerns were not unfounded (see chapter 4).

Advice from the NHF to treatment centers focused on decreasing patient anxiety and providing AIDS education for families. General AIDS education in schools and communities, as a means of primary prevention of prejudice toward hemophiliacs, was not a priority of the NHF, nor has it been strongly supported by hemophilia parent groups. While gay rights groups sought out public forums to warn against unsafe sexual practices and increase federal funding for research and health care, the NHF quietly tried to decrease fears among hemophiliacs without trying to draw public attention.

The Division of Maternal and Child Health (DMCH), the NHF, and individual comprehensive hemophilia centers have quickly recognized the need for expanding psychosocial services to the hemophilia population. In 1986, the CDC made available to the homophilia centers through DMCH $2.5 million for the development of risk-reduction programs and psychosocial services. In 1987, CDC support was increased to $3.5 million, and the 1988 budget has allocated $6.3 million. This funding has and will continue to affect the nature of comprehensive core teams. Before the CDC's funding of hemophilia centers, only 7% had a full-time mental health professional on staff. This figure is dramatically increasing. For example, the five comprehensive hemophilia centers in the Department of Health and Human Services Region VI (Texas, Oklahoma, and Arkansas) have more than doubled their mental health staff in the past 12 months. Currently, three of the five centers have increased their staff to include a full-time psychologist.

PSYCHOSOCIAL PREVENTION
AND INTERVENTION STRATEGIES

Wanted. A psychiatrist, psychologist, clinical social worker, nurse clinician, public health professional, educator, or physician's assistant to work with hemophilia patients and their families. Necessary skills include developing, implementing, and evaluating public and patient education programs about AIDS, conducting individual, family, and group therapy, educational and neuropsychological assessment, allocating financial and emotional resources for pediatric

AIDS patients and families, conducting and evaluating stress management seminars for health care professionals, families with hemophilia, hospital staff, and school nurses. Applicants must have
experience in dealing with chronic and terminal illnesses in children.
An understanding of the medical model, the political structure of
hospitals, basic immunology, hematology, and virology concepts
are very useful. Applicants need own transportation for state travel
(home visits) and be willing to be on call 24 hours per day. Salary:
$18,000–$40,000 (depending on academic degree and experience).

This exaggerated advertisement illustrates the wide variety of skills
necessary if a single professional is to meet the needs of the pediatric
hemophilia population and hemophilia centers. From an inspection of
this advertisement, one can identify three basic areas in which intervention is necessary: 1) providing AIDS education to families; 2) providing
stress management for health care workers, hemophiliacs, and family
members; and 3) providing psychological services to HIV-positive and
pediatric AIDS patients and families. A prerequisite for successfully ac-
complishing these services, however, is the mental health professional's
ability to gain the trust and respect of the hemophiliac's comprehensive
health care system.

Many hemophilia centers are seeking mental health professionals to
join their core team to provide services to their patients. The resulting
shift in the composition of the core team may not be entirely welcomed
by the patients or all staff members. More often than not, the person
designated to provide psychosocial services will be someone new to the
hemophilia center or someone who has not previously been a member
of the core team. It is likely that a new member to the comprehensive
team will be viewed with mistrust, which may be openly expressed by
the patients and their families and covertly expressed by the more experienced comprehensive team members, who see their roles and responsibilities changing.

The task of the new member is twofold. First, the mental health professional must assist members of the team in defining their own roles and responsibilities and clarifying how these duties relate to the overall goals of the team. An understanding of the concerns and issues outlined above should sensitize the mental health professional to the potential sense of loss of roles, function, and relationships patients and core team members may be experiencing.

Second, the mental health professional must establish a trusting relationship with the patient population. The hemophiliac's history would suggest that he (and his parents) had relied on a single contact person through which they received health care services. The mental health professional's task will involve obtaining sensitive information not previously in the domain of hemophilia care, information, for example, on sexual behavior, relationships with relatives, and so on. As one parent stated to her son's nurse coordinator, "What do you expect me to say to some psychologist I don't know when he asks if I have any psychological problems? I tell him 'Hell no!' "

Both the comprehensive team and the patient need to be educated about what services the mental health professional can and cannot provide. A likely way to accomplish this is for the team first to consider carefully and to agree on the new roles of each member of the team. Then, the family's contact person (usually the nurse coordinator) can educate the family about the availability of new services and resources.

Another possible avenue to gaining the trust and acceptance of the pediatric hemophilia population is to become associated with the NHF chapters. There appears to be great variability across the nation in the strength of local chapters. If these parent and patient groups are active, the incoming mental health professional may profit from going to their meetings and observing their activities. Like anyone else, hemophilia patients and families need reassurances that the mental health professional is truly concerned about their well-being.

AIDS Education
Until a cure for AIDS or a vaccine against the disease is found, the primary goal for the mental health professional is to prevent the spread of

HIV infection. For mental health professionals working with children with hemophilia, this requires educating the patient and his family about the virus and how it is transmitted. Home safety infusion needs to be reiterated to the patients and parents. Proper cleaning of spilled body fluids needs to be taught. Sexual counseling for adolescents is extremely necessary. Compliance with recommended health behaviors has been and continues to be a major concern for mental health professionals.

Families with a child who is not experiencing any AIDS-related symptoms may not be pleased to find that a greater emphasis has been placed on AIDS education and prevention during comprehensive evaluations. The statement "The hemophilia clinic has turned into an AIDS clinic" has been made by parents of both HIV-positive and HIV-negative children. Thus, there is a need to tailor teaching about HIV, AIDS, stress management, and school problems to the affected individuals and families. Other strategies to provide up-to-date information about AIDS and how to prevent the spread of HIV to other family members have included mailing NHF and local treatment center newsletters and digested research reports, holding educational workshops, and making presentations at parent group meetings. All these methods of disseminating information are encouraged by the NHF.

The clinical observations that some families are ambivalent about or resistant to discussing AIDS, HIV, and sexual practices may appear to be inconsistent with the needs assessments suggesting that patients and parents want more information about these topics (Brondolo et al., 1986; Mason et al., in press). One explanation for this discrepancy may be that parents and patients are ambivalent about the new demands AIDS has placed on them and the subsequent shift in emphasis they observe in their treatment centers. Furthermore, Agle et al. (1986) and Brondolo et al. (1986) have suggested that the initial levels of distress and panic have subsided and that families are now trying to return to a state of normalcy. However, patients and families frequently admit that they are currently experiencing an undercurrent of concern that creeps into their awareness at various times. This sets the stage for the devel-

84

opment of ambivalence toward the hemophilia center. Similar reactions are commonplace among pediatric cancer patients. When patients are not in the clinic or hospital for chemotherapy, they can avoid thinking about their situation. Returning to the clinic forces them to recognize the seriousness and uncertainty of their medical condition.

Psychological Services to Patients with AIDS and HIV Infection

The mental health professional needs to establish a network of support for those patients with AIDS and to prepare such a network for those who may later develop AIDS. Helping the family of a pediatric hemophiliac with AIDS involves interventions at many different levels. Unlike other childhood terminal illnesses such as leukemia, a powerful social stigma is associated with AIDS, and many concerns about transmission of the HIV are being expressed by school administrators, parents of the patient's classmates, and others. The mental health professional not only is faced with helping a family prepare for the death of one of its members but also must serve as the family's advocate in addressing the concerns and fears of those who have, in the past, served as support systems for the family.

Stress Management

The mental health professional is also faced with assisting families who have a child who is HIV positive and asymptomatic. For these families, there is tremendous uncertainty about what will happen, when it will happen, how they will behave if and when it happens, and, finally, how to continue living in the present in the midst of the unknown future.

General stress management techniques may offer families cognitive, behavioral, and psychophysiological techniques to cope with daily life stresses. Recent literature on stress management has focused on the ability to cope with the continual small stressors of daily living as a more effective way to learn to cope with anxiety. By presenting stress management programs that focus on how to handle daily life events, concerns and fears about AIDS are put in perspective as one of the many challenges of daily living. Thus, the mental health professional can contribute to rebalancing the focus of the comprehensive care center. This focus also allows families to leave the treatment center with stress-reduction strategies that do not always focus on AIDS.

Offering stress management strategies for treatment center staff may also be an appropriate task for the mental health professional. However, providing these services presents potential conflicts. Provision of psychological services to both the patient and the staff places the mental health worker in a dual relationship with the staff. It may be difficult to be both a consultant/therapist to the team and a member of that team. The mental health professional, as a team member, may be best utilized only as a provider to the patient. Consultation services outside the team may well serve the needs to provide psychological services to the team, *including* the mental health professional on that team.

SUMMARY

Position wanted. My present employment will be cut to half time owing to decreased need for psychological services as a result of a successful vaccine and treatment for AIDS. I am a clinical psychologist with extensive experience working as a team member on a hemophilia treatment center team. Have provided individual, family, marital, and group therapy for HIV-positive children and children with AIDS. Knowledge of educational, psychodiagnostic, and neuropsychological testing. Have experience working with medical staff, school administrators, teachers, and parents. Enjoy working in a multidisciplinary setting, providing stress management, crises intervention, and networking. Looking for same in new job. Will send vita on request.

It is hoped that a successful treatment and vaccine for HIV infection will be found in the future and that the need for psychologists working with HIV-positive and AIDS patients and families will diminish. Until that time, psychologists can play an important role in helping children, adolescents, and families cope with the uncertainty of HIV exposure.

REFERENCES

Agle, D. P. (1964). Psychiatric studies of patients with hemophilia and related states. *Archives of Internal Medicine, 114*, 76–82.

Agle, D., Gluck, H., & Pierce, G. F. (1986). The risk of AIDS: Psychologic impact on the hemophilic population. *General Hospitals Psychiatry, 9*, 11–17.

Agle, D. P., & Mattsson, A. (1968). Psychiatric and social care of patients with hereditary hemorrhagic disease. *Modern Treatment, 5*, 111–124.

Allgeier, E. R., & Allgeier, A. R. (1984). *Sexual interactions*. Lexington, MA: Heath.

Brondolo, E., Clemow, L., & Saidi, P. (1986, September). *Assessment of psychosocial needs concerning AIDS in hemophiliacs, their relatives, and staff*. Paper presented at the 38th annual meeting of the National Hemophilia Foundation, Washington, DC.

Browne, W. J., Mally, M. A., & Kane, R. P. (1960). Psychosocial aspect of hemophilia: A study of twenty-eight hemophilic children and their families. *American Journal of Orthopsychiatry, 30*, 730–740.

Centers for Disease Control. (1982). Pneumocystis carinii pneumonia among persons with hemophilia A. *Morbidity and Mortality Weekly Report, 31*(27), 365–367.

Centers for Disease Control. (1987). HIV infection and pregnancies in sexual partners of HIV-seropositive hemophilic men—United States. *Morbidity and Mortality Weekly Report, 36*(35), 593–595.

Centers for Disease Control. (1988a). Update: Acquired immunodeficiency syndrome (AIDS)—worldwide. *Morbidity and Mortality Weekly Report, 37*(18), 286–295.

Centers for Disease Control. (1988b). Safety of therapeutic products used for hemophilia patients. *Morbidity and Mortality Weekly Report, 37*(29), 441–444, 449–450.

Curran, J. W., Lawrence, D. N., Jaffe, H., Kaplan, J. E., Zyla, L. D., Chamberland, M., Weinstein, R., Lui, K., Schonberger, R., Spira, T. J., Alexander, W. J., Swinger, G., Amman, A., Solomon, S., Auerbach, D., Mildvan, D., Stoneburner, R., Jason, J., Haverkos, H. W., & Evatt, B. L. (1984). Acquired immuno-

87

deficiency syndrome (AIDS) associated with transfusions. *New England Journal of Medicine, 310*(2), 69–75.

Davis, K. C., Horsburgh, C. R., Hasiba, U., Schocket, A. L., & Kirkpatrick, C. H. (1983). Acquired immunodeficiency syndrome in a patient with hemophilia. *Annals of Internal Medicine, 3,* 284–286.

DiClemente, R. J., Zorn, J., & Temoshok, L. (1986). Adolescents and AIDS: A survey of knowledge, attitudes and beliefs about AIDS in San Francisco. *Public Health Briefs, 76*(2), 1443–1445.

Dilley, J. W., Ochitill, H. N., Perl, M., & Volberding, P. A. (1985). Findings in psychiatric consultation with patients with acquired immune deficiency syndrome. *American Journal of Psychiatry, 142,* 82–86.

Directory of hemophilia treatment facilities. (1986). New York: National Hemophilia Foundation.

Elliott, J. L., Hoppes, W. L., Platt, M. S., Thomas, J. G., Patel, I. P., & Gansar, A. (1983). The acquired immondeficiency syndrome and mycobacterium avium—intracellulure bacteremia in a patient with hemophilia. *Annals of Internal Medicine, 98,* 290–293.

Eyster, M. E., Goedert, J. J., Sarngadharan, M. G., Weiss, S. H., Gallo, R. C., & Blattner, W. A. (1985). Development and early natural history of HTLV-III antibodies in persons with hemophilia. *Journal of the American Medical Association, 253*(15), 2219–2223.

Faulstich, M. E. (1987). Psychiatric aspects of the acquired immune deficiency syndrome. *American Journal of Psychiatry, 144,* 551–556.

Fischl, M. A., Dickinson, G. M., Scott, G. B., Klimas, N., Fletcher, M. A., & Parks, W. (1987). Evaluation of heterosexual partners, children and household contacts of adults with AIDS. *Journal of the American Medical Association, 257,* 640–644.

Gallo, R. C. (1987). The AIDS virus. *Scientific American, 258,* 47–56.

Goldman, D. S. (1985, May 2). Hemophilia treatment and research. *National Hemophilia Foundation,* pp. 1–4.

Goldsmith, J. C., Moseley, P. L., Monick, M., Brady, M., & Hunninghake, G. W. (1983). T-lymphocyte subpopulation abnormalities in apparently healthy patients. *Annals of Internal Medicine, 98,* 294–296.

Goldsmith, M. F. (1986). Hemophilia, beaten on one front, is beset on others. *Journal of the American Medical Association, 256*(23), 3200.

Goldy, F. B., & Katz, A. H. (1963). Social adaptation in hemophilia. *Children, 10*(5), 189–193.

Handford, H. A., Mayes, S. D., Bagnato, S. J., & Bixler, E. O. (1986). Relationships between variations in patients' attitudes and personality traits of hemophilic boys. *American Journal of Orthopsychiatry, 56*(3), 424–434.

Hanford, H. A., Mayes, S. D., Bixler, E. O., & Mattison, R. E. (1986). Personality traits of hemophilic boys. *Development and Behavioral Pediatrics, 7*(4), 224–229.

Hargraves, M. A., Jason, J. M., Chorba, T. L., Holman, R. C., Dixon, G. R., Eastham, J. C., Brownstein, A. P., Heine, P., Agle, D. P., & Evatt, B. L. (1986). Hemophiliac patients' knowledge and educational needs concerning AIDS. (Available from Centers for Disease Control, Division of Host Factors, Atlanta, Ga 30333).

Hilgartner, M. W., Aledrot, L., & Giardina, P. J. V. (1985). Thalassemia and hemophilia. In N. Hobbs and J. M. Perrin (Eds.), *Issues in the care of children with chronic illness* (pp. 299–323). San Francisco: Jossey-Bass.

Huszti, H. C., Olson, R. A., & Mason, P. J. (1987, November). *Survey of school nurses and school teachers knowledge of AIDS.* Paper presented at the annual meeting of the Oklahoma Psychological Association, Oklahoma City, OK.

Jones, P. (1984). *Living with hemophilia:* 2nd English edition. Boston: MTP.

Katz, A. H. (1963). Social adaptation in chronic illness: A study of hemophilia. *American Journal of Public Health, 53*(10), 1666–1675.

Lawrence, D. N., Jason, J. M., Bouhasin, J. D., McDougal, J. S., Knutsen, A. P., Evatt, B. L., & Joist, J. H. (1985). HTLV-III/LAV antibody status of spouses and household contacts assisting in home infusion of hemophilia patients. *Blood, 66*(3), 703–705.

Levine, P. H. (1985). The acquired immunodeficiency syndrome in persons with hemophilia. *Annals of Internal Medicine, 103*, 723–725.

Liebling, L. G., Wertz, D. C., Sorenson, J. R., Kessler, L., & Heeren, T. C. (1986, September). AIDS *education for health care providers.* Paper presented at the 114th annual meeting of the American Public Health Association, Las Vegas.

Luban, N. L., Kelleher, J. F., & Reaman, G. H. (1983). Altered distribution of T-lymphocyte subpopulations in children and adolescents with haemophilia. *Lancet, 1*, 503–505.

Ludlam, C. A., Tucker, J., Steel, C. M., Tedder, R. S., Cheingson-Popov, R., Weiss, R. A., McClelland, D. B. L., Philip, I., & Prescott, R. J. (1985). Human T-lymphotropic virus type III (HTLV-III) infection in seronegative hemophiliacs after transfusion of factor VIII. *Lancet, 2*, 233–236.

Markova, I., McDonald, K., & Forbes, C. (1980). Impact of hemophilia on child-rearing practices and parental cooperation. *Journal of Child Psychology and Psychiatry and Allied Disciplines, 21*, 153–162.

Mason, P. J., Olson, R. A., Meyers, J. G., Huszti, H. C., & Kenning, M. (in press). AIDS and hemophilia: Implications for interventions with families. *Journal of Pediatric Psychology*.

Mattsson, A., & Gross, S. (1966). Adaptational and defensive behavior in young hemophiliacs and their parents. *American Journal of Psychiatry, 122*, 1349–1356.

Meyer, P. R., Modlin, R. L., Powars, D., Ewing, N., Parker, J. W., & Taylor, C. R. (1983). Altered distribution of T-lymphocyte subpopulations in lymph nodes from patients with acquired immunodeficiency-like syndrome and hemophilia. *Journal of Pediatrics, 103*(3), 407–410.

Mulhern, R., Crisco, J., & Camitta, B. (1981). Patterns of communication among pediatric patients with leukemia, patients, and physicians: Prognostic disagreements and misunderstanding. *Journal of Pediatrics, 99*, 480–483.

National Institute of Allergies and Infectious Disease Study Group. (1980). *Sexually transmitted disease summary and recommendations* (Report No. 81–2213). Washington, DC: Department of Health, Education, and Welfare, of National Institutes of Health.

Olch, D. (1971). Personality characteristics of hemophiliacs. *Journal of Personality Assessment, 35*, 72–79.

Piot, P. (1987, June). *The natural history and clinical manifestations of HIV-infection.* Paper presented at the third International Conference on AIDS, Washington, DC.

Pool, J. G., & Shannon, A. E. (1965). Production of high-potency concentrates of antihemophilic globulin in a closed bag system: Assay in vitro and in vivo. *New England Journal of Medicine, 273*, 1443–1447.

Poon M., Landay, A., Prasthofer, E., & Stagno, S. (1983). Acquired immunodeficiency syndrome with pneumocystis carinii pneumonia and mycobacterium avium-intracellular infection in a previously healthy patient with classic hemophilia. *Annals of Internal Medicine, 98*, 287–290.

Ragni, M. V., Tegtmeier, G. E., Levy, J. A., Kaminsky, L. S., Lewis, J. H., Spero, J. A., Bontempo, F. A., Handwerk-Leber, C., Bayer, W. L., Zimmerman, D. H., & Britz, J. A. (1986). AIDS retrovirus antibodies in hemophiliacs treated with factor VIII or factor IX concentrates, cryoprecipitate, or fresh frozen plasma: Prevalence, seroconversion rate, and clinical correlations. *Blood, 67*(3), 592–595.

Redfield, R. R., & Burk, D. S. (1988). HIV-infection: The clinical picture. *Scientific American, 259*, 90–98.

Smith, P., & Levine, P. (1984). The benefits of comprehensive care of hemophilia: A 5-year study of outcomes. *American Journal of Public Health, 74*, 616–617.

Surveillance of hemophilic-associated acquired immunodeficiency syndrome. (1986). *Journal of the American Medical Association, 256*(23), 3205–3206.

Survey of non-U.S. hemophilia treatment centers for HIV seroconversions following therapy with heat-treated factor concentrates. (1987). *Journal of the American Medical Association, 257*(13), 1706–1709.

Tross, S. (1986, November). *Psychosocial problems in AIDS spectrum disorders.* Workshop seminar presented at the Carle Medical Communications' Psychosocial Interventions in Cancer and AIDS, Denver, CO.

Varni, J. W. (1981). Behavioral medicine in hemophilia arthritic pain management: Two case studies. *Physical Medicine and Rehabilitation, 62*, 183–187.

Varni, J. W., Gilbert, A., & Dietrich, S. L. (1981). Behavioral medicine in pain and analgesia management for the hemophilic child with factor VIII inhibitor. *Pain, 11*, 121–126.

Volberding, P. (1985). The clinical spectrum of the acquired immunodeficiency syndrome: Implications for comprehensive patient care. *Annals of Internal Medicine, 103*, 729–733.

•

CHAPTER FOUR

The Schooling of Children with AIDS: The Development of Policies

MARSHA B. LISS

No other aspect of pediatric acquired immunodeficiency syndrome (AIDS) has generated more controversy, tension, and highly volatile emotional encounters than rumors that a child with AIDS is about to enroll or has enrolled in school. In response to headlines and news broadcasts across the country, parents, children, and school administrators have reacted to the current controversy even when no afflicted child was involved. "What if . . . " has become the basis for school board meetings and community involvement. In some communities, the questions have led to the calm development of policy. In others, the mere consideration of the issue convinced parents that there already was a problem when none existed.

Now that it is virtually certain that blood and blood products will no longer be sources of transmission of the virus for transfusion recipients and hemophiliac children (see the discussion in chapter 1 of the prevalence of pediatric AIDS and the development of the virus), popular opinion assumes that the schooling issue is not critical. This assumption is based on the idea that children born of intravenous drug users or other human immunodeficiency virus (HIV) positive mothers will not live long enough to attend school. However, as HIV infection spreads through the heterosexual population, there will be more cases of children infected with HIV (Bottoroff, 1985). As the medical field increases its knowledge about the virus and develops more sophisticated treatment techniques that delay or prevent progression from seropositive to AIDS, there will inevitably be more infected children reaching school age. Thus, the question of schooling HIV-infected children is far from moot.

This chapter will describe how school placement decisions have been and are being made for HIV-infected children. In order to understand the policy development process, I will first discuss the methods of transmission of HIV infection, which methods, if any, occur in the school setting, and published recommendations on the subject. Then I will examine the most publicized cases of HIV-infected children, those that have become the focus of public policy decisions as well as judicial review. A consideration of case law involving schooling decisions for children with other diseases (herpes and hepatitis) will form the background for this examination. Next, opinions of school district administrators and physicians about the schooling of children with AIDS will be presented. The problems faced by these groups and their interaction with the community at large is important in understanding the decisions that have been made. Finally, I will review the development of legislative responses to the AIDS crisis as it relates to school placement and consider responses to past epidemics.

Ultimately, I come to three principal conclusions. (1) School districts need to develop systems and procedures to deal with emerging diseases and health concerns as they arise, before they attract media attention and stimulate public fear. (2) The cases of children with AIDS/HIV should not be referred to the courts because of time and confidentiality issues involved. (3) Education is essential in guiding the public and decreasing panic and fears.

Is the Virus Likely to be Transmitted in the School Setting?

The Centers for Disease Control (CDC, 1985) and the American Academy of Pediatrics (AAP; 1986, 1987, 1988) report that there is no evidence HIV infection is transmitted in day-care, preschool, or public school settings. They further believe that the types of behaviors grade school children generally exhibit in school are not likely to transmit the virus. Current medical information indicates that activities such as spitting, kissing, sharing food, and breathing on someone are unlikely to transmit the disease: "Transmission via th[ese] route[s] will be as rare as contracting syphillis from the proverbial toilet seat" (Church, Allen, & Stiehm, 1986, p. 426). The risk of contracting AIDS in school has been compared to "the risk of being struck by lightening when you walk out the front door in the morning" (Partida, 1986, p. 1046).

However, some common activities are likely to transmit the virus. For instance, the childhood custom of becoming blood brothers with a best pal (*District 27 Community School Board v. Board of Education of the City of New York,* 1986) should be strongly discouraged between children exposed in any way to the virus. Of course, it should also be discouraged between children known to be carrying hepatitis or any other infectious disease. Also, the possible risks of HIV transmission associated with bloody fights should be considered a basis for discouraging such actions, although the actual risk remains unknown (Partida, 1986). Obviously, the best way to prevent the spread of infectious disease in all children is to prevent practices likely to transmit the infection.

Other potentially risky behaviors include handling fecal material and biting that leads to the breaking of skin and bleeding. However, since saliva contains only a small concentration of probably inactive HIV, the possibility of HIV transmission on contact with an infected child's saliva is considered highly remote, and precautions recommended to be taken after contact with infected saliva are therefore extremely conservative. The "normal first aid techniques applicable to any human bite—i.e., washing with soap and water followed by the application of alcohol" (p. 172)—are sufficient to destroy any virus that is

95

present (Schwarz & Schaffer, 1985). The main concern remains blood-blood contact between children, which is unlikely to occur with biting as a young child's bite usually does not pierce the skin (*District 27 Community School Board v. Board of Education of the City of New York*, 1986).

Initially, the CDC (1985) recommended that HIV-infected children below preschool age should not attend day-care centers or be placed in other group care situations. Similarly, while recognizing that the chance of HIV transmission among preschoolers was remote, the AAP (1986, 1987) recommended that decisions regarding enrollment of an infected preschooler or day-care child be made on a case-by-case basis, taking into account the child's control of body excretions, his or her exhibition of biting, and the presence of oozing skin lesions. A more recent AAP policy statement (1988) on pediatric guidelines for schools indicated that "no studies in the literature or cases reported to the Centers for Disease Control suggest transmission of HIV by urine, feces, saliva, tears or sweat. Similarly, no studies or reports have suggested transmission of HIV in school or day care settings" (p. 1). Hand washing alone is now considered sufficient for non-blood-containing bodily fluids (urine, feces, vomit, tears, and nasal-oral secretions). Additionally, the report notes that, while theoretically HIV could be transmitted through biting or oozing skin lesions, there are no reports of this mode of transmission of the virus. The AAP recommends that infants be admitted to day-care facilities on a case-by-case basis and that children be admitted if they display appropriate health, neurological development, and behavior.

School attendance also presents a threat to HIV-infected children. Not only is it possible that the infected child will infect others, but the infected child himself may be exposed to common childhood illnesses (e.g., chicken pox, colds) that his weakened immune system cannot handle and that are therefore potentially fatal (Bittle, 1986).

What Has Been the Response by the Courts and Schools?
There is very little case law on pediatric AIDS. At least eight cases (in Queens, NY; Swansee, MA; Kokomo, IN; Carmel, CA; Atascadero,

CA; Orange County, CA; Plainfield, NJ; Arcadia, FL) have made headlines across the country, but only two (those in New Jersey and New York) have reached judicial review and become published cases on which courts and the public can rely.[1] Before turning to the pediatric AIDS cases, I will lay a foundation by examining the outcome of cases involving other infectious diseases (e.g., herpes and hepatitis).[2] The tendency in all the court cases has been toward the enrollment of the children in school classes.

Herpes and Hepatitis: Burris (1985) notes that only relatively recently have courts begun to use medical information when deciding school placement cases. One model for making decisions in health law suggests a two stage process: assessment of the medical risk and determination that the plan to be adopted is the least restrictive. Both the Rehabilitation Act (1973) and the Education for All Handicapped Children Act (1975) were developed to ensure that handicapped individuals receive proper treatment and that their handicaps are not cause for discrimination. The cases involving children with infectious diseases decided under the Rehabilitation Act show that states may not interfere with or alter regular education and school attendance on "any basis less than valid medical necessity" (Burris, 1985, p. 495). "Medical necessity" means certain risk to the ill child or a high likelihood of transmission of the disease within the school setting.

---

1. Not all judicial decisions are published. Those that are not published do not appear in the judicial reviews and cannot be used as precedent by other courts. Thus, only those that are published (or reported) carry weight. However, unless the decision is from the same court (or from a higher court in the same jurisdiction), the decision, while of interest, may not necessarily be of substantial value in the judge's rendering of a decision.

2. There have been several cases concerning the education of children with poliomyelitis and the requirement of vaccination of children wishing to attend public school (In the Matter of Elwell, 55 Misc. 2d 252, 284 N.Y.S.2d 924 [1967]; McCartney v. Austin, 57 Misc. 2d 525, 293 N.Y.S.2d 188 [1968]; Davis v. State of Maryland, 294 Md. 370, 451 A.2d 107 [1982]). However, these cases have generally concerned exemption from immunization on the basis of religious beliefs, not the right to education in regular classes. Additionally, it should be noted that the polio virus is transmitted much more easily than HIV is. Moreover, unlike HIV, polio can be spread by airborne means.

In Council Bluffs, Iowa (*Council Bluffs Education Association v. Council Bluffs Community School District,* 1984), a young child with herpes was admitted to school; this decision was subsequently challenged by parents in a panic "colored by fears and misinformation" (Burris, p. 500). The court's proposed solution was either isolation of the child or daily examination of the child at school. This case clearly reflects a failure of the court to make a decision based on integrative objective medical criteria; rather, it gave way in the face of community pressure. Such a decision stigmatizes the child inappropriately and imperils the child's social development.

The courts have also ruled on hepatitis B, which is transmitted in ways similar to HIV only more easily. Hepatitis B is a virus with a long incubation period. The disease, once the virus is activated, may result in sufficient damage to the liver to be fatal. In *New York State Association for Retarded Children, Inc. et al., v. Carey et al.* (1978), the Board of Education had decided to isolate all handicapped children (mentally retarded) who had active hepatitis B or were carriers of the virus. At trial and on appeal (1979), the court noted that the "health hazard posed . . . was [less] than a remote possibility . . . the activities that occur in classroom settings were not shown to pose any significant risk that the disease would be transmitted" (1979, p. 652).

The Court of Appeals also noted that isolation of the children would stigmatize them and deprive them of the activities in which children normally participate. Segregation of the children, the court noted, would violate the Constitution, state statutes, and the Education for All Handicapped Children and Rehabilitation acts. Both courts also stressed that administrative review would relieve public panic and reduce the need for court intervention in the future. The decision balanced the importance of education with the likelihood of disease transmission and resulted in the enrollment or continued enrollment of the children in their regular school classes.

Pediatric AIDS: In situations involving the school attendance of children with AIDS where school officials educated the public and involved the community in decision making, panic was reduced, fears were diminished, and supportive environments evolved. However, in those situations where the public was not involved in policy-making, where education was limited, and where there was a cloak of secrecy, panic, fear, emotional reactions, and public displays of hostility were evinced. In the less volatile situations, the media have served as a public health educator, helping to decrease concern, reduce tension, and avoid hasty, uninformed, or misinformed decision making by publishing updated information and interviews with Department of Health officials.

The first school district knowingly to allow a student with AIDS to attend school was that of Swansee, Massachusetts (Kirp, 1987a). The school system's reaction to the problem provides an example of the sensitivity that communities can proactively show in such situations. School officials and teachers knew that a teenage boy in the system had contracted AIDS, but they chose not to make an issue of it, and his identity was not made public until his death. When a school official was asked to comment on the rumor that a child with AIDS was enrolled, the reporter was asked to consider the psychological effect of such a disclosure. Eventually, the rumor was published, and tensions erupted. School board and town meetings, however, helped the community band together and support the family rather than isolate or shun them and their son, and the boy was allowed to continue attending school. Throughout, the press acted responsibly, neither mentioning the boy's name nor seeking information about the family. Even now, only the boy's first name has been released. The boy remained actively involved in high school and social activities until his death.

On November 26, 1985, the guardian of a young HIV-infected hemophiliac boy, Channon Phipps, went to court in Orange County, California, to ask that Channon be readmitted to school (*Phipps v. Saddleback Valley Unified School District,* 1986). The school had placed him in a home-tutoring program after his guardian had voluntarily advised the school district that Channon had tested positive for exposure to HIV. At first, tutoring was irregular and lasted only approximately 2 hours per week. The quality and quantity of the instruction increased dramatically, however—from 2 to 4 hours per week to 10 hours per

week—when the suit was filed. Even so, the guardian felt that home tutoring was socially isolating the boy and that Channon was missing a
great deal by not being in a classroom with peers.

The family maintained that the school board decision was capricious
and arbitrary and that Channon's due process rights had been violated.
In February 1986, the judge ordered an examination of the boy by the
director of epidemiology and disease control of the County Department of Public Health, who concluded that it was safe for both Channon and the other children for Channon to be readmitted to school
("AIDS Virus," 1986). The school district was therefore ordered to
readmit the boy. In conjunction with the county director of public
health, the school district sent out health care packets about AIDS to the
school. Some parents protested and refused to send their children to
school. The school district, however, chose not to appeal the decision.
Channon returned to school the following week and has continued to
attend to this date.

A somewhat different situation obtained in Kokomo, Indiana
(*White v. Western School Corp.*, 1986). Ryan White was 14 years old—
post—elementary school—when he was diagnosed with AIDS and removed from school. Just as in the case of Channon Phipps, the county
health administrator determined that the boy posed no threat to other
students, and Ryan was readmitted to school. He has since become a
symbolic figure in the fight for the civil rights of AIDS patients. An
American Civil Liberties Union lawyer commenting on the case as it
developed remarked, "Ryan White will take it as far as he can. Hopefully
he'll live that long" ("School Counsel," 1985).

In one sense, Ryan was fortunate since the case proceeded no further
and he was not subjected to continued legal battles. However, parents
of the other children protested outside the school and the White's
home, and hostile comments were made to the family through the mail
and by telephone. Some students were willing to socialize with Ryan,
but most of the community was unsympathetic. The Whites subsequently moved to another school district, and the hostility they encountered in Kokomo was not repeated.

Still another scenario was enacted in Atascadero, California, when the school district tried to formulate an AIDS policy. After public debates and discussions with authorities, the school's ad hoc AIDS placement committee developed detailed guidelines that were more conservative than those of the CDC. Under the guidelines, a 5-year-old boy infected with HIV was allowed to enroll in kindergarten. Unfortunately, after his enrollment, he bit a classmate. The bite did not break the skin, and the bitten child's parents shrugged off the incident. But the community panicked and demanded action. The infected child was suspended, the placement committee reconvened, and psychological assessments of the boy's aggressive behavior were ordered. A federal district court judge determined (in the first such decision at that level) that, under the school district's guidelines, the boy was allowed to attend school (*Thomas v. Atascadero Unified School Dist.*, 1986). The school board was relieved that the case went to court because "the judgment had taken matters out of the hands of the administration and the school board, absolving them of responsibility" (Kirp, 1987b, p. 12) and allowing them to retain the community's trust.

Sometimes the process of discussion and action takes place too slowly to benefit the child. In Carmel, California, a grade school boy infected with HIV was kept from attending school and received home instruction; he died before any action was taken to ensure his entry into the normal school and social milieu. The family noted (Kirp, 1987a) that the rejection their son experienced was the most difficult aspect of the illness for him to deal with.

The only two cases to result in published court opinions were filed at approximately the same time in early 1986. The first, *District 27 Community School Board v. Board of Education of the City of New York* (1986), resulted from heated community picketing and debate in Queens, New York, when the information was leaked that an unidentified girl with AIDS had been attending school "somewhere in the district" for several years.[3] The court listened to 5 weeks of expert testimony on studies of

---

3. For extensive discussion of this case, see Weiner (1986) and Schwarz and Schaffer (1985).

transmission of the disease and the effects of casual contact within the family. Relying on the medical experts, equal protection claims, the Education for All Handicapped Children and Rehabilitation acts, and the social implications of exclusion and testing, the court found no justification for testing all children or for excluding HIV-infected school age children.

The court then recommended enrollment of HIV-infected children on a case-by-case basis, as the CDC (1981, 1982, 1985) had outlined. The court also recognized that to exclude HIV-infected children who have developed symptoms of AIDS and not those who are seropositive but asymptomatic would be futile as well as discriminatory under the Rehabilitation Act. It determined that all infected children could remain in school and that the current hygiene and first-aid policies were adequate (Schwarz & Schaffer, 1985). In addition, the court determined that decisions regarding notification and identification of the child should rest with the review board of the school system but that surveillance methods that compromise the child's privacy should be avoided. It is important to note that the furor over the enrollment diminished even before the case reached the courts. The lesson for other school districts was clear—devise a policy before it is needed, when there is concern but no emergency or tension, and inform the public of what decision is being made and why.

In the second published case, *Board of Education v. Cooperman* (1987), two New Jersey school board actions were appealed. In one action, the school had denied enrollment to a preschool girl with AIDS, placing her instead on home instruction. In the second action, a kindergarten girl with AIDS-related complex (ARC) and her 9-year-old uninfected brother were denied admission to school. In reviewing the cases, the New Jersey Supreme Court considered the importance of education with peers for social and cognitive development and determined that hearings investigating the overall health of a child needed to be held before the decision to exclude that child could be made.

The New Jersey cases represent the highest level of appeal that cases have reached to date. The final decision remanded the cases to the lower courts to conduct full hearings in accordance with the court's recommendations. One of the New Jersey Supreme Court Judges indicated that the children would be readmitted to their schools and that school attendance would be the policy followed for all HIV-infected children in the state. The preschool child was placed in a class for handicapped children because of her neurological deficits; the other children were enrolled in regular classes.

In the summer of 1987, the media covered the story of the three Ray boys from Arcadia, Florida (see, e.g., "The Other AIDS Epidemic," 1987). The boys were infected with HIV as a result of treatments for hemophilia. They were initially excluded from school. But, after examining the policies of other communities and gathering extensive medical information on AIDS, the school district overturned its decision and allowed them to reenroll in school. Unfortunately, the school board made no attempt to educate either the community or the school staff. The community reacted by protesting the boys' school attendance, protests that culminated in the firebombing of the Rays' home on August 28, 1987. The family has since moved to another community, where the boys were automatically enrolled and accepted in school without incident. That community has received information from the district and health officials to educate and allay fear.[4]

It is clear that even well-articulated policies are not sufficient if the policies and the information behind them are not disseminated to the public. The difference between what happened in Swansee, Massachusetts, and Arcadia, Florida, may be one of lack of communication of information and community empathy. The public receives much of its information from informal sources such as the media. It is important that the media report on the positive adjustment of infected children and their school communities while minimizing stories that increase

4. It should be noted that there are many cases of HIV-infected children in another Florida city, Miami. Many of these children have attended school in Miami with little or no public protest, panic or litigation.

public panic and misinformation. If the public receives only one side of the story, then it is that much more difficult for positive actions to be taken (Liss & Younkin, 1987).

Many of these cases have attracted extensive media coverage (see, e.g., "AIDS," 1985; "The Fear of AIDS," 1985; and "Kids with AIDS," 1987). Clearly, such attention has made anonymity for these children impossible. How much privacy can Ryan White of Channon Phipps have left after their pictures have been flashed across the country on television screens and printed in newspapers and magazines? They will always be identified and stigmatized as "AIDS" carriers or patients or, as a recent article suggests, as bearers of the "new scarlet letter(s)" (Church et al., 1986).

Such branding might be avoided if children remain unidentified in media reports and court records, and the best way to remain unidentified is to avoid legal intervention. Decisions about whether to allow HIV-infected children to attend school require the integration of medical information, not legal analyses. Legal analysis and the adversarial nature of the judicial system serve only to compromise the family's privacy and confidentiality and disrupt the normal routine of a potentially or currently ill child. These issues might be better addressed elsewhere than in court. Already, regulations at several levels of government have been developed or proposed to provide services or protection against discrimination to AIDS patients.

Additional concerns about the psychological and social development of HIV-infected children are raised by the issues of media attention and anonymity. The AIDS cases pursued so far have taken from several months to over a year to resolve, and during that time the children involved have been kept away from what should be normal activities—school attendance and the accompanying interactions with peers. The importance of social interaction is recognized even by peers of the children with AIDS. A friend of the boy in Swansee, Massachusetts, said, "It wouldn't feel right if he were at home, if he couldn't communicate with his friends. He belongs here, it's his home" (Kirp, 1987a, p. 16).

Regardless of the final decision in a case, however, or the statements of medical authorities, some parents may continue to feel uncomfortable about the HIV-infected child attending school with their children or hostile toward the child's family if he or she has been identified. Some parents will discourage their children from playing with, sitting near, or even interacting in any way with a child they know to be infected. Only if the child's identity is not known can the school environment be kept as near normal as possible. These publicized cases that I have reviewed here raise most of the issues of concern in discussions of the need for balance—the balance between "the benefits of an unrestricted setting" and the risk of transmission of the disease (CDC, 1985, p. 519).

What Do School Administrators Think?
A Survey of Changing Attitudes

Reflections of Societal Concerns: In this section, I will outline some of the approaches taken and the attitudes adopted by school districts toward the school placement question. The process by which school districts developed policies is important if we are to understand public opinion and the acceptance of HIV-infected children in schools. Twenty school district administrators in two large Southern California counties were contacted during 1986 in order to determine their knowledge about and attitudes toward AIDS. The districts differed in size (encompassing from 4 to 25 elementary schools), income level (some serving predominantly lower-class blue-collar communities and others upper-middle-class white-collar communities), and ethnic/racial composition (containing large and small proportions of minority families). As a result, the sample was very heterogeneous and likely to represent the range of reactions of school districts in other parts of the country. In addition, while there may be differences across the country in terms of parents' values and general beliefs, health concerns that may affect children are likely to evoke common emotional reactions from parents.

The superintendent of each school district was first contacted to determine the appropriate administrators (directors of pupil services, health care coordinators, or the superintendents themselves) to interview. Interviews were then conducted using a semistructured format. While the same topics and information were covered in each interview, the order of questions and the amount of time spent on each topic differed, depending on the interviewee's willingness to discuss the topics and how involved the individual district was in developing policy and educational programs about AIDS. Interviews lasted 20–75 minutes. In all cases, anonymity of the district and administrator was maintained. Information was collected regarding the health care decision-making process in general and the effect that parental pressure has had on the administration. Permission was also obtained during the interview to administer questionnaires to the grade school principals to assess their knowledge about and attitudes toward AIDS. (For a discussion of the principal questionnaire data, see Liss & Younkin, 1987.) Generally, the more well developed the state or the district's policies, the more the principals knew about AIDS and the more positive their attitudes toward dealing with an HIV-infected child in their schools.

During the data collection phase, the first court case in California (*Phipps v. Saddleback Valley Unified School District,* 1986) was decided. This decision appeared to have a major impact on the responses. Administrators interviewed before the decision was handed down were more interested in obtaining information than in discussing their own concerns. Their cautiousness and concern over public reaction led to refusals by school boards or superintendents to allow principals to participate. Following the decision in the Phipps case, school district personnel were more willing to participate and often volunteered to assist in administering the project. Several superintendents were so interested in sensitizing their principals to the issues that they volunteered to duplicate, distribute, and return the questionnaires themselves.

Clearly, school district officials felt more comfortable discussing AIDS and AIDS policy because they now had judicial precedent favoring the enrollment of HIV-infected children to rely on. Open discussion of the subject was also encouraged by positive media coverage of the decisions. Such support enabled school districts to take positions with which some parents in their communities might disagree. Weiner

(1986) observed a similar shift in attitudes during the height of the controversy in Queens. Coverage at first focused on public panic and the extraordinary measures suggested to isolate the virus or those carrying it (e.g., quarantines, special medical care). However, public attention eventually turned to the search for a cure, the provision of services to the afflicted, and the rights of AIDS patients. The result was that, the more people knew about AIDS, the more compassionately and reasonably they could deal with such issues as school admission ("AIDS—Knocking," 1985).

School Districts' Responses: On being questioned, the school districts either (1) refused to discuss the subject, (2) were concerned solely with legal liability, (3) were concerned primarily with community response to their actions, or (4) gave an informed, educated reply. These responses reflect neither ethnic nor socioeconomic differences among districts.

Those administrators who avoided the issue entirely generally were curt, sought information without revealing any policies, were evasive, and avoided follow-up conversations. Meetings with them were, not surprisingly, brief—less than 20 minutes. They indicated their districts would have no problems because there would be no cases of HIV infection in their communities—a conclusion based on the presumably socially acceptable behaviors of parents, few student problems, highly involved parent-teacher associations, and a low incidence of contagious diseases. Clearly, these administrators were not well informed about HIV transmission and demographics.

Administrators in the second group, those who emphasized financial and legal liability, were more concerned with the bureaucratic consequences of the presence of an HIV-infected child in the district. What if a teacher or a playmate contracted AIDS from a student, or what if a child contracted AIDS from a teacher? They referred to increases in liability insurance in general and to the types of activities that have been curtailed because of the increases in insurance costs. These attitudes, while not enlightened, are indicative of the continuing debates over an educational institution's responsibilities. Diseases transmitted by means of readily observed activities can be easily managed. However, a disease such as AIDS, which is transmitted by such usually private acts as sharing needles or engaging in sexual contact, are much more difficult for schools to manage (Mawdsley, 1986). The administrators concerned with liability believed that parents would want absolute guarantees that the virus would not be transmitted between children. They were also concerned with whether confidentiality could be maintained if they chose to participate in the project. These concerns are to some extent legitimated by recent trends in litigation: segregation of AIDS children might involve "legal problems under the [Education for All Handicapped Children Act] or a tort theory of right to privacy," but then again if action is not taken suits alleging failure to provide a safe environment might be brought (Mawdsley, 1986).

Administrators concerned mainly with community response represented school districts that had already discussed the issue but had decided not to adopt any formal policies. They indicated that, while they did not personally object to the attendance of HIV-infected children in their schools, they did not want to be responsible for that decision and preferred to pass responsibility along to the courts. They focused their attention instead on minimizing chaos and panic. They felt that, if they were confronted with the problem of an infected child, their initial response would be to refuse admission and to offer home tutoring. Then, should parents appeal the decision in court and the court rule that the child should be admitted to school, they would not be responsible for the consequences. Such an attitude is likely to lead to school-district shopping by parents and panic when a case does arise (Weiner, 1986).

Administrators who gave a well-informed and educated response showed a concern for the social development of the child as well as a recognition of the need to educate the district's parents. The districts they represented developed policies before they were faced with the problem of an HIV-infected child. In the process, the administrators attended conferences for health care professionals, gathered information from the CDC and other agencies, presented detailed reports to the school board, outlined the CDC suggestions for schools to follow, held mandatory in-service sessions at each school to educate the staff, and implemented programs to educate parents. The policies they developed were based on the CDC guidelines (1985), outlined a case-by-case approach with periodic review, and excluded only children too ill to attend school of any kind, disabled children whose hygiene needs might increase the risk of transmission, and children prone to drooling or biting. (The 1985 CDC guidelines propose different activities for neurologically impaired children and preschoolers.)

Almost all the administrators contacted in the latter days of data collection fell into the fourth category, those who gave a well-informed response. Many of these districts were developing programs to educate both parents and school personnel. Two of the representatives to the California State Task Force on AIDS came from school districts in this category, indicating their high degree of commitment to solving the problems presented by AIDS. Others of these administrators have represented their districts throughout the country at AIDS awareness programs and planning sessions.

A focus on balancing needs and risks is clearly evident in the CDC and AAP guidelines as well as in decisions made by physicians, school districts, and the courts. Children who are too ill to attend school should not be classified with children whose symptoms are in remission. The latter are able to attend class and interact with peers with no risk to the other children and only minimal risks to themselves. The decision to keep a child home is put in the hands of the child's physician and parents.

Physicians' Perspectives

In this section, I will outline comments from school and hospital physicians, focusing on their recommendations for the schooling of HIV-infected children at the preschool and elementary school levels. These comments were elicited during interviews conducted during the same time period as the interviews with administrators were. The semistructured format concentrated on types of policies advocated for schools, methods of transmission, attention to health care policies in schools in general, and the professional's involvement in the treatment of patients with HIV infection.

One interviewee, a school district staff physician whose district was in the process of policy development, felt that the most important aspect was the maintenance of as normal a life and schedule for an HIV-infected child as possible. He noted that, if parents do not want their child in class with an HIV-infected child, then the healthy child, not the infected child, should be shifted to another class.

The physicians at Children's Hospital of Los Angeles (Childrens-LA) are interesting because of their recommendations regarding education as well as their provision of information to families of infected children. They believe that HIV-infected children should be allowed to attend preschool, elementary, and secondary schools as long as they are healthy, in control of their body secretions, and not prone to behaviors such as biting.

The physicians observed that HIV-infected children must, however, face other restrictions in life. They may become seriously ill in the near future if they are not currently ill. Those who are asymptomatic but are seropositive will need to be told, when they are old enough (at least by puberty), that they will always have the uncertain risk of becoming seriously ill. Their condition and abilities may become further impaired, they may require repeated hospitalization, and, as a result, their regular activities, such as schooling, may be interfered with. Adolescents will have to learn that they can transmit the virus during sexual relations. Recognizing the need for guidance in these areas, the American Psychological Association (1987) and the U.S. Department of Health and Human Services (1987) have published pamphlets aimed at people providing support services for individuals infected with HIV.

The physicians note, however, that AIDS is not nearly as easily transmitted as hepatitis. They note also that precautions taken regarding AIDS may not only prompt schools to reexamine and update their health care policies and educational programs but also assist in the prevention of other infectious diseases. Universally, the physicians recommend that high-risk practices (becoming blood brothers, all contact with fecal matter, or persistent slobbering) be curtailed or approached with appropriate precautions (e.g., the use of gloves, cleansing with bleach solutions, or hand washing after elimination in the case of fecal material—Black, 1986; Price, 1986).

Some physicians believe that the school nurse should know about an AIDS diagnosis in case of illness or accidents but that there is no reason for classroom teachers to know. They recognize, however, that it would be difficult to maintain confidentiality. Church et al. (1986) propose that necessary precautions should involve informing the principal, the teacher, and the school nurse. They also suggest the development of better precautionary methods of handling any and all situations. These recommendations are similar to those of the CDC and the AAP that confidentiality should be maintained and that schools should adopt more stringent routine sanitary procedures since there may be infected but unidentified children in many school districts throughout the country.

What Examples from History Can Assist in Decision Making?
Acquired immunodeficiency syndrome is not the first disease to trigger panic and public concern. Nor is it the first disease to be the object of legal decisions. Neither, unfortunately, is it likely to be the last. Epidemics have often resulted in "a paralyzing effect" ("The Fear of AIDS," 1985, p. 23) that is sometimes far worse than the disorder itself. Leprosy (Roark, 1986) and bubonic plague (Abramson, 1985; Albury, 1985), for example, resulted in the blaming or scapegoating of portions of the population. Cholera and polio epidemics have also invoked fear in the population (Albury, 1985). Reactions to such diseases often involve quarantine, banishment, torture, and, at the very least, stigmatization and isolation.

While it seems unlikely that children with AIDS will be stereotyped or branded as scapegoats the way homosexuals have been, some children, especially hemophiliac adolescents, may have to deal with both the stigma of the disease and people's suspicions that they are gay. As earlier cases indicate, many of the children have been considered "untouchables."

Most recent concerns have been over herpes and hepatitis in children. Prior to enactment of the Education for All Handicapped Children Act, school systems would have opted merely to exclude any sick child or carrier from school. Herpes and hepatitis provide examples of how infectious diseases can be handled in school systems.

Throughout history, epidemics have also been sources of literary and artistic inspiration, and AIDS has been no exception. There has been a great deal of effort and care to avoid stereotyping, to increase public sensitivity, and to decrease myths about the disease in the airing of movies, television series episodes, and documentary programs on AIDS. Despite that care, there are also examples of media blunders that contribute to negative stereotypes and attitudes.

Legislative Issues

Legislation has been enacted in some states (e.g., California, New York) to protect the identity of AIDS patients and thereby to prevent stigmatization or discrimination. The major impetus for these bills was the fear that AIDS would be considered a problem primarily of the homosexual population and therefore used to justify discrimination against gay men and women. Los Angeles Municipal Code, Ordinance includes sections referring specifically to education, employment, and housing. Section 45.86 specifically states, "It shall be an unlawful educational practice for any person to . . . deny admission or to impose different terms or conditions on admission" because of a diagnosis of HIV infection.

One federal statute, the Education for all Handicapped Children Act, might be applicable to decisions involving the school attendance of HIV-infected children, especially given the recent Supreme Court decision (*School Board of Nassau County, Florida v. Arline,* 1987) that the protections provided under the Rehabilitation Act extend to communicable diseases. Both the Rehabilitation and the Education for all Handicapped Children acts address discrimination against the handicapped. Ms. Arline, a schoolteacher, carries the tuberculosis virus; most of the time she is free of symptoms and is not in a communicable state.

However, she does have episodes during which the virus is active and capable of being transmitted. The U.S. Supreme Court ruled that her rights to employment were protected under the Rehabilitation Act. It then defined a handicapped person as anyone with a communicable disease whose rights and access to services (employment, education) would be jeopardized if they were not afforded protected under the act.

Jones (1986) suggests that similar arguments could be made regarding the Education for All Handicapped Children Act and HIV-infected children. Jones also advocates considering these children on a case-by-case basis as well as balancing collective and individual rights. On this analysis, children would be considered handicapped only if they were severely affected by the disease; at that point, however, such serious illness might preclude school attendance, rendering the question moot. If the HIV-infected child does not have special needs, then she or he does not fit the act's definition of handicapped, and she or he should not be excluded from the classroom. There are additional cautions to be considered since, according to recent case law (*Board of Education of the Hendrick Hudson Central School District v. Rowley,* 1982), the quality of the education to be provided is not that which would maximize the child's potential but would merely provide rudimentary or minimal skills and knowledge (*Board of Education of Hendrick Hudson Central School District v. Rowley,* 1982; Jones, 1986). Thus, guidelines are needed that indicate not only that the HIV infected should be allowed to attend school but also that the education provided them should be commensurate with their abilities, not merely a minimal intervention.

Conclusion

There is a great deal more that can be done as more is learned about the AIDS virus, more cases on the schooling subject are decided, and public opinion becomes less volatile. It is hoped that as knowledge is gained and public opinion changes, attitudes and policies within the school systems will change as well. In time, positive community actions may become the norm, and media treatment of the issues may become less sensational and more informative. Such developments would greatly assist community adjustment.

Three policy concerns can be identified on the basis of the history of panic and resulting stigma regarding disease, the state of transmission of the AIDS virus and comparisons of it to hepatitis, and issues of confidentiality. First, education must be recognized as an important process at all levels—not only to foster the social and cognitive growth of children but also to provide sufficient information to allay the fears of adults. The only way to dispel fear and suspicion is through education—of staff, parents, and health care professionals. Second, schools need to develop broader policies and procedures that provide for some system of review when any new health concern develops. Third, it should be recognized that the courts are not the ideal setting to resolve problems concerning the schooling of HIV-infected children. Decisions made in the offices of physicians and school district administrators are more likely to protect the confidentiality of the infected child and serve the best interests of all the children involved.

In the past, the failure of public health and educational policies has led to psychological crises (in the cases of, e.g., herpes, hepatitis, and polio). The court and public health responses to children with AIDS represent a departure from earlier strategies and seem likely to help stem the panic. The school placement issue has evoked strong reactions from communities, yet, "even in this emotionally charged context, the Constitution requires that policymakers ground their decisions in reality" ("The Constitutional Rights," 1986, p. 1292) and provide for the education of children with AIDS, AIDS-related complex, and HIV infection.

Burris's (1985) model, described earlier, suggests that, after the medical information is assessed, decisions need to be made that are based on the benefits to the child of school participation. How, then, are these decisions to be made, by whom should they be made, and how can they be made without inciting public panic? A tentative proposal is to establish review boards composed of parents, physicians, mental health professionals, and school district personnel. Rather than convening only when a crisis arises, such panels could meet on a regular basis to assess the current state of knowledge and review how policies are working. We need to recognize that AIDS is not the first disease to concern the schools and that it will not be the last. The lesson from the media's attention to and treatment of AIDS is that mechanisms are needed to ensure the continuous examination of health care policies and continuing efforts at public education. These mechanisms need to include exercises assisting educators in alerting their students to and educating them about unsanitary and unnecessary risk-taking behaviors. "It's an auspicious time for school nurses to help revamp all of the school's hygienic practices" ("AIDS Knocking," 1985, p. 13; see chapter 5 for an extended discussion of this issue).

REFERENCES

Abramson, H. (1985, October 31). New generation of "Typhoid Marys" face ostracism, jail for having AIDS. *Los Angeles Daily Journal*, p. 18.

AIDS. (1985, August 12). *Newsweek*, pp. 20–29.

AIDS—knocking at the schoolhouse door. (1985, November–December). *School Nurse*, pp. 8–19.

AIDS virus should not keep student from class—official. (1986, February 12). *Los Angeles Daily Journal*, sec. 2, p. 1.

Albury, W. R. (1985). Historical reaction to "new" diseases. *Australian Journal of Forensic Science, 18*(1), 5–12.

American Academy of Pediatrics. (1986). School attendance of children and adolescents with human T lymphotropic virus III/lymphadenopathy-associated virus infection. *Pediatrics, 77*(3), 430–432.

American Academy of Pediatrics. (1987). Health guidelines for the attendance in day-care and foster care settings for children infected with human immunodeficiency virus. *Pediatrics, 79*(3), 466–469.

American Academy of Pediatrics. (1988, July). Pediatric guidelines for infection control of HIV (AIDS virus) in hospitals, medical offices, schools, and other settings. *AAP News*, pp. 8–10.

American Psychological Association. (1987, September). Mental health care in AIDS treatment goal of APA lobby. *American Psychological Association Monitor*, p. 26.

Bittle, E. H. (1986). Private rights v. public protection: AIDS in the classroom. *Compleat Lawyer, 7*, 7–9.

Black, J. L. (1986). AIDS: Preschool and school issues. *Journal of School Health, 18*, 560–566.

Board of Education of the City of Plainfield v. Cooperman & Board of Education of the Borough of Washington v. Cooperman. Nos. A–45–46. N. J. Sup. Court (April 15, 1987).

Board of Education of the Hendrick Hudson Central School District v. Rowley. 458 U.S. 176 (1982).

Bottoroff, S. (1985, October 7). School counsel tackle problem of AIDS children. *Los Angeles Daily Journal*, pp. 1, 17.

Burris, S. (1985). Fear itself: AIDS, herpes and public health decisions. *Yale Law and Policy Review, 3*, 479–518.

Centers for Disease Control. (1981). Pneumocystis pneumonia—Los Angeles. *Morbidity and Mortality Weekly Report, 30*, 250–252.

Centers for Disease Control. (1982). Possible transfusion-associated acquired immune deficiency syndrome (AIDS)—California. *Morbidity and Mortality Weekly Report, 31*, 652–654.

Centers for Disease Control. (1985). Education and foster care of children infected with human T-lymphotropic virus type III/lymphadenopathy-associated virus. *Morbidity and Mortality Weekly Report, 34*, 517–521.

Church, J. A., Allen, J. R., & Stiehm, E. R. (1986). New scarlet letter(s), pediatric AIDS. *Pediatrics, 77*(3), 423–427.

City of Los Angeles, California, Municipal Code. Article 5.8 (amended by Ordinance No. 85–160289).

The constitutional rights of AIDS carriers. (1986). *Harvard Law Review, 99*, 1274–1293.

Council Bluffs Education Association v. Council Bluffs Community School District. No. 84–66–W slip opinion (S. D. Iowa, December 31, 1984).

District 27 Community School Board v. Board of Education of the City of New York. 130 Misc. 2d 398 (February 11, 1986).

Education for All Handicapped Children Act of 1975. 20 U.S.C. 1401 et seq.

The fear of AIDS. (1985, September 23). *Newsweek*, pp. 18–25.

Jones, N. L. (1986). The Education for All Handicapped Children Act: Coverage of children with acquired immune deficiency syndrome (AIDS). *Journal of Law and Education, 15*(2), 195–206.

Kids with AIDS. (1985, September 7). *Newsweek,* pp. 50–59.

Kirp, D. L. (1987a). *Ordinary heroes.* Unpublished manuscript.

Kirp, D. L. (1987b). *Ryan's story: How a five-year-old boy taught a California town about* AIDS. Unpublished manuscript.

Liss, M. B., & Younkin, S. (1987, August). *Pediatric* AIDS: *The relationship between knowledge and policy.* Paper presented at the meeting of the American Psychological Association, New York.

Mawdsley, R. (1986). Privacy rights of AIDS victims. *Education Law Reporter, 31,* 697–707.

New York State Association for Retarded Children, Inc. et al., v. Carey et al. 466 F. Supp. 479 (1978).

New York State Association for Retarded Children, Inc. et al., v. Carey et al. 612 F. 2d 644 (1979).

The other AIDS epidemic. (1987, September 3). *New York Times,* sec. A, p. 26.

Partida, G. A. (1986). AIDS: Do children with AIDS have a right to attend school? *Pepperdine Law Review, 13,* 1041–1061.

Phipps v. Saddleback Valley Unified School District. No. 474981 (Orange County Superior Court, California, 1986).

Price, J. H. (1986). AIDS, the schools, and privacy issues. *Journal of School Health, 56*(4), 137–140.

Rehabilitation Act of 1973. 29 U.S.C. 794 et seq.

Roark, A. C. (1986, February 23). AIDS adds to history of epidemics. *Los Angeles Times,* pp. 1, 20, 21.

School Board of Nassau County, Florida v. Arline. (1987, March 3). *Law Week, 55,* 4245.

School counsel tackle problems of AIDS children. (1985, October 2). *Los Angeles Daily Journal,* p. 1.

Schwarz, F. A. O., & Schaffer, F. P. (1985). AIDS in the classroom. *Hofstra Law Review, 14,* 163–191.

Thomas v. Atascadero Unified School Dist. No. 886–609AHS(BY) (C. D. Cal., November 17, 1986).

U.S. Department of Health and Human Services. *Coping with* AIDS. Rockville, MD: National Institute of Mental Health.

Weiner, R. (1986). AIDS: *Impact on the Schools.* Washington, DC: Capitol Publications.

White v. Western School Corp. No. I. P. 85–1192–C (N. D. Ind. 1985).

•

CHAPTER FIVE

Educating Children and Youth about AIDS

SALLY E. DODDS

MARILYN VOLKER

HELEN F. VIVIAND

The purpose of this chapter is to define strategies that can be used by public schools to provide information and education to children and adolescents about the prevention of acquired immunodeficiency syndrome (AIDS) and the promotion of healthier lives. Though the schools are not the only or always the preferred route for educating children about AIDS, their role as the institution primarily responsible for education is pivotal in the understanding and prevention of this epidemic.

Sound AIDS prevention education can occur only after schools establish appropriate policies regarding such other AIDS-related concerns as the inclusion or retention of human immunodeficiency virus (HIV) infected children in the classroom. Despite sufficient existing federal and state laws that require free and uniform public education, equal access, and least restrictive educational environments, and despite clear recommendations from the Centers for Disease Control and the American Medical Association, AIDS evokes strong emotions in the public school setting. Administrators, teachers, and parents struggle to balance the right of the few with those of the many. Furthermore, to provide education specific enough to speak directly to the behaviors that transmit this deadly virus is to provoke a confrontation between issues of health and safety and issues of morality.

There was no national comprehensive plan or document to assist the schools in the development of their own AIDS education and prevention programs prior to 1988. Out of urgency, many school districts in the country began developing policies and procedures about AIDS and AIDS education. In December 1986, the U.S. Conference of Mayors (1987) conducted a survey of 73 of the country's largest school districts and 25 state school agencies to assess the degree to which AIDS policies and education were already being developed or implemented in the nation's schools. Of the local school districts, 54% were already providing some form of AIDS education to public school students. A small number of local school districts, especially those located in the metropolitan areas with the highest number of AIDS cases (New York, San Francisco, Los Angeles, Miami, and Houston), initiated AIDS education programs early in the epidemic. Programs in these cities include such components as teacher training, curriculum guides, and educational materials for students and staff. The information these programs provide to students is detailed, typically including the definition of AIDS, its causes and symptoms, routes of transmission, treatment, prevention (including safer sex information), and civil rights issues. The experiences of these cities can provide guidance to other districts whose programs are still in the planning stages.

This chapter focuses on the dilemmas faced by schools attempting to educate their students about AIDS. In a major metropolitan area with a high incidence of AIDS, we have worked extensively in assessing the institutional parameters of AIDS curriculum development and in preparing instructional and noninstructional staff for the delivery of that curriculum. One of us is a public school employee who co-chairs the local school board's AIDS task force. The other two work for a community

AIDS service organization—one is a certified sex educator with a broad base of experience in educating children about human sexuality, and the other is a social worker with a background in medical education. It is our fundamental belief that AIDS information and education must focus on the prevention of an epidemic in the context of positive interpersonal and sexual relationships and that it must consider the needs and concerns of the persons most involved in the lives of children—parents and teachers.

Specifically, a program of information and education for children on AIDS should consider the following strategies. (1) It should be developed with the school system in the context of prevailing community/family values and in cooperation with parents, educators, and others. (2) It should begin as early as possible in the schools, continue throughout the entire course of schooling, and be integrated into a variety of related curricular content areas. (3) It should address the critical need for adequate teacher preparation in the delivery of content, discussion of sensitive issues and concerns, and utilization of available resources. (4) It should include objectives and cognitive content that are developmentally appropriate and enhancing to the psychosocial/psychosexual development of the child. (5) It should foster an understanding of body integrity and safety, disease prevention, and positive health promotion, particularly as they relate to human sexuality and drug abuse. (6) It should acknowledge and include the range of potentials of human sexuality. (7) It should use relevant, specific, age-appropriate language. (8) It should encourage and support attitudes, values, and behaviors that are consonant with responsible decision making both interpersonally and as regards society. (9) It should include a means for evaluating the effectiveness of the program and the curriculum.

Three documents have guided the development of this chapter: *The Surgeon General's Report* (Koop, 1986), *Confronting* AIDS (National Academy of Science, 1986), and the Centers for Disease Control guidelines (1988). These bold statements provide a challenge to educators to provide accurate information about the behaviors that transmit the

AIDS virus in ways that do not alienate those who need to hear it. Wherever possible, statements from these sources will be cited to underscore the strategies listed above.

STRATEGY I

The surgeon general has observed, "Those of us who are parents, educators and community leaders, indeed all adults, cannot disregard this responsibility to educate our young. The need is critical and the price of neglect is high. The lives of our young people depend on our fulfilling our responsibility. . . . The threat of AIDS can provide an opportunity for parents to instill in their children their own moral and ethical standards. . . . The appearance of AIDS could bring together diverse groups of parents and educators with opposing views on the inclusion of sex education in the curricula" (Koop, 1986, pp. 5, 31).

Within any community, the role of the schools is broad and powerful. Beyond imparting knowledge and skill, the school extends its role to include the institutionalization of regional values. And, in any community, there is no single set of values; rather, there is a rich blend reflecting the diversity of race, ethnicity, religion, and historical traditions within it. Thus, local school boards are in a unique position to provide educational leadership in the face of the AIDS epidemic and to promote positive public health attitudes. However, the extent to which school boards meet the challenges of developing AIDS policies and curricula depends on the local level of fear about all aspects of the disease, or AIDS phobia, which is predicated on the fear and misunderstanding of such emotionally charged topics as contagious and infectious diseases, death and disfigurement, sexuality and sexually transmitted disease, and drug abuse.

In general, to begin to meet the AIDS challenges being faced by the schools, the entire school system must go through the difficult process of desensitization of heavily value-laden issues and acquisition of AIDS-specific information, especially data on epidemiology and future trends for the region. The process of desensitization must allow ample time for debate, discussion, and communication of emotionally charged topics.

Typical issues to be included are the extent of the school's role in public health and sex education, the extent to which descriptive language about sexual behavior can be specific, realistic perceptions of the level of sexual activity and drug use among children and adolescents in the district, and questions of liability about the provision of sensitive information.

Ample time must also be allocated for the process of acquisition of information. Some fundamental AIDS content areas, in need of frequent repetition, are definition of the spectrum of HIV infection, the clinical course of HIV infection, ways that viruses in general and AIDS specifically are transmitted, differentiation between behaviors that transmit the virus and groups at risk, and methods of reducing the risk of HIV infection. Once these content areas have been delineated, curriculum designers can begin to draft a basic AIDS curriculum, targeting three groups seen to be appropriate—students, employees, and parents. After developing the initial curriculum, the designers must be prepared to continue the development process, redefining and revising the curriculum to include greater specificity and a broader range of issues as comfort with the subject increases, scientific knowledge develops, and the urgency of the epidemic becomes more apparent.

These desensitization and acquisition processes should be initiated by planning, self-study, and education at the highest level, that of the school board itself. Creation of an AIDS task force, responsible to the superintendent, is a good first step. The membership of this task force deserves careful consideration to ensure democratic representation and consensus building as well as provision of state-of-the-art information about the AIDS epidemic, so that the board can define its role and develop appropriate policies. The task force should represent all major school components, including administration, elementary and secondary education, adult education, special education, vocational education, the Equal Employment Opportunity Commission, labor unions, personnel, the school board attorney, and parent-teacher groups. It should also include experts about AIDS and AIDS-related problems, such as physicians, public health officials, AIDS community service organization representatives, the media, and others. The U.S. Conference of Mayors survey found that 80% of school districts have worked with or are currently working with local or state health departments and that 50% have worked with various community organizations, including AIDS service organizations, gay service organizations, and the American Red Cross. Also participating on the task force should be individuals who reflect the unique racial and ethnic subpopulations of the community. Finally, the board must ensure that adequate financial and staff resources are allocated for the task force to perform its duties.

Curriculum is but one AIDS-related concern to be addressed by school boards. The task force needs a clear mandate to develop policy recommendations not only in curriculum development but also in such areas at the employment of HIV-infected personnel and the education of HIV-infected children. Over half—58%—the respondents in the USCM survey reported having policies on the management of students and employees with AIDS, and 72% currently conducting AIDS education programs also have AIDS management policies (see chapter 4.)

As one of its first orders of business, the task force should clearly formulate its objectives and then decide on a time frame within which to complete those objectives. Some of those objectives could include the following.

1. A comprehensive educational program might be arranged for the task force itself, using the best available AIDS experts in the community, that allows adequate time to discuss feelings and concerns related to AIDS issues. The focus of the program should be on the knowledge, attitudes, and values of members of the task force themselves, with a major goal being fear reduction. Too often, this critical step is not included with professional and scholarly people. In addition to surveying information about the transmission of HIV and the virus's effects, members should determine the scope of the problem in the district, articulate the diversity of religious and ethnic values of the community, and identify available internal and external resources to address the identified problems. Time might also be set aside for each task force member to evaluate

his or her own risk of exposure to HIV. While such reflection is generally silent, resultant anxiety may prompt a variety of reactions, including asking detailed questions about viral transmission, making negative and hostile comments abut socially stigmatized behaviors, and taking rigid positions in debate. Task force chairpersons must be prepared to recognize and cope with these reactions so as to facilitate the educational process.

2. The task force might collect and review AIDS policies, procedures, curricula, and educational materials from other school districts in other parts of the country. A diversity of materials allows task force members to assess the available choices and to provide a basis for formulating criteria to evaluate materials.

3. Issues and concerns raised by the review of such information and materials might be identified and discussed.

4. The applicability and/or modification of such materials for the school district's unique needs might be discussed.

5. A statement outlining the task force's philosophy might be drafted to guide the continued development of AIDS policies and educational/information programs. Of course those statements should be sent through appropriate channels for review and adoption.

6. Policies, procedures, and curricula might be drafted, along with recommendations for their implementation, and sent through appropriate channels for review and adoption.

7. A plan might be developed to disseminate all statements made by and all materials collected by the task force. Concerned parties receiving this information should include the school board, chief administrators, principals, instructional and noninstructional (e.g., custodians, food-service workers) staff, parents and parent-teacher groups, the union, and the media. The dissemination should take into account the specific informational needs and skill levels of the target audiences. Custodians and food-service workers will have very different concerns from classroom teachers about risk of exposure and may want to know in detail about sanitation and infection control techniques. Classroom teachers, on the other hand, may have concerns about presenting such emotion-

ally laden material to young people and may therefore need information about an appropriate format (see strategy 3 below).

Once these objectives have been met, the task force must maintain a vigilant and responsive role in the continuing process of AIDS information dissemination. When AIDS becomes more real and tangible within a particular school (as when an infected child or teach is actually identified in the classroom), there is an ongoing process of reeducation, reinforcement of ideas and strategies, and clarification of feelings. No longer is AIDS an abstract, hypothetical situation. Support mechanisms for staff at every level and strong position statements that are legally valid, endorsed by upper administration, the legal division, and labor management, must be anticipated and developed early in the planning process.

STRATEGY 2

Currently, schools have a unique challenge (as well as federal encouragement)—to integrate AIDS education into existing curricula in a developmentally sound manner. The surgeon general has stated, "Education about AIDS should start in early elementary school and at home so that children can grow up knowing the behavior to avoid to protect themselves from exposure to the AIDS virus. . . . Education concerning AIDS must start at the lowest grade possible as part of any health and hygiene program" (Koop, 1986, pp. 531).

From the elementary grades to high school, educational curriculum subcommittees need not only to develop specialized curricula for AIDS education but also to determine how and where they will be integrated into existing related classes. The USCM survey found the range of contexts for AIDS education in the districts surveyed to include sex education/family life, health education, drug abuse prevention, general science/biology, home economics, social studies and human ecology, and life management skills. Nearly 90% of the existing AIDS programs were integrated into health education classes, and about half were part of the sex education/family life curriculum (a substantial number of districts utilized both contexts).

The survey did not assess the role of specialized after-school organizations and clubs in AIDS education efforts. These clubs can provide unique opportunities for students to learn about AIDS issues and to become involved in projects to educate themselves while contributing to their communities. Relevant organizations include the debate, future teachers, health service occupations, science, and Key clubs.

The implementation of AIDS education programs in elementary schools has lagged behind that in the higher grades. The USCM data show that the majority of AIDS education is occurring at the junior and senior high school levels. At the time of the survey, 90% of the districts with existing AIDS education programs offer them in the tenth grade and 60% in the ninth grade. Only a small number (10) of the school districts were offering or planning to offer AIDS education at the elementary school level.

In the earliest grades, information that can be generalized to AIDS can be introduced to set the foundation for later, more specific AIDS education. San Francisco, for example, provides education about contagious diseases in grades 1–4; in grade 5, students are taught about the human reproductive system, maturation, and development. Having had this background, children may begin to learn about sexually transmitted diseases, including AIDS. Many basic health education concepts about reducing the risk of transmission of infections are already covered in elementary school curricula and are easily understood by young children (for further discussion, see strategy 4 below).

From the third grade through high school, information more directly related to AIDS can be progressively incorporated into science, health or physical education, and sex education classes. At successive grade levels, AIDS-specific information can be reintroduced and discussed in an increasingly complex manner, including a question-and-answer format that ensures that students' very personal concerns are addressed.

STRATEGY 3

Central to the success of AIDS education is an educator who provides a safe environment for discussion, engenders trust, demonstrates comfort with the material, and avoids editorializing, eroticizing, and moralizing. Regardless of the specialization of the person selected to provide that education (health educator, science teacher, school psychologist/social worker, guidance counselor, physical education or home economics teacher), he or she must be accepted by school officials, by parents, and, most important, by the students themselves. Some necessary qualities are ease with the material, the ability to answer questions in a nonjudgmental manner, and the ability to elicit a variety of feelings and values to use in the process of decision making.

In an attempt to gain some insight into the approach of teachers with responsibility for communicating information about AIDS to their students, eight teachers of a tenth-grade life management course (in which AIDS is covered) in the Dade County (Florida) Public Schools were surveyed. Questions were asked about preparation, curriculum, training, materials, and feelings about teaching the topic of AIDS. On the whole, the teachers felt well prepared to teach an AIDS curriculum component. However, this feeling was based on a personal commitment to researching and understanding the topic rather than on any official training and curriculum received from the school system. Rarely did these teachers adhere to the developed curriculum guide; many felt that it was outdated although it was less than a year old. Most relied on outside resources, such as the Dade County Public Health Unit, Health Crisis Network, Inc. (a local AIDS service organization), and the Centers for Disease Control. All the teachers expressed comfort in discussing the topic and seemed to be emphasizing the clarification of behavior and values rather than life-styles and risk groups. Though abstinence is the only risk-reduction strategy approved by the Dade County Public Schools, several of the teachers described other methods in their discussion of prevention techniques. Most of the teachers spent a week on the component and utilized a variety of supplemental instructional materials, including films and videos, speakers, brochures, new articles, a puppet show, and an anonymous question box.

Persons teaching AIDS curricula should be knowledgeable about basic aspects of the virus and its transmission and should receive updated information as new data become available. They also need to understand the most effective methods for presenting information and creating learning opportunities (e.g., puppets, trivia questions, poster contests, etc.) that are developmentally appropriate (see strategy 4 below). Teachers could also benefit greatly from workshops in human sexuality, led by a qualified professional, to explore their own feelings and values about sexual thoughts, feelings, and behaviors. Allowing students to express their own values without adult judgment is a skill developed only through practice and self-awareness. To discuss with students the sources of conflict among personal values as well as the risks associated with certain behaviors and life-styles requires a delicate balance between delivering facts and maintaining an openness for dialogue about consequences of personal choices and actions. Death and dying issues may also need to be discussed. Effective teacher preparation would include the opportunity to prepare questions and practice answers on all aspects of AIDS and AIDS-related issues with a group of peers.

Frequently overlooked in teacher preparation is the need to identify, address, and reduce the teachers' own fears, for example, anxieties about infectious diseases, feelings of inadequacy and of being poorly prepared when presenting sensitive and emotionally charged subject matter, and, perhaps, their own possible exposure to HIV infection. Teachers willing or expected to assume the responsibilities of AIDS education deserve adequate preparation. To demonstrate the complexity of the teacher preparation process, we provide the following description of one school system's response to placing HIV-infected children in the classroom.

In Dade Country, Florida, where twin sisters with AIDS-related complex were being mainstreamed, a comprehensive orientation and preparation program was conducted. Four months before the children actually began school, a district administrator, a school district attorney, the president of the teachers union, and the education director of the local AIDS service organization met with the school principal and selected staff. Together they determined a need to introduce the mainstreaming of the infected children, without identifying who those children would be, to the entire staff and to the parent-teacher association. These meetings were arranged. Teachers were given the opportunity to voice their concerns and fears. Although most were supportive or neutral, some were not and stated that they would ask for a transfer if children with AIDS were placed in their classrooms. In a bold move, the district administrator, with support from the union president, stated that teachers had a right to request a transfer but that, unless other justification was demonstrated, this situation did not warrant transfer. They further stated that very concerned teachers might reconsider their desire to remain employed by the school system if they felt the situation to be too threatening.

Somewhat unique to this school district is its multiethnic, multilanguage community. To meet the needs of parents at the school, separate sessions were held simultaneously—one for Haitian Creole-speaking parents, one for Spánish-speaking parents, and one for English-speaking parents. Interestingly, parents voiced fewer concerns and seemed less frightened than had been anticipated and were initially more supportive than the teachers.

The next step was to plan a series of meetings with the specific classroom teachers who would be directly involved with the children, including the physical education teacher, the assigned guidance counselor, and the teacher aides. Another outside resource was added to the team—a pediatric AIDS social worker from the medical center who knew the children and their family. At this level, the teachers spoke from the heart. They asked what specific words they could use to explain the problem of the twins to other children if they were hostile and what they should say if irate parents of another child appeared at the classroom door demanding to take their own child home. They discussed ways of modeling accepting behaviors in the classroom and ways to use the many issues raised by AIDS as teaching opportunities. One teacher asked about how to handle a situation where, for example, one of the twins was playing softball and perspiring while holding the ball and another child refused to take the ball. The teachers as a group suggested

that the teacher hold the ball before passing it on, thus actively modeling appropriate behavior.

In order to maximize AIDS education, teachers should be aware of
community resources that can assist, reinforce, and provide models for
the classroom. Examples of these valuable resources are local AIDS service organizations, local public health department personnel, the
American Red Cross, local medical associations, and such federal agencies as the U.S. Public Health Service and the Centers for Disease Control. Awareness of and access to existing brochures and audiovisual
materials appropriate to the classroom is important. Resources must be
identified and evaluated for children and adolescents with respect to
their trustworthiness, credibility, accuracy, accessibility, and assur-
ances of confidentiality.

STRATEGY 4

The designers of any educational program must consider the cognitive
level of the children they are trying to reach in order to gauge the material appropriately. Linking the AIDS curriculum to already existing
curricula in related areas can help assure that concepts and explanations
are introduced that are developmentally appropriate and consider the
child's level of psychosocial development. These kinds of issues will be
important considerations in the design of any AIDS curriculum. Flavell
(1985) provides an extensive overview of problem-solving strategies,
concepts, and explanations that can be expected to be within the range
of children of different ages. The following represents our own interpretation and extension of the Flavell's analysis.

The very young elementary school child, younger than 7 or 8 years
of age, will have difficulty with detailed logical explanations but nevertheless should be able to understand simple functional or cause-effect
relations among observable objects and events. More abstract explanations of disease processes will be beyond the grasp of a child this young.
Analogies with familiar situations in the child's life may be effective
in teaching basic health concepts and rules of infection control.

The child in the middle school years (from the third grade to the sixth or the seventh) will be able to understand concrete explanations and relations of a fairly complicated nature, especially if they are supported with easily understood graphic and three-dimensional models. The adolescent in junior and senior high will become increasingly skillful in appreciating others' perspectives and will become capable of understanding concepts such as multiple causation and probabilities.

Before considering approaches and information appropriate to different ages and grades, a basic AIDS education program should be developed. One sample outline of a comprehensive program would include (1) a definition of AIDS; (2) an overview of virology and immunology; (3) a discussion of the causative virus; (4) the effects of the virus on the immune system; (5) the course of the disease and stages of HIV infection; (6) the number and percentage of afflicted people currently at each stage; (7) possible co-factors that may hasten the progression of the disease; and (8) a discussion of the physical and emotional aspects of each stage.

A special effort should be made to make students aware that they may already be interacting with people infected with the virus but that such contact poses no danger if no risk behaviors are involved. Discussion of virus transmission and risk reduction should follow, emphasizing the specific behaviors that allow the infection to be passed from person to person rather than generalized risk groups (see strategy 7 below). To provide a positive focus to any discussion, sound information and principles of health promotion should be discussed. Finally, information on available resources for AIDS information and counseling should be shared with students. Obviously, not all this information will be provided at all grade levels. At the youngest ages, the focus will be more on providing some very basic information on diseases and infection control, immune system functioning, protection of ourselves and others, and correct names for body parts and genitals. To varying degrees, these content areas can then be related to AIDS in a general way. Some awareness of interpersonal issues can also be fostered, starting at a young age

132

(see strategy 8 below). Most of these elements can be incorporated into existing curricula.

Many basic health education concepts about the reduction of transmission of infection are already part of elementary school curricula, are easily understood by children, and can be the basic building blocks of AIDS education. Examples of some basic infection control concepts are covering your nose when you sneeze, washing your hands with soap and water, washing your hair and body, brushing your teeth but not using someone else's toothbrush, not drinking out of someone else's glass or cup, and throwing away trash in proper containers. Emphasis on the relation of health life-styles and nutrition to the immune system is also appropriate at early ages. The immune system and its key components can be discussed and visually presented to second or third graders. For example, children can understand an explanation such as, "When you get a cold, there are fighter cells and protector cells that go to work to keep the cold germs from hurting you." Beginning education about drug and alcohol use is also appropriate in the discussion of healthy life-styles.

By the time a child is approaching adolescence (the fifth or sixth grade), he or she will be ready to understand fairly complex concepts of health and illness. The need for AIDS education also becomes more urgent at that time, as the National Academy of Science (1986) notes in its report *Confronting AIDS*: "Special educational efforts must be addressed to teenagers, who are often beginning sexual activity and also may experiment with illicit drugs. Sex education in the schools is no longer advice about reproductive choice, but has now become advice about a life-or-death matter. Schools have an obligation to provide sex and health education, including facts about AIDS, in terms that teenagers can understand" (p. 11).

The outline of a comprehensive program provided above can be expanded by the sixth grade to include highly AIDS-specific information about transmission, sexuality, and reduced-risk behaviors. It will be critical to address precise sexual and drug-related behaviors that transmit the virus. Both boys and girls should understand their own and the opposite gender's body parts, functions, and sexual response cycle (ejaculatory fluids and vaginal/cervical secretions) so that issues about transmission and specific risk behaviors can be understood. Options for protection ranging from abstinence to correct condom usage should be explored. As noted earlier (U.S. Conference of Mayors, 1987), San Francisco teaches its fifth graders about the human reproductive system, maturation, and development and then introduces material on sexually transmitted diseases, including AIDS. Discussion of healthy life-styles, the immune system, and the effects of drugs and alcohol is also appropriate for this age group after the basic background on physiology has been provided.

The objection is frequently raised that a discussion of sexuality and sexual behavior, even in the context of AIDS education, may encourage young people to engage in activities for which they are too immature. While such a possibility is of concern, there are some grounds for making decisions about what sexually related information will be appropriate at different ages. An area of special relevance to AIDS and one highly integrated with the child's cognitive and psychosocial development is his or her own psychosexual development. Some key concepts with which curriculum designers and teachers should be familiar are gender identity, gender constancy, sex roles, sex typing, and sexual orientation. The following overview of these issues is drawn in part from the synthesis of theory and research on sex typing presented by Aletha Huston (1985) in the latest *Handbook of Child Psychology*.

One of the child's first major psychosexual developmental tasks is the establishment of gender identity, that is, recognition of self and others as male or female. Gender identity is usually established by age 3. The young child sees gender identity as a function of external characteristics such as length and style of hair, clothing, and physical size and so fails to recognize its constancy over time. Gradually, between the ages of 3 and about 8 or 9, the full identification of self and others as either male or female becomes stable.

Concurrently, the child is developing knowledge of sex-typed behaviors (i.e., activities perceived to be associated with one sex more than the other—boys play with trucks; girls play with dolls) and sex roles (i.e., general unified patterns or sets of behaviors and responsibilities associated with one sex more than the other—men are soldiers; women are nurses). The child is rigid about sex-typed behaviors and roles and allows little flexibility in the behaviors, activities, and occupations that he or she considers appropriate for each gender. Conformity to rules and roles is very important, and there appears to be a polarization of masculine and feminine sex roles as mutually exclusive in the child between 5 and 7 years of age (Flavell, 1985).

The beginning of flexibility in sex-typed behaviors and roles can be observed at age 8 or 9 as the child develops gender constancy. The child recognizes those characteristics that are primary and criterial to gender identity (e.g., genitalia) and those that are secondary (e.g., physical appearance such as hairstyle). Some of the implications of these developmental trends relevant to teaching children about AIDS and sexuality are discussed below.

Since gender identity and gender constancy are the earliest psychosexual developments, a foundation for later education efforts can be laid by providing both boys and girls with appropriate terminology for both male and female genitalia. For children in the early elementary school grades, the context for the use of accurate names is one of anatomy and physiology, not sexual behavior. Appropriate words for genitalia and related body parts are *penis, scrotum, testicles, anus, clitoris, vagina, breasts,* and *nipples.* Using accurate terminology in everyday school situations (see strategy 7 below) at these young ages creates an atmosphere of comfort and familiarity that will allow teachers to discuss appropriate behavior in relation to genitalia—for example, "We cover our genitals in public places. Where are your public body parts? Your private body parts?" A discussion of sexual exploitation and the right to say no to inappropriate touching of genetalia (e.g., Stranger Danger programs) will naturally follow, and the student will also have been prepared for future discussion of more complex and sensitive issues.

Discussion of sex-typed roles and behaviors and their origins can begin in the elementary school years as youngsters are first beginning to make such distinctions reliably. Taking into account the young child's cognitively limited understanding of these dimensions of behavior, the teacher can begin to set the stage for a consideration of a wider range of alternatives and perspectives than what is typically represented in prevailing sexual stereotypes. These discussions may help lead to a more open attitude about sexual orientation when the issue becomes relevant and is included in AIDS curricula in early adolescence (see strategy 6 below).

STRATEGY 5

Although issues related to this strategy have been addressed in the previous section, an understanding of body integrity and safety deserves special emphasis. In educating young children about AIDS, concepts that underscore and enhance AIDS prevention are also ones that foster a positive self-concept. Children need to develop the attitudes and skills necessary to say no to situations they understand as being unacceptable to their safety. The Stranger Danger programs are good examples of this skill-building approach. In them, children learn acceptable and unacceptable touching as it relates to both familiar and unfamiliar persons and the ability to say no. Children are also taught that it is appropriate to tell a responsible adult of an incident of unacceptable touching, that they should not to be ashamed and "keep secrets." These strategies teach children appropriate limit setting on body contact and the avoidance of anxiety-producing silence. Similar programs, such as Just Say No to Drugs, convey equally powerful messages when used as an organizing theme in drug abuse awareness programs at school. Learning these strategies in massive, school-wide campaigns also encourages normative behavior standards among peers. These limit-setting activities can be broadened to consider all risks related to targeted problems; for example, it can be pointed out that excessive use of drugs and alcohol may lead to impaired judgment, greater sexual activity, and lack of concern for such basic needs as food and rest.

At the same time, a positive approach to encouraging healthy bodies can be developed through education focused on nutrition, good hygiene practices, and care in sexual relationships. The National Academy of Sciences has stated, "In addition to knowing which sexual activities are risky, people also need reassurance that there are sexual practices that involve little or no risk. For example, unprotected sexual intercourse between individuals who have maintained a sexual relationship exclusively with each other since 1978 can be considered essentially free of risk for HIV transmission, assuming that other risk factors are absent. An integral aspect of an education campaign must be the wide dissemination of clear information about those behaviors that do not transmit the disease . . . latex condoms have been shown under laboratory conditions to limit passage of HIV. They should be more widely available and more consistently used. Young people, early in their sexually active lives, and thus less likely to have been infected with HIV, have the most protection to gain from the use of condoms" (1986, p. 10).

STRATEGY 6

The surgeon general has stated, "There is now no doubt that we need sex education in schools and that it must include information on heterosexual and homosexual relationships. . . . There are a number of people, primarily adolescents, that do not yet know that they will become homosexual or become drug abusers and will not heed the message. They must be reached and taught the risk behaviors that expose them to infection with the AIDS virus" (Koop, 1986, p. 29).

For adolescents, preoccupation with sexuality is a given; adolescence is a period characterized by uncertainty and ambivalence. In this time of exploring their own sexuality, adolescents are extremely vulnerable, and it is because of this vulnerability that it is timely and crucial to introduce AIDS prevention education. Adolescent obsession with sexuality is played out in the use of stylish clothing, jewelry, makeup, and hairstyle. Adolescence is often a time for acting out sexuality by touching, talking, and practicing. Frequently, there is confusion about sexual orientation and experimentation about what it means to be heterosexual, homosexual, or bisexual. A few experiences of one type do not define one's sexuality, but the psychological adjustment of youths has frequently been impaired through both a lack of understanding and a lack of validation.

It is a great irony that homosexuality has traditionally been side-stepped in sex education. Avoiding this issue leaves many adolescents feeling isolated and ashamed to accept, acknowledge, or express same-sex feelings and also excludes a whole category of young people from AIDS education. Such exclusion may create a denial system in which some adolescents may be placed at a higher risk because they feel the information given does not apply to them. Many students will be beginning to develop an awareness of their sexual orientation in early adolescence after gender constancy has been established. A discrepancy between personal feelings and classroom messages that focus only on heterosexual orientation and relationships can add to the stress and confusion that an adolescent with a developing homosexual identification will experience. In addition, if the adolescent has labeled himself or herself as gay and does not identify with any of the heterosexual examples used in classroom discussions, he or she may, at great risk, judge that the material is "not relevant to me."

This lack of validation will do little to enhance the adolescent's self-esteem and may erode a self-concept that otherwise might be strong enough to set limits in risky situations. Sex education should not be presented value free. Without eroticizing human sexuality, and by introducing content according to the sexual readiness of the young person (see strategy 4 above), teachers can discuss the necessary responsibilities to self and others, regardless of same- or opposite-sex interactions. Statements of inclusion could be used in discussion of sexual behavior—for example, "When two people have sexual intercourse, a man and a woman, or two men, or two women . . . "—and the appropriate behavior described or point made. It is critical to present information to adolescents about same- and opposite-sex behaviors, thoughts, and feelings in a positive and inclusive way.

STRATEGY 7

The National Academy of Sciences has stated, "If an education campaign is to change behavior that spreads HIV infection, its message must be as direct as possible. Educators must be prepared to specify that in-tercourse—anal or vaginal—with an infected or possibly infected per-son, and without protection of a condom is very risky. They must be willing to use whatever vernacular is required for that message to be understood. Admonitions to avoid 'intimate bodily contact' and the 'exchange of bodily fluid' convey at best only a vague message" (1986, p. 10).

There is a midpoint between obtuse language and vulgarity (includ-ing words for body parts and sexual practices). It should be possible to be precise without being offensive. A brochure developed by students for students under the auspices of the New York Public Health Depart-ment, for example, describes anal intercourse as "sex in the behind," an apt and relatively communicative description that is not offensive. Words used should reflect a knowledge of the colloquialisms and slang of the region, with a careful distinction made between what is and what is not appropriate. These points apply not only to sexual terms but also to terms related to drugs and drug paraphernalia.

The teacher will want to be certain to use vocabulary that students can understand. To assume that all adolescents will know the meaning of such terms as *penis, semen, vaginal/cervical fluids, oral/vaginal/anal intercourse* is shortsighted—even if their behaviors involve the body parts and activities referred to. Appropriate terms should be defined, and teachers should make sure that their students understand those definitions. It is not, however, necessary to use the students' vernacular. Obviously, the teacher must be comfortable using sexually explicit lan-guage and discussing the thoughts, behaviors, and feelings of a wide va-riety of people.

It may make sense to postpone discussion of such potentially titillat-ing and hence disruptive topics until later in the school year, when class group dynamics are known and the teacher can gauge students' reac-tions and when people are more open and comfortable with each other. Use of an anonymous suggestion box may also be useful in providing a channel for questions that students are too embarrassed to ask aloud in the presence of others. Since the context in which information is deliv-ered can make a big difference, the teacher will want to consider whether certain kinds of information should be presented in lecture format, small group discussion, or even one-to-one interactive discussion that may allow use of the individual student's own vocabulary. Regardless of which context is used, the teacher will have to establish a rapport and create a level of comfort that supports open communication.

Clearly, there is a need to be sensitive to a child's level of development and understanding when communicating ideas. To a very young child, who is already more than happy to say no to medicine, talk about drugs may only conjure up thoughts about aspirin and cough syrup and create more confusion than good.

How information is presented can also affect how effectively the basic message is communicated. It is important to note, for example, that not all homosexual men are at risk for AIDS, only those who engage or have engaged in specific behaviors that allow viral transmission. Focusing on risk groups may interfere with students' identification of their own risk behaviors because they may not identify themselves with a specific risk groups even though they may engage in similar behaviors. For example, a young boy who experiments sexually with other boys but does not define himself as gay as a result of this activity, because of stereotypes he holds about what it means to be gay, may not recognize that the information being presented is relevant to him if specific risk behaviors are not described.

In areas of the country with high concentrations of racial and ethnic minorities, special attention must be given to the choice of educational strategies and language relevant to the young people in these communities. Case statistics show that blacks and Hispanics are overrepresented among persons with HIV infection. Yet there is a widespread belief in these communities that AIDS affects only gay white men. Using information and education strategies designed for white, heterosexual, non-drug-using audiences simply will not be sensitive to the differences in values, beliefs, and practices of minority communities. One potentially effective strategy for reaching minority teenagers has been the use of "rap." "Rap" is a form of rhyming with rhythm that is familiar to many black and Latin teenagers in urban inner cities. The Baltimore

AIDS service organization, HERO, has produced a rap record about AIDS prevention that is aired on local rock radio stations that target black teenagers in particular. In San Francisco, health educators sponsored a rap contest to reach teenagers and to have teenagers reach each other with AIDS prevention information. The contest, held in local youth centers throughout the country, was organized under the slogan "Rap'n Down Drugs, STD and AIDS." The contest winner, by Riff and Raff, follows:

D-I-S-E-A-S-E × 3
Disease get protection and use sex safely.
Use condom, use jells or just say no.
AIDS is claiming victims like the cocaine blow.
It's a heavy situation so don't take this light.
Don't throw your life away for a toss in the night.
Respect yourself protect yourself and act like you care,
Just because you use protection doesn't mean you're a square.
Contraceptives make a difference they might keep you alive,
So if sex is what you're into you should keep a supply.
And don't rely on lucky vibes cause the odds are against
Any team that tries to play without a solid defense.
You're blowing crack, blowing caine, and you're blowing the pipe,
You're blowing bank, blowing money and blowing your life.
If you insist on using dope and you use a syringe
Just use the needle once and never use it again.

STRATEGY 8

Acquired immunodeficiency syndrome is associated with a number of stigmatized issues and activities: sexually transmitted diseases (STD), promiscuity, homosexuality/bisexuality, prostitution, drug abuse, contagious/infectious disease, wasting, and death. The effective teacher will want to assist children in dealing with AIDS issues in a positive manner, one that facilitates tolerance and understanding of others and responsible decision making for self and others.

The child can be helped to overcome fear of or disgust for persons with AIDS or at risk for AIDS. Just as able-bodied children can be prepared to accept disabled or handicapped children being mainstreamed into public schools (e.g., opportunities to ride in a wheelchair or listen through a hearing aid), empathy for an HIV-infected person can be fostered at an early age. An important perspective-taking concept that can be introduced is the awareness that disease processes have real effects on specific people (e.g., "Daddy got wet in the rain and got a cold," or, "Can you remember when you might have eaten something to make your stomach hurt?"). However, it is important to help the child recognize that individuals cannot always be in control of becoming ill or being in accidents. Most people with HIV infection have become infected unknowingly. They do not deserve to contract a fatal disease because they may have unknowingly engaged in behaviors found later to be associated with AIDS. To help the young child identify feelings about the disruptive effects of diseases on normal patterns of activity and interaction, emphasis on the person who has become ill is a key strategy. The ill person's feelings about not being able to go out and play or go to work can be discussed.

Role models that are relevant to children and youths are important resources that can be drawn on to promote responsible attitudes and actions. They can include rock stars, cartoon characters, athletes, actors, radio disc jockeys and personalities, youth organizations, and churches. A group that is highly influenced by the media, teenagers may develop more open and responsible attitudes and behaviors as a result of well-placed media messages. The use of acceptable role models for both males and females of various racial and ethnic groups is essential if the message is to be communicated that all people need information in order to be responsible and assertive in making decisions about engaging in activities that may place them at high risk for infection with the virus.

Yarber (1987), who has developed an AIDS curriculum with support from the Centers for Disease Control, has commented, "Negative social attitudes formerly called 'social diseases' have been associated with

STD. People who have contracted them were subject to scorn and ridicule because of their link to promiscuity and illicit sex. Consequently, many persons who contracted STD felt shame and guilt. These feelings often interfered with the individual's practice of positive health behaviors. Education about STDs should attempt to overcome these negative attitudes by emphasizing a mature attitude that assumes responsibility for one's own health and the health of others. Hence, instruction should be directed toward acceptance of these responsibilities as specified in the desired behavioral outcomes" (p. 108).

Yarber (1987) cites a series of decision-making steps that should facilitate positive behavior toward good health as it is related to prevention, acquisition, transmission and disposition of STD . These include "decisions about when, how and with whom to engage in sexual behavior; decisions specific to health promotion if sexual behavior includes genital contact; decisions in response to suspected illness; decisions in response to diagnosed disease; decisions related to other people" (p. 107). Each step is a critical one, and the omission of discussion of any of them may be hazardous to the health of the adolescent or young adult. It is important that the adolescent be aware of the options available at each step and know which ones promote good health and which ones jeopardize it (Yarber, 1987).

The ability to make sound decisions is based on the ability to acquire adequate information and frequently relies on the availability of informed others with whom to share feelings and concerns. When emotionally laden material has been presented in a mature, factual, and specific manner, and when significant adults have modeled an openness and willingness to discuss the concerns of young people, they will be better prepared to set limits and to communicate to their partners their responsible choices without embarrassment or fear of humiliation.

Adolescents need skill development in several areas, including (1) assessment of accuracy and reliability of information gained from various sources, including peers, of a potential partner's past and present behaviors and his or her responsibility toward one's self; (2) decision

143

making about relationships, including criteria for selection of potential partners (addressed in a manner that acknowledges, for different individuals, the possibility of same- or opposite-sex relationships); (3) communication about one's own and the other's values and concerns; and (4) negotiation about acceptable behaviors and responsibility toward self and others. To acquire and practice these skills, adolescents must be provided a safe, trusting environment that allows them to express a variety of feelings and values regarding these issues. There should be opportunities to practice communication strategies about interpersonal decision making with sufficient time allowed for questions and answers (including anonymous questions) in small and large groups.

The responsibilities of both boys and girls need to be addressed in discussions of sex roles and risk reduction to avoid stereotyping of decision making on the basis of gender alone. The same messages should be delivered to both sexes about shared responsibility in decision making about sexual and drug activity and risk behavior reduction.

Because there will be concerned individuals and critics who fear that AIDS education promotes sexuality, including homosexuality, responsible decision making must be emphasized. As noted earlier, AIDS education can not be value free. The goal of AIDS education, however, is to foster the development of responsible adults capable of making informed decisions that consider their own good and the good of others. The alternative—keeping children and adolescents in ignorance when they are surrounded by many irresponsible sources of misinformation and temptations to engage in risky behaviors—would only be a foolish and shortsighted avoidance of a significant issue in the lives of children.

STRATEGY 9

Accountability will soon become an issue for AIDS education and information programs, which means that their effectiveness must be evaluated. This chapter should have made clear that our goals and objectives for these programs, which influence evaluation strategies, extend beyond the development of a written curriculum available in a prepackaged format. There are central issues that affect the very fabric of our society. Acquired immunodeficiency syndrome provides us all with an opportunity to address some of these issues with our children in a significant and meaningful way.

Any evaluation plan should include an assessment of attitudes, knowledge, and behaviors (this latter category is especially controversial and difficult, particularly in the areas of sexual activity and drug use among students) both prior to the delivery of the program and then afterward. There have already been some general attempts to assess high school students' attitudes and knowledge (e.g., DiClemente, Zorn, & Temoshok, 1986). There have been surprising findings of major gaps in understanding about modes of transmission of the AIDS virus and effective means of protection, even in a city (San Francisco) where AIDS awareness would be expected to be at its highest. Such studies point to the need for careful targeting of our audiences. Simply making information about AIDS available does not mean that people are hearing and understanding it.

At a more specific level, each AIDS curriculum should have a pretest/ posttest component built into it so that the changes in knowledge and understanding occurring as a result of the education activities can be assessed. There remain a number of areas, such as developing the ability to make responsible decisions, that are much more difficult to assess and can probably be judged only on the basis of subjective feedback from students on how useful the activities have been in their own personal lives.

The issues at stake, the health and well-being of our children and youths, are too critical for us to fail in our responsibility to listen to how they are hearing us and to determine whether the basic messages are being communicated. We are confronted with a dread disease and epidemic, but we are also provided with an opportunity for communication that can lead to much more meaningful and harmonious lives for our children in the future. How we choose to respond now will have major implications for many years to comes. Dr. June Osborn, dean of the School of Public Health at the University of Michigan, has given us the challenge: "The ways we meet this epidemic will dictate the ways we meet the next. Surely there will be another."

REFERENCES

Centers for Disease Control. (1988). Guidelines for effective school health education to prevent the spread of AIDS. *Morbidity and Mortality Weekly Report, 37,* (Suppl. 2).

DiClemente, R. J., Zorn, J., & Temoshok, L. (1986). Adolescents and AIDS: A survey of knowledge, attitudes and beliefs about AIDS in San Francisco. *American Journal of Public Health, 12,* 1443–1445.

Flavell, J. H. (1985). *Cognitive development.* Englewood Cliffs, NJ: Prentice-Hall.

Huston, A. C. (1985). Sex-typing. In E. M. Hetherington (Ed.), P. Mussen (Series Ed.), *The handbook of child psychology: Vol. 4.* Socialization, personality and social development (4th, pp. 387–468). New York: Wiley.

Koop, C. E. (1986). *Surgeon general's report on acquired immune deficiency syndrome.* Washington, DC: U.S. Department of Health and Human Services.

National Academy of Science. (1986). *Confronting AIDS: Directions for public health, health care, and research.* Washington, DC: National Academy Press.

U.S. Conference of Mayors. (1987, January). Local school districts active in AIDS education. *AIDS Information Exchange, 4,* 1–10.

Yarber, W. L. (1987). Sexually transmitted diseases and young adults. *Educational Horizons, 65*(3), 106–109.

•

CHAPTER SIX

Prevention of
Pediatric and Adolescent
AIDS

HEATHER C. HUSZTI
DALE D. CHITWOOD

In the absence of effective treatments and vaccines for acquired immunodeficiency syndrome (AIDS), prevention programs are the only way to control the epidemic. The primary mode of pediatric AIDS transmission is perinatal, currently accounting for 77% of all pediatric cases (Centers for Disease Control [CDC], 1988). To slow the further spread of pediatric AIDS, prevention programs must target the women at highest risk for human immunodeficiency virus (HIV) infection who could consequently give birth to HIV-infected children. This chapter will discuss the specific target groups of high-risk women and adolescents and give examples of possible risk-reduction programs directed toward each of these groups. Impediments to the use of risk reduction behaviors among each high-risk group will be discussed. The current state of knowledge about intervention strategies will also be addressed.

Prior to the discussion of any specific programmatic recommendations, however, some general issues important to consider in the development of AIDS prevention programs will be reviewed. A brief overview of theories of preventive health behaviors will also be presented. Although each disease presents its own unique issues, there are some general theories of preventive health behavior that apply to AIDS. Therefore, a review of past prevention research can be beneficial in the design of AIDS prevention programs.

When attempting to design an AIDS prevention program, it is important to understand the social structure of the high-risk group the program is designed to reach. Prevention of AIDS is not a unitary concept. The most frequent types of high-risk behaviors differ among risk groups, and, even more important, the factors that reinforce these high-risk behaviors differ across populations. The factors that might motivate the sexual partner of an intravenous drug user (IVDU) to become pregnant may be quite different from those that would motivate the sexual partner of a hemophiliac. In order to be successful, prevention programs must address and modify the specific beliefs and attitudes that motivate and maintain the performance of high-risk behaviors within the specific target population. Therefore, program elements that are successful with one group may or may not succeed with another high-risk group. Collaboration between professionals who are experienced with specific high-risk populations and can identify some of the important social factors and professionals with expertise in the promotion of preventive health behavior may be necessary to design effective AIDS prevention programs.

The need to reduce the further spread of pediatric and adolescent AIDS is so great that interventions are being made immediately (Drotman, 1987). However, it is crucial that the effectiveness of the various prevention efforts mounted by a program be evaluated simultaneously with its implementation. Assessment of a program's effectiveness may be problematic because of confounding variables and a lack of resources and time. However, only a thorough outcome assessment can identify which of a program's components are effective. The results of these assessments can then lead to the further refinement of existing prevention programs.

Prevention programs are so urgently needed that there is often little time to ground interventions thoroughly in theories of health behavior. The programs are also often in a state of flux at the time evaluations are being conducted. Consequently, many existing programs may implicitly incorporate elements of various health prevention theories without clearly identifying a theoretical base. However, theories about preventive health behaviors should not be forgotten. Theoretical frameworks are important to the development of prevention programs. Programs are often more coherent and can be more easily evaluated when a specific theoretical base underlies the program. Efforts are currently under way to provide additional theoretical frameworks through a review of previous studies (Des Jarlais & Friedman, 1988). These ongoing, concurrent efforts will help to provide a framework for the further development of prevention programs.

THEORIES OF PREVENTIVE HEALTH BEHAVIORS
Researchers have explored a number of variables that might predict the performance of various preventive health behaviors. Certainly, knowledge of the appropriate precautions to take is not sufficient to produce long-term behavioral changes, although it may be a necessary component. The prevention of HIV infection is no exception to this rule. For example, in one survey of IVDUs, 75% knew that AIDS was transmitted through the sharing of drug injection equipment, but only 40% reported changing their behaviors to avoid contracting AIDS (Kleinman et al., 1987).

Among the more prominent theories of preventive health behavior is the Health Belief Model (HBM) (Rosenstock, 1966). The model postulates that people are most likely to practice preventive behaviors if they feel that they are susceptible to the disease, that the disease will have serious consequences if contracted, and that preventive behaviors are both possible to perform and offer effective protection and if some event happens to motivate the performance of preventive behavior, such as the early warning signs of a heart attack (Chen & Land, 1986). Additionally, the more barriers that are perceived to achieving compliance with recommended behavioral changes, the less likely it is that the preventive behavior will be performed. Although the model postulates a causal relation between these variables and the subsequent performance of health behaviors, most studies of the model are retrospective, rather than prospective, in nature (Chen & Land, 1986). Therefore, it is difficult to assess precisely which factors predict an individual's practice of preventive behaviors.

Rogers (1985; Maddux & Rogers, 1983; Rogers & Mewborn, 1976) has proposed a model similar to the HBM known as protection motivation theory. Protection motivation theory focuses on how individuals process and react to fear-arousing messages. Rogers proposes that fear-arousing messages, such as information about disease prevention, contain three major components: the noxiousness of the event, the probability it will occur, and the effectiveness of possible preventive behaviors. Maddux and Rogers (1983) suggested an additional intrapersonal variable, how confident the individual is of his or her ability to perform the recommended preventive behaviors. According to protection motivation theory, the likelihood of the use of preventive behaviors is determined by the relative strength of each of the fear message's components. Although Rogers's model suggests that the components combine in an additive fashion, he also suggest that, when individuals are confronted with real threats, they may behave more irrationally (Rogers, 1985). The HBM and protection motivation theory are very similar, although the latter focuses on the message's component parts, while the former focuses on the individual's internal perceptions. However, much of the research on the two models has produced similar results.

Several studies (Emmons et al., 1986; Rogers & Mewborn, 1976; Simon & Das, 1984) have found that, the greater the perceived efficacy of preventive options, the more likely that preventive behaviors would be performed. One study, based on the HBM, assessed the correlations between the variables of the HBM and the likelihood that the participants, students at a New York City university, would go for asymptomatic checkups for sexually transmitted diseases (STDS) (Simon & Das, 1984). The individual's perception that the recommended behaviors were effective in preventing the disease was the most important predictor of the likelihood of taking preventive action. It was also found that the frequency of obtaining asymptomatic checkups was related to the subjects' perceptions that they were personally susceptible to the disease, that there were few barriers to obtaining checkups, and that asymptomatic checkups lead to health benefits.

A recent review (Job, 1988) of the use of fear in health promotion campaigns suggested that effective messages appear to have three main components. These components are, a relatively low level of induced fear so that individuals do not have to use denial mechanisms to cope with that fear, a concentration on the short-term benefits of preventive behaviors that allows individuals to see some immediate result from behavioral changes, and the teaching of the specific skills necessary to implement the recommended preventive health behaviors. Job also suggests that care should be taken to make sure that the performance of the recommended preventive health behaviors does eliminate the fear aroused by the prevention message; otherwise, the recommended behaviors will not be performed.

It is interesting that studies exploring the factors that actually motivate individuals to change their attitudes about and/or performance of preventive behaviors indicate that the perceived seriousness of the disease has little effect on either attitudes or behavior (Chen & Land, 1986; Maddux & Rogers, 1983; Rogers & Mewborn, 1976; Simon & Das, 1984). Ironically, given the results of the previous studies, the cornerstone of many preventive health programs is detailed information about the seriousness of the disease. This dichotomy between past research and the content of current prevention programs only reinforces the need for the developers of prevention programs to be aware of past preventive health research. With the urgent need for effective prevention programs, we must not repeat the mistakes of the past.

PEDIATRIC AIDS PREVENTION
The Problem

Programs that could curb a further increase in the incidence of pediatric AIDS must focus on the problem of perinatal transmission, the primary route of HIV infection to young children. Approximately three-quarters (78%) of all cumulative pediatric AIDS cases in the United States (CDC, 1988) have been attributed to transmission from an infected mother. The rate of perinatal transmission from infected mothers is undetermined, but an estimate of 40%–50% is plausible on the basis of existing data (Friedland & Klein, 1987; Scott et al., 1985; CDC, 1985). The second leading mode, transfusion with contaminated blood or blood products, now accounts for 13% of pediatric cases, and infection from contaminated factor concentrate accounts for another 6%. With the advent of blood donor screening and the heat treatment of factor concentrate, the number of pediatric AIDS cases caused by contaminated blood products should decline (Grossman, 1988). The cases that are being reported presently are primarily those of individuals infected prior to blood donor screening procedures.

Recent studies have found high rates of HIV infection in newborns at inner-city hospitals (Hoff et al., 1988; Landesman, Minkoff, Homan, McCalla, & Sijin, 1987). One study at a Brooklyn, New York, hospital that serves an inner-city population found a 2% seroprevalence rate among newborns (Landesman et al., 1987). Almost one-quarter of the women (24.6%) in the entire sample had self-identified risk factors, and 4.7% of the sample were seropositive.

A disproportionate number of pediatric AIDS cases occur in Black and Hispanic children. Although Blacks represent 12% and Hispanics 6% of the U.S. population, 58% of pediatric AIDS cases are among Black children and 22% among Hispanic children (CDC, 1986). The geographic distribution is also striking, with more than 50% of pediatric AIDS patients residing in New York, New Jersey, or Florida, usually in inner cities. Since perinatal transmission is the primary mode of pediatric AIDS transmission, it is not surprising that the ethnic and geographic distribution of women with AIDS is similar to the pattern of pediatric AIDS. The cumulative incidence of AIDS among minority women is 10 times that for white, non-Hispanic women (unpublished data for 1987 from the National Institute on Drug Abuse).

About 90% of the mothers of children infected via perinatal transmission are IVDUs or the heterosexual partners of IVDUs. At least half of all women with AIDS are IVDUs themselves. Female IVDUs are known to have a relatively high rate of pregnancy (Ralph & Spigner, 1986). One recent study of clients of methadone programs reported an average family size of almost two children per client, and about one-quarter of the adults expected to have at least one additional child (Friedman, Des Jarlais, & Sotheran, 1988).

Another 20% of women with AIDS do not inject drugs but are heterosexual partners of IVDUs. This risk group accounts for approximately two-thirds of all female heterosexual AIDS cases. A study of male IVDUs in New York found that 80% of these men had their primary sexual relationships with women who were not IVDUs (Des Jarlais, Friedman, & Strug, 1986). In Miami, a study of IVDUs in treatment reported that 61% of all male IVDUs were heterosexual partners of one or more women who did not inject drugs (Chitwood et al., 1988). Because men often do not tell female sexual partners that they are IVDUs, it is probable that the proportion of heterosexual AIDS cases attributable to infection through a sexual partner who has used intravenous drugs is even greater than the reported 65% (Des Jarlais, Chamberland, Yancovitz, Weinberg, & Friedman, 1984). In all, the number of female heterosexual partners of IVDUs has been estimated to be at least half the size of the IVDU population (Des Jarlasi et al., 1984), which would make these women the third largest risk group for AIDS in the United States, behind gay men and IVDUs.

These facts reinforce the concern that IVDUs, who represent the most rapidly increasing transmission category for AIDS, are the primary bridge for the transmission of HIV into the heterosexual, non-drug injecting female population. Although the incidence rate of reported AIDS cases among heterosexual partners and children is lower than that among IVDUs, the rate appears to be following an exponential increase similar to that of IVDU cases (Friedman et al., 1988).

These data signal a clear warning. In the absence of effective treatments and vaccines, risk reduction/prevention programs must be initiated to control the epidemic. Because the perinatal route is the principal mode of pediatric AIDS transmission, one key approach to the prevention of viral transmission to young children must be the development and implementation of intervention programs that target women of child-bearing age who are infected by HIV or are at high risk for becoming infected. The general goals of prevention programs for high-risk women are to stop the use of intravenous drugs or to stop the sharing of needles or syringes, to increase the practice of safer sex behaviors, and to avoid pregnancy if HIV antibody positive. The specific goals of prevention programs vary according to the targeted population.

WOMEN AT RISK FOR HIV INFECTION
Women Who Inject Drugs

There are two distinct groups of women who inject drugs, those in treatment programs and those not in treatment programs. Because each group raises unique issues, they will be discussed separately.

The Treatment Outcome Prospective Study (TOPS) has indicated that about 30% of the clients in treatment programs are women (Hubbard et al., 1983). Between 1975 and 1985, the percentage of women entering methadone maintenance programs increased from 24% to 34% (unpublished data for 1987 from the National Institute on Drug Abuse). In 1987 and 1988, 36% of all treatment clients in Miami who entered an epidemiologic study of HIV infection were women (Chitwood et al., 1988). Existing drug treatment resources need to be utilized as efficiently as possible to reach clients who are at highest risk for exposure to or transmission of HIV. Community-based methadone maintenance programs are in an excellent position to expand these prevention efforts.

Effective programs must provide a setting to help clients eliminate or reduce their drug or needle use and high-risk sexual behaviors. All programs should provide education and counseling about HIV transmission and behavioral training on how to eliminate the sharing of nonsterile needles and syringes and unprotected sexual behavior. Both components appear to be necessary. For instance, in one study, 93% of IVDUs in treatment clinics knew that sharing drug equipment can spread AIDS. However, the IVDUs in the survey did not know what to use to clean their equipment effectively; 87% had cleaned their works (needle and syringe) after the last use but had used an ineffective method, such as water (Flynn et al., 1987). For those clients who desire HIV antibody testing, confidentiality must be guaranteed and pre- and posttest counseling made available.

All treatment programs ought to develop intervention modules that address the needs of the family of IVDUs. It is important that programs for the prevention of pediatric AIDS be able to respond to the interpersonal and sociocultural contexts of the users (Cohen, 1987). Enhanced treatment programs aimed at preventing AIDS will be most effective if they also provide counseling and education for the sexual partners of their drug-injecting clients. Information about HIV transmission through sexual behavior must be provided in a format that encourages safer sexual practices such as training in the proper use of condoms and increasing the appeal of condoms. The special needs of pregnant IVDUs and their sexual partners should be addressed in the treatment program in which drug use and risk behavior reduction services are provided. Unfortunately, few traditional drug treatment services are designed to address the needs of families of IVDUs.

Programs should also be designed to provide aftercare or tapering services to those women clients who can function effectively on low doses of methadone or who can abstain entirely from drugs (Zackon, McAuliffe, & Chiron, 1985). These types of services will permit the reallocation of resources to provide more intensive services to other female treatment clients who are at greater risk for contracting or spreading HIV. The aftercare program model may include professionally led recovery training sessions, peer-led fellowship meetings, drug free social and community activities, and a network of ex-addicts to provide guidance to the clients.

Female IVDUs who are not in formal drug treatment programs can be difficult to reach. Unfortunately, traditional treatment programs, while helpful, do not reach most high-risk women because the vast majority of IVDUs do not participate in them. It is estimated that, for each person in treatment, there are at least seven others who are not in treatment, and women tend to be underrepresented within the treatment client population (Chitwood & Morningstar, 1985). Watters, Newmeyer, Feldman, and Biernacki (1986) found that two-thirds of 101 not-in-treatment IVDUs they interviewed had not been in a treatment program in the past 5 years.

The reasons for this are rooted in the availability, accessibility, and acceptability of programs. Treatment is not available for many IVDUs who cannot afford to pay for care. In several cities, waiting lists exist for admission to treatment programs. Some IVDUs have reported that treatment is not accessible because treatment hours or locations are not compatible with their work or family schedules. Treatment is avoided by some IVDUs because they find it too stigmatizing (Chitwood & Morningstar, 1985). If possible, treatment programs should attempt to address the elements that keep IVDUs away.

In addition, aggressive community-based outreach programs to IVDUs who are not in treatment are needed to address the problem of HIV transmission and pediatric AIDS. Most programs of this type operate with a four-tiered health promotion theme about needle use (Ginzburg et al., 1988): (1) do not use drugs; (2) if you will not stop using drugs, do not inject drugs; (3) if you will not stop injecting drugs, stop sharing needles; and (4) if you will not stop sharing needles, use medically sound methods to disinfect the injecting equipment.

At least two basic, complementary approaches that have been developed to reach not-in-treatment IVDUs are currently being evaluated (unpublished data for 1987 from the National Institute on Drug Abuse). One approach is to provide active IVDUs on the street with basic education, risk-reduction training, and the supplies (e.g., bleach, condoms) essential to practice specific reduction behaviors. Professionally trained indigenous community health outreach workers enter the social networks of needle users, promote needle/syringe hygiene and safer sexual behaviors, and educate, counsel, and train IVDUs in the street or at storefront locations where drug use is prevalent. The focus of the intervention is, of necessity, simple and is based on ethnographic and survey data that indicate that IVDUs are very concerned about AIDS. The earliest programs of this type were initiated in San Francisco (Watters, 1987), New York (Des Jarlais, Friedman, & Hopkins, 1985), and Chicago (Wiebel & Fritz, 1987). Initial evaluations of these programs suggest that those programs that include specific information about treatment program options and demonstrate risk reduction behaviors are successful in increasing the use of treatment programs and safer injection behaviors (McAuliffe et al., 1987).

However, the available data suggest that these programs are not as successful in increasing the use of safer sexual behaviors (Kleinman et al., 1987). The reasons for the difficulty in achieving sexual behavior changes are unclear. Additional research is needed to understand what factors maintain the practice of risky sexual behaviors. As more is understood about those factors, prevention programs can address and change them.

A second approach provides alternative risk reduction programs at an assessment center that is not affiliated with a formal drug treatment program. An early example of this model has been initiated in Miami at a medical center located in an area frequented by IVDUs for primary and emergency health care (McCoy et al., 1988). The assessment center provides pretest counseling, antibody testing, posttest counseling, and risk reduction behavior training for IVDUs and their sexual partners. Program outcome evaluation will be important in determining the effectiveness of these programs.

Sexual Partners of IVDUs

Women who do not inject drugs but are the sexual partners of male IVDUs constitute a large, hidden population of women who are at risk for giving birth to an infected child. Many are unaware that their sexual partners inject drugs. Even among those who know that their partners are IVDUs, very few have ever been involved with their partners in a drug treatment program and may not have received information about their risk. The women in this group are very diverse and are difficult to identify and access.

One of the earliest AIDS prevention efforts among hig-risk women, including sexual partners of IVDUs, was undertaken in San Francisco (Cohen, 1987). Project AWARE (Association for Women's AIDS Research Education) has developed prevention programs that are rooted in mutual respect and recognition between project staff and women at high risk. Total confidentiality and supportive conditions have enabled staff to access sexual partners, learn about specific sexual practices of both prostitutes and other women, and develop specific strategies to reduce high-risk sexual behavior.

There are also community programs under way in a number of cities that are reaching out to minority women and men, who often run the highest risk of using intravenous drugs or being the sexual partners of IVDUs (Deresiewicz, 1988). These programs use volunteers who go out into the community to educate those at high risk for HIV infection. The emphasis is placed on educating minorites about the behaviors that place them at risk to contract AIDS. These groups might not receive this information otherwise or might not trust primarily homosexual or government groups. Minority community groups also provide AIDS education within the context of relationships, accepting responsibility, and empowering their audience. Although these groups are performing a needed service, there has been little systematic evaluation of their effectiveness. Such an evaluation is crucial to determine if additional services or programs are needed to increase compliance with preventive behaviors.

Pregnant Women

All women in high-risk groups should be counseled to be tested for antibodies for HIV prior to deciding whether to become pregnant. Although this is sound policy, in reality most pregnancies of IVDUs are unplanned (Ralph & Spigner, 1986), and these women are seldom aware of their HIV infection risk. Women who are pregnant and who either inject drugs or are sexual partners of IVDUs are in need of immediate AIDS education and tertiary prevention services.

Not only the unborn child is affected by AIDS, however. There is also reason to believe that pregnant women who are seropositive or have

AIDS-related complex (ARC) are at increased risk for developing AIDS (Grossman, 1988; Murphy, 1988). Pregnancy is linked with the suppression of immunity, especially cell-mediated immunity. This is particularly true during the last trimester, and such suppression contin- ues up to 3 months after delivery. It is thought that this decreased immunity may also place a seropositive, pregnant woman at increased risk for developing AIDS (CDC, 1985). High-risk women therefore should be counseled to be tested for antibodies to HIV during the first trimester of pregnancy. Those who are positive should receive counseling about their options, including terminating the pregnancy. Those women who elect to have the child will need assistance in identifying the social services available to them.

Education about effective birth control options and training in their use should be available to all high-risk women after the birth of a child. Women who have already delivered a seropositive child need to be aware of their continued risk to deliver another seropositive child at each additional pregnancy. Ongoing groups at some centers also provide emotional support, education, and problem-solving techniques for HIV-positive women, both mothers and nonmothers (Wagner, Greenberg, Higgins, Norris, & Taylor, 1987).

All the services discussed in this section should be available wherever prenatal health care is provided. These services are particularly important at medical centers that serve large numbers of high-risk women.

IMPEDIMENTS TO CHANGE

As discussed earlier, women at high risk present some difficult challenges. Most AIDS prevention programs have been conducted with predominantly white, well-educated, middle to upper socioeconomic status, homosexual males. This group also had preexisting social networks available to use as vehicles for AIDS prevention messages. Intravenous drug users and their sexual partners often come from minority groups, are frequently of low socioeconomic status, have little education, and do not belong to readily identifiable social networks. Therefore, it is not realistic to expect that prevention programs that were successful in modifying homosexual males' unsafe sexual behaviors will be equally successful with IVDUs and their sexual partners.

The majority of women in the two highest risk groups are members of ethnic minority groups. Intervention programs must be not only tailored to women but also culturally and linguistically appropriate for the norms of Black, Hispanic, and other ethnic minority groups as well as for white women. Many women in minority communities may view AIDS as a disease that affects only gay males (Deresiewicz, 1988).

An additional consideration in designing prevention programs for women may be the perception that love makes unsafe injections or sexual practices with a primary sexual partner acceptable. For instance, prostitutes may use condoms consistently with clients but not with nonpaying sexual partners (Day, War, Wadsworth, & Harris, 1987). The nonuse of condoms is seen as a way to delineate between work and pleasurable relationships. Therefore, women's perceptions of when condom use is acceptable and necessary need to be altered before condoms will be used consistently.

Additionally, socially and economically disadvantaged women who inject drugs or are heterosexual partners of IVDUs are often unable to change their risk behavior because they do not believe that they can control any important aspect of their lives, including their health (Mayes & Cochran, 1988). Women IVDUs who are in a sexual relationship are likely to be with a man who is also an IVDU. The drug distribution system is male dominated for the most part, and a woman who uses drugs is frequently dependent on a man for her drug supply (Chitwood & Morningstar, 1985). Therefore, many women avoid initiating the topics of not sharing needles or using condoms with their primary male partners out of fear that they will be rejected, humiliated, physically abused, or abandoned or that they will lose their drug supply. Feelings of powerlessness, helplessness, and depression diminish their ability to take active control of their lives. Prevention programs need to empower these women to enable them to assume control over their health. The behavior changes necessary to prevent heterosexual and perinatal transmission of HIV will require at times a disruption of sexual relationships; on other occasions, a decision may be made not to have children. Women must have a sense of control over their lives in order to make and implement their decisions.

The majority of drug treatment programs are not geared toward the needs of women, particularly women with children, making it difficult for many women to enter treatment programs willingly. One of the most important factors for effective intervention is that the risk reduction program be developed within the context of genuine concern for the well-being of women who inject drugs or are the sexual partners of men who are IVDUs. New techniques that are sensitive to the unique needs of women must be developed in order to reach these high-risk groups successfully.

ADOLESCENTS

Different subgroups of adolescents represent varying degrees of risk. Two groups at highest risk for HIV infection are male homosexual adolescents and adolescent runaways who live on the streets. Among 18–24-year-olds with AIDS, 79% have been reported to have contracted it through homosexual activity (Hein, 1988). Because the symptoms of AIDS may not appear for 5–7 years after initial infection with HIV, these young adults may have been infected as younger adolescents. There are not any reliable statistics on the rate of infection in adolescents who live on the street. However, this group is potentially at high risk because many survive by engaging in prostitution and often use intravenous drugs. Specialized prevention programs need to be developed to reach both of these groups.

Homosexually oriented adolescent males represent special challenges to the development of successful prevention programs. Homosexuality still carries a social stigma, and, consequently, individuals may be unwilling to openly identify themselves as homosexual. This denial makes it difficult to identify those male adolescents who should be the targets of prevention services. Males who deny their homosexuality may also deny the risks associated with gay sexual behavior.

An organization that attempts to provide a safe and supportive place for gay and lesbian youths to socialize has developed a prevention program for adolescent males (Martin & Hetrick, 1987). The Institute for the Protection of Lesbian and Gay Youth, Inc., stresses overall health education programs in a group setting. Information about AIDS prevention is incorporated into the overall health education program and is discussed in group and individual counseling, educational, and social sessions. Although this type of program appears to be an ideal way to encourage the practice of preventive behaviors, it must be empirically assessed before its effectiveness can be known. Additionally, not all communities offer similar social groups that could provide prevention services. In these communities, additional sensitive educational approaches must be developed, perhaps using adult male homosexual role models to deliver the educational programs.

Adolescents who have run away from home can be a particularly difficult group to reach. They are often suspicious of adults and resist using social services. They are also likely to run away from placements in shelters or foster homes. The use of peer counselors to educate runaways about the risk of AIDS, a program modeled on the approach used with IVDUs, may prove to be effective. Additionally, shelters and medical centers that are used by runaways could institute informal AIDS prevention programs to alert these high-risk adolescents to their personal risk. Expanded social services may help this group reduce or eliminate risky behaviors, such as prostitution as a means of economic support.

Adolescents in general are also at risk for HIV infection because of the sexual and drug experimentation that is common in this age group. Many of the sexual and drug use behaviors that will later place them at high risk will be learned in adolescence. If safer behaviors can be learned before risky habits start, adolescents may be less likely to be infected as adults. Although there are no reliable statistics on HIV infection rates among adolescents, data on the prevalence of other STDs in this population can be sobering. Estimates are that 1 of every 7 adolescents has had an STD. Among sexually active persons, STD rates are higher for 10–19-year-olds than for any other age group. Many of the risk factors for other STDs, such as having multiple sexual partners, are also risk factors for HIV infection.

Adolescents' cognitive developmental stage can also increase their risk for HIV infection. Adolescents ten to believe that they are invulnerable to negative consequences (Elkind, 1967). Therefore, they may not be able to acknowledge their personal susceptibility to AIDS. Melton (1988) suggests that because of their age, adolescents have rarely had any personal experience with the health consequences of their behavior. Peers, who are an extremely important influence in adolescence, may also subtly or blatantly encourage participation in high-risk behaviors.

Surveys of adolescents' knowledge about AIDS indicate that they are generally unaware of their risk. One study found that only 15% of sexually active adolescents had changed their behavior to avoid contracting AIDS (Strunin & Hingson, 1987). Of those who had changed their behavior, only 20% had adopted methods that were effective. The majority were "more careful" in selecting partners, perhaps believing that they could readily identify HIV-infected individuals. Another survey found that 61% of adolescents believed that they were not the kind of person who is likely to get AIDS (DiClemente, Zorn, & Temoshok, 1986). The first step in risk reduction programs for adolescents, and other high-risk populations, is to address the issue of who is truly at risk of contracting AIDS.

As with adults, adolescents' awareness of recommended behaviors does not always lead to compliance. The results of a study of sexually active adolescents followed over a 1-year period indicated that, despite an awareness that condoms can prevent the spread of STDs, condom use decreased over the year (Kegeles, Adler, & Irwin, 1988). The authors suggest that, although adolescents may cognitively recognize the value of using condoms, they may not acknowledge a personal susceptibility to STDs that would necessitate the use of condoms. Effective education programs may need to increase adolescents' sense of personal susceptibility. Adolescents' attitudes about condom use also need to be improved. Females perceived that males had more negative attitudes toward condom usage than they actually did and may therefore be unlikely to insist on the use of condoms for fear of rejection by the males. If condom use were perceived more positively, condoms might be used more frequently.

An increasing number of AIDS prevention programs have been introduced in the schools. In his report on AIDS, Surgeon General Koop (1986) recommended that "education about AIDS should start in early elementary school and at home so that children can grow up knowing the behavior to avoid to protect themselves from exposure to the AIDS virus" (p. 5). Several studies have examined the effects of these programs. Students who participated in educational programs have increased their knowledge about AIDS (DiClemente et al., 1987; Huszti, Clopton, & Mason, 1988; Miller & Downer, 1987) and increased their positive attitudes toward persons with AIDS (Huszti et al., 1988; Miller & Downer, 1987).

Although increasing knowledge about AIDS and positive attitudes toward persons with AIDS are useful, the primary goal of AIDS education programs for adolescents is to increase the use of preventive behaviors. It is difficult to assess adolescents' actual participation in high-risk and preventive behaviors through schools because of the controversial and sensitive nature of those behaviors. However, some measure of adolescents' behaviors or attitudes is necessary to determine the effectiveness of prevention programs. One study evaluated adolescents' attitudes toward practicing preventive behaviors before, immediately after, and 1 month after a 1-hour prevention program (Huszti et al., 1988). Attitudes were significantly more positive following the program, but the change was small. All positive effects had disappeared at the 1-month follow-up. Because behavioral information could not be collected, it is difficult to draw firm conclusions from the data. However, current education programs do not appear to be sufficient to encourage long-term changes in preventive behaviors.

If further research confirms that current educational programs do not encourage the use of preventive behaviors, then other prevention programs must be developed. One promising approach used cognitive-behavioral techniques to facilitate pregnancy prevention in high school students (Schnike, Blythe, & Gilchrist, 1981). Students were instructed in basic reproductive and contraceptive knowledge and learned problem-solving skills specifically relating to birth control issues and both verbal and nonverbal communication skills. Posttest scores indicated that the group who received training showed increased knowledge, problem-solving techniques, and social skills in opposite-sex interactions. The 6-month follow-up data indicated that the training group had significantly better attitudes toward family planning, greater habitual use of contraception, greater protection at last intercourse, and less reliance on ineffective forms of birth control.

Certainly, the data from this program are promising. Similar training techniques might be used in AIDS prevention programs for both adolescents and adults. More skills are involved in using safer sex techniques than simply knowing that a condom should be used. Knowledge of health recommendations is useless without the accompanying skills that are necessary to implement the behaviors. Persons at high risk for HIV infection must be able to recognize the possible consequences of their choices and be comfortable in assertively communicating their choice for risk-reducing behavior to potential partners. Individuals must also be comfortable with the behavioral skills needed, and therefore explicit instructions in how to use condoms or sterilize needles are needed.

GENERAL RECOMMENDATIONS FOR AIDS PREVENTION PROGRAMS

Although, as discussed above, each high-risk group presents its own unique problems, some general points may be useful to consider when developing programs to reduce the risk of the transmission of HIV for women and adolescents. The bulk of the research on the prevention of the spread of HIV has been conducted with adult homosexual men. Although the factors maintaining high-risk behavior may be different for homosexual men than for homosexual adolescents or heterosexual risk group members, some of the information gained from studies of homosexual men may be usefully applied to other populations.

Studies examining the variables associated with the continued practice of high-risk behaviors in adult homosexual males have identified a number of associated factors. A denial of any personal risk of HIV infection has been associated with the continued practice of high-risk behavior (Emmons et al., 1986; McKusick, Coates, Wiley, Morin & Stall,

1987; Valdiserri et al., 1988). A negative attitude toward condoms has also been associated with the continued practice of high-risk behavior (Valdiserri et al., 1988), as has the use of drugs and/or alcohol during sexual activity (McKusick et al., 1987; Seigel, Chen, Mesagno, & Christ, 1987; Stall, McKusick, Wiley, Coates, & Ostrow, 1986; Valdiserri et al., 1988). This latter finding may be directly applicable to IVDUS' sexual behavior as well. Even when individuals know the proper preventive behaviors and intend to use them, they may return to previously used, high-risk behaviors when under the influence of drugs. The age of participants also appears to have an effect on the practice of safer sex. Younger men appear to be less likely to use preventive measures (Doll, Darrow, O'Malley, Bodecker, & Jaffe, 1987; McKusick et al., 1987; Pollak, Schiltz, & Lejeune, 1987; Valdiserri et al., 1988).

The results of studies examining the influence of HIV antibody test results on the practice of safer sexual behaviors have been mixed. The results of one study suggested that taking an HIV antibody test, regardless of the results, is associated with a greater reduction in the number of sexual partners (Van Griensven et al., 1987). Other studies have found that the test results influence the practice of safer behaviors. Men who learned that they were seropositive were more likely to reduce the number of their sexual partners than were men who learned that they were seronegative (Van Griensven et al., 1987; Willoughby et al., 1987). Still other studies have found no association between antibody status and sexual behavior (Calabrese, Harris, & Easley, 1987; Pollak et al., 1987). Currently, the results of the antibody screening test cannot be conclusively linked to any changes in the use of risk reduction practices.

In designing AIDS risk reduction programs, it is important to address and modify both the factors that serve to initiate the use of preventive health behaviors and those factors that encourage the long-term use of these behaviors. These factors may not be identical. A study of homosexual men found that those subjects who perceived themselves to be at risk for HIV infection and had high levels of self-efficacy were most likely to initiate the use of risk reduction behaviors (Emmons et al.,

1986). At a 1-year follow-up, the greatest predictor of continued practice of preventive behaviors was membership in a social system that reinforced the use of preventive behaviors. A study of the risk reduction behaviors of IVDUs showed a similar association between sustained behavioral change and the perception that friends were also practicing preventive behaviors (Friedman et al., 1987). In addition to modifying intrapsychic variables, prevention programs may need to encourage changes in entire social systems to support the continued practice of preventive behaviors once they have been initiated.

Second, program developers should keep in mind that there is a difference between a reduction in the practice of high-risk behaviors and an increase in the practice of preventive behaviors. Surveys of risk reduction behaviors among homosexual men indicate that the major changes in sexual behavior have been a decrease in risky behaviors, such as reducing the number of sexual partners, without a corresponding increase in the use of safer sexual behaviors, such as increasing the use of condoms (Martin & Hetrick, 1987; Van Griensven et al., 1987; Willoughby et al., 1987). Whether this same pattern will be found in heterosexual risk groups is unclear. Although any decrease in high-risk behaviors is welcome, there are some disturbing implications about this pattern of behavior changes. One hypothetical statistical model suggests that the reduction of sexual partners, in an already infected cohort, is not as effective in preventing HIV infection as the increased use of condoms (Fineberg, 1988). Additionally, it can be difficult for people to maintain abstinence from formerly pleasurable behaviors if no appealing alternative activities are substituted.

One interesting study on prevention education compared four different types of AIDS prevention programs (Quadland, Schattls, Schuman, Jacobs, & D'Eramo, 1988). Outcome was assessed by the self-report of participation in different sexual activities. Participants completed questionnaires prior to their participation in the programs and again 2 months later. The four types of prevention programs compared provided either basic information about safer sex guidelines, complete information about HIV and its effects in addition to safer sex guidelines, a positive and appealing discussion of safer sexual activities, or a positive and appealing presentation of safer sexual activities using explicit visual stimuli. Results indicated that the full educational program that presented information about HIV and its effects and safer sex guidelines encouraged the greatest reduction in the practice of unsafe behaviors. However, this type of educational program did not encourage participants to increase their use of safer behaviors. The presentation of safer sexual activities using erotic visual stimuli was most effective in increasing the practice of safer behaviors but did not greatly decrease the performance of risky sexual behaviors. The authors concluded that some degree of anxiety must be introduced to encourage participants to acknowledge their personal susceptibility to the disease and the necessity of avoiding certain behaviors to reduce their risk of HIV infection. Although this increased anxiety may cause individuals to reduce their high-risk behaviors, it does not encourage the performance of safer alternative behaviors. Participants must also be presented with appealing alternative behaviors. Thus, a total prevention program may need to use the two components together, combining education about the disease with the presentation of attractive, viable alternative behaviors.

Although an increase in personal anxiety about HIV infection may be important in encouraging the initiation of preventive behaviors, anxiety can be raised to dysfunctional levels. For example, in one study of homosexual males' high-risk and preventive sexual behaviors (Emmons et al., 1986), men with a moderate level of self-perceived risk of HIV infection were most likely to practice preventive behaviors. However, men with the highest degree of self-perceived risk did not make recommended changes. The authors suggest that too high a level of anxiety about personal susceptibility may promote feelings of fatalism, that infection is inevitable, and that nothing can change that fact. As a result, preventive behaviors are not practiced.

An alternative explanation may be that messages that arouse high levels of fear may be ineffective in stopping behaviors that are commonly used by the target population to reduce anxiety (Job, 1988). In other words, when anxiety is increased, individuals use their typical coping responses to reduce that anxiety. For example, when messages about AIDS are heard, anxiety may be increased, and IVDUs who use drugs to alleviate anxiety will use the drugs to reduce their anxiety about AIDS. Ironically, this behavior ends up increasing their risk of HIV infection by placing them in a state in which recommended behavioral patterns are disregarded (Stall et al., 1986). Interestingly, the results of one study of homosexual men in San Francisco found a positive relation between subjects' agreement with the statement "I use hot anonymous sex to relieve tension" and having had more than three anonymous sexual partners in the prior month (McKusick, Horstman, & Coates, 1985). Perhaps messages about the threat of AIDS served to increase this group's fear and anxiety, leading them to use sexual intercourse to alleviate that fear, thereby increasing the very activity the fear message was supposed to reduce.

A program to reduce the spread of STDs may offer some important directions for the development of AIDS risk reduction programs. A sexually transmitted disease clinic used television-quality, soap-opera-style videotaped vignettes to encourage clinic patients to increase their compliance with medical regimens (Solomon & DeJong, 1986). These tapes were effective. A similar tape was developed to increase condom usage. The videotape portrayed a young woman who is supported by her friends in her attempts to change her boyfriend's attitudes toward using condoms. The boyfriend's attitudes are eventually changed. The disadvantages of condoms were discussed as well as the advantages. The goal of the videotape was to influence the subjects through the use of attractive and believable role models. Preliminary analyses of pre- and postfilm attitude surveys suggest that the videotape increased positive attitudes toward condom usage. Analyses of behavioral changes are currently under way. The study was conducted using a poor, nonwhite, inner-city population similar to groups that are currently at a disproportionately high risk of developing AIDS. This type of intervention may be particularly effective with poor, minority populations who have received little AIDS prevention education but are at the highest risk of contracting AIDS.

It is important to remember that AIDS prevention may raise different issues for women than for men. The majority of risk reduction programs have been developed for males, and the majority of resources for HIV antibody positive individuals are also oriented toward males. Although many elements of prevention programs can serve both males and females, program developers need to recognize women's unique needs. Women who are HIV antibody positive are facing the chance of developing a potentially fatal illness and may feel a need to have a child in order to leave a part of themselves behind after they die (Buckingham & Rehm, 1987). Female sexual partners of HIV-infected males may feel a similar pressure from their partners to have a child. Female partners of IVDUs often see having a child as a way to maintain their primary sexual relationship. Women in high-risk groups may also be parents, and successful prevention programs ought to address the needs of their children. Not only do high-risk women face psychosocial problems, but they often also lack effective parenting skills. The occurrence of HIV infection, ARC, or AIDS in these women or their children places an extraordinary burden on their families, who have difficulty coping even before the advent of infection. Comprehensive prevention programs need to recognize and address these issues in order to be successful in preventing the further spread of pediatric AIDS. They might benefit from previous studies on increasing females' use of contraceptives. Many of the issues pertinent to increasing the use of preventive sexual behaviors, such as the use of condoms, are similar to those raised by the issue of effectively using contraceptives.

EVALUATION

A vital element of any prevention package is an evaluation of its effectiveness. Past research has indicated that expected or logical outcomes are not always found. Just because a program intuitively sounds as if it should increase the use of preventive behaviors does not mean that it actually has any effect at all. Given the necessity of encouraging the use of preventive behaviors, it is essential that resources be spent on programs that are proven to be effective. Evaluation of prevention programs should assess the factors that maintain the use of risky behaviors in the various high-risk populations and the factors that encourage the initiation and maintenance of preventive behaviors. With the continued evaluation of which elements of prevention programs are most effective, prevention programs can continue to be refined to obtain the most effective programs possible.

REFERENCES

Buckingham, S. L., & Rehm, S. J. (1987). AIDS and women at risk. *Health and Social Work, 10,* 5–11.

Calabrese, L. H., Harris, B., & Easley, K. (1987, June). Analysis of variables impacting on safe sexual behavior among homosexual men in an area of low incidence for AIDS. Paper presented at the Third International Conference on AIDS, Washington, DC.

Centers for Disease Control. (1985). Recommendations for assisting in the prevention of perinatal transmission of human T-lymphotropic virus type III/lymphadenopathy-associated virus and acquired immunodeficiency syndrome. *Morbidity and Mortality Weekly Report, 34,* 721–732.

Centers for Disease Control. (1986). AIDS among Blacks and Hispanics—U.S. *Morbidity and Mortality Weekly Report, 35,* 655–666.

Centers for Disease Control. (1988). AIDS weekly surveillance report. *Morbidity and Mortality Weekly Report, 38,* 810.

Chen, M., & Land, K. C. (1986). Testing the health belief model: LISREL analysis of alternative models of causal relationships between health beliefs and preventive dental behavior. *Social Psychology Quarterly, 49,* 45–60.

Chitwood, D. D., Comerford, M., McCoy, C. B., Trapido, E. J., Page, J. B., McBride, D. C., & Inciardi, J. (1988, June). Epidemiology of HIV among intravenous drug users in south Florida. Paper presented at the Fourth International Conference on AIDS, Stockholm, Sweden.

Chitwood, D. D., & Morningstar, P. C. (1985). Factors which differentiate cocaine users in treatment from non-treatment users. *Internation Journal of Addictions, 20,* 449–459.

Cohen, J. B. (1987, September). Three years' experience promoting AIDS prevention among 800 sexually active high risk women in San Francisco. Paper presented at the National Institute of Mental Health/National Institute on Drug Abuse research conference *Women and* AIDS: *Promoting health behaviors,* Bethesda, M. D.

Day, S., Ward, H., Wadsworth, J., & Harris, J. R. W. (1987, June). Attitudes of female prostitutes in London to barrier protection. Paper presented at the Third International Conference on AIDS, Washington, DC.

Deresiewicz, W. (1988). Against all odds: Grassroots minority groups fight AIDS. *Health Policy Advisory Center, 18,* 4–11.

Des Jarlais, D. C., Chamberland, M. E., Yancovitz, S. R., Weinberg, P., & Friedman, S. R. (1984). Heterosexual partners: A large risk group for AIDS. *Lancet, 2,* 1346–1347.

Des Jarlais, D. C., & Friedman, S. R. (1988). The psychology of preventing AIDS among intravenous drug users: A social learning conceptualization. *American Psychologist, 43,* 865–870.

Des Jarlais, D. C., Friedman, S. R., & Hopkins, W. (1985). Risk reduction for the acquired immunodeficiency syndrome among intravenous drug users. *Annals of Internal Medicine, 103,* 755–759.

Des Jarlais, D. C., Friedman, S. R., & Strug., D. (1986). AIDS and needle sharing within the IV-drug use subculture. In D. Feldman & T. Johnson (Eds.), *The social dimension of* AIDS: *Methods and theory* (pp. 111–125). New York: Praeger.

7DiClemente, R. J., Pies, C. A., Stoller, E. J., Haskin, J., Oliva, G. E., & Rutherford, G. W. (1987, June). Evaluation of a school-based education curricula in San Francisco. Paper presented at the Third International Conference on AIDS, Washington, DC.

DiClemente, R. J., Zorn, J., & Temoshok, L. (1986). Adolescents and AIDS: A survey of knowledge, attitudes, and beliefs about AIDS in San Francisco. *American Journal of Public Health, 76,* 1443–1445.

Doll, L. S., Darrow, W., O'Malley, P., Bodecker, T., & Jaffe, A. (1987, June). Self-reported behavioral change in homosexual men in the San Francisco City clinic cohort. Paper presented at the Third International Conference on AIDS, Washington, DC.

Drotman, D. P. (1987). Now is the time to prevent AIDS. *American Journal of Public Health, 77,* 143.

Elkind, D. (1967). Egocentrism in adolescence. *Child Development, 38,* 1025–1034.

Emmons, C. A., Joseph, J. G., Kessler, R. C., Wortman, C. B., Montgomery, S. B., & Ostrow, D. G. (1986). Psychosocial predictors of reported behavioral change in homosexual males at risk for AIDS. *Health Education Quarterly, 13*, 331.

Fineberg, H. V. (1988). Education to prevent AIDS: Prospects and obstacles. *Science, 239*, 592–596.

Flynn, N. M., Jain, S., Harper, S., Bailey, V., Anderson, R., & Acuna, G. (1987). Sharing of paraphernalia in intravenous drug users (IVDU): Knowledge of AIDS is incomplete and doesn't affect behavior. Paper presented at the Third International Conference on AIDS, Washington, DC.

Friedland, S. R., & Klein, R. D. (1987). Transmission of the human immunodeficiency virus. *New England Journal of Medicine, 317*, 1125–1135.

Friedman, S. R., Des Jarlais, D. C., & Sotheran, J. L. (1988). AIDS health education for intravenous drug users. In R. Galea, B. F. Lewis, & L. A. Baker (Eds.), *AIDS and IV drug abuse: Current perspectives* (pp. 199–214). Owings Mills, MD: National Health Publishing.

Friedman, S. R., Des Jarlais, D. C., Sotheran, J. L., Garber, J., Cohen, H., & Smith, D. (1987). AIDS and self-organization among intravenous drug users. *International Journal of Addictions, 22*, 201–220.

Ginzburg, H. M., French, J., Jackson, J., et al. (1988). Health education and knowledge assessment of HIV diseases among intravenous drug users. In R. Galea, B. F. Lewis, & L. A. Baker (Eds.), *AIDS and IV drug abuse: Current perspectives* (pp. 185–197). Owings Mills, MD: National Health Publishing.

Grossman, M. (1988). Children with AIDS. In I. B. Corless & M. Pittman-Lindeman (Eds.), *AIDS: Principles, practices and politics* (pp. 167–173). Cambridge, MA: Hemisphere.

Hein, K. (1988, March). AIDS in adolescence: Exploring the challenge. Paper presented at the National Invitational Conference on Adolescent AIDS, New York.

Hoft, R., Berardi, V. P., Weiblen, B. J., Mahoney-Trout, L., Mitchell, M. L., & Grady, G. F. (1988). Seroprevalence of human immunodeficiency virus among childbearing women. *New England Journal of Medicine, 318*(9), 525–530.

Hubbard, R. L., Allison, M., Bray, R. M., Craddock, S. G., Rachal, J. V., & Ginzburg, H. M. (1983). An overview of client characteristics, treatment services and drug treatment outcomes for outpatient methadone clinics in the treatment outcome prospective study (TOPS). In J. R. Cooper, F. Altman, B. S. Brown, & D. Czechowicz (Eds.), *Research on the treatment of narcotic addiction* (Treatment

Research Monograph Series, DHHS Publication No. ADM 83–1281, pp. 714–751). Rockville MD: National Institute on Drug Abuse.

Huszti, H. C., Clopton, J. R., & Mason, P. J. (1988). Effects of an AIDS educational program on adolescents' knowledge and attitudes. Paper submitted for publication.

Job, R. F. S. (1988). Effective and ineffective use of fear in health promotion campaigns. *American Journal of Public Health, 78,* 163–167.

Kegeles, S. M., Adler, N. E., & Irwin, C. E. (1988). Sexually active adolescents and condoms: Changes over one year in knowledge, attitudes and use. *American Journal of Public Health, 78*(4), 460–461.

Kleinman, P. H., Friedman, S. R., Mauge, C. E., Goldsmith, D. S., Des Jarlais, D. C., & Hopkins, W. (1987). Beliefs and behaviors regarding AIDS: A survey of street intravenous drug users. Paper presented at the Third International Conference on AIDS, Washington, DC.

Koop, C. E. (1986). *Surgeon general's report on acquired immune deficiency syndrome.* Washington, DC: U.S. Department of Health and Human Services.

Landesman, S., Minkoff, H., Holman, S., McCalla, S., & Sijin, O. (1987). Serosurvey of human immunodeficiency virus infection in parturients. *Journal of the American Medical Association, 258,* 2701–2703.

McAuliffe, W. E., Doering, S., Breer, P., Silverman, H., Branson, B., & Williams, K. (1987, June). An evaluation of using ex-addict outreach workers to educate intravenous drug users about AIDS prevention. Paper presented at the Third International Conference on AIDS, Washington, DC.

McCoy, C. B., Chitwood, D. D., McCoy, V., Trapido, E. J., Page, J. B., McBride, D. C., Inciardo, J., & Cummerford, M. (1988, June). Implementation and evaluation of an HIV risk reduction program for intravenous drug abusers. Paper presented at the Fourth International Conference on AIDS, Stockholm, Sweden.

McKusick, L., Coates, T. J., Wiley, J. A., Morin, S. F., & Stall, R. (1987, June). Prevention of HIV infection among gay and bisexual men: Two longitudinal studies. Paper presented at the Third International Conference on AIDS, Washington, DC.

McKusick, L., Horstman, W., & Coates, T. J. (1985). AIDS and sexual behavior reported by gay men in San Francisco. *American Journal of Public Health, 75,* 493–496.

Maddux, J. E., & Rogers, R. W. (1983). Protection motivation and self-efficacy: A revised theory of fear appeals and attitude change. *Journal of Experimental Social Psychology, 19*, 469–479.

Martin, A. D., & Hetrick, E. S. (1987). Designing an AIDS risk reduction program for gay teenagers: Problems and proposed solutions. In D. G. Ostrow (Ed.), *Bio-behavioral control of AIDS* (pp. 137–152). New York: Irvington.

Mays, V. M., & Cochran, S. D. (1988). Issues in the perception of AIDS risk and risk reduction activities by Black and Hispanic/Latina women. *American Psychologist, 43*, 949–957.

Melton, G. B. (1988). Adolescents and prevention of AIDS. *Professional Psychology: Research and Practice, 19*, 403–408.

Miller, L., & Downer, A. (1987, June). Knowledge and attitude changes in adolescents following one hour of AIDS instruction. Paper presented at the Third International Conference on AIDS, Washington, DC.

Murphy, J. S. (1988). Women with AIDS: Sexual ethics in an epidemic. In I. B. Corless, & M. Pittman-Lindeman (Eds.), *AIDS: Principles, practices and politics* (pp. 65–79). Cambridge, MA: Hemisphere.

Pollak, M., Schiltz, M. A., & Lejeune, B. (1987, June). Safer sex and acceptance of testing: Results of the nationwide annual survey among French gay men. Paper presented at the Third International Conference on AIDS, Washington, DC.

Quadland, M. C., Schattls, W., Schuman, R., Jacobs, R., & D'Eramo, J. (1988). The 800 men study: A systematic evaluation of AIDS prevention programs. Unpublished manuscript.

Ralph, N., & Spigner, R. C. (1986). Contraceptive practices among female heroin addicts. *American Journal of Public Health, 76*, 1016–1017.

Rogers, R. W. (1985). Attitude change and information integration in fear appeals. *Psychological Reports, 56*, 179–182.

Rogers, R. W., & Mewborn, C. R. (1976). Fear appeals and attitude change: Effects of a threat's noxiousness, probability of occurrence, and the efficacy of coping responses. *Journal of Personality and Social Psychology, 34*, 54–61.

Rosenstock, I. M. (1966). Why people use health services. *Milbank Memorial Fund Quarterly, 44*, 94–127.

Schnike, S. P., Blythe, B. J., & Gilchrist, L. D. (1981). Cognitive-behavioral prevention of adolescent pregnancy. *Journal of Counseling Psychology, 28*, 451–454.

Scott, G. B., Fischl, M. A., Klimas, N., Fletcher, M. A., Dickinson, G. M., Levine, R. S., & Parks, W. P. (1985). Mothers of infants with the acquired immunodeficiency syndrome: Evidence for both symptomatic and asymptomatic carriers. *Journal of the American Medical Association, 253,* 363–366.

Siegel, K., Chen, J. Y., Mesagno, F., & Christ, G. (1987, June). Persistence and change in sexual behavior and perceptions of risk for AIDS among homosexual men. Paper presented at the Third International Conference on AIDS, Washington, DC.

Simon, K. J., & Das, A. (1984). An application of the health belief model toward educational diagnosis for VD education. *Health Education Quarterly, 11,* 403–418.

Solomon, M. Z., & DeJong, W. (1986). Recent sexually transmitted disease prevention efforts and their implications for AIDS health education. *Health Education Quarterly, 13,* 301–316.

Stall, R., McKusick, L., Wiley, J., Coates, T. J., & Ostrow, D. G. (1985). Alcohol and drug use during sexual activity and compliance without safe sex guidelines for AIDS: The AIDS Behavior Research Project. *Health Education Quarterly, 13,* 359–371.

Strunin, L., & Hingson, R. (1987). Acquired immunodeficiency syndrome and adolescents: Knowledge, beliefs, attitudes, and behaviors. *Pediatrics, 79,* 825–828.

Valdiserri, R. O., Lyter, D., Leviton, L. C., Callahan, C. M., Kingsley, L. A., & Rinaldo, C. R. (1988). Variables influencing condom use in a cohort of gay and bisexual men. *American Journal of Public Health, 78,* 801–805.

Van Griensven, G. J. P., Tielman, R. A. P., Goudsmit, J., Van der Noordaa, J., DeWolf, F., & Coutinho, R. A. (1987, June). Effect of HIVab serodiagnosis on sexual behavior in homosexual men in the Netherlands. Paper presented at the Third International Conference on AIDS, Washington, DC.

Wagner, B., Greeberg, R., Higgins, B., Norris, H., & Taylor, J. (1987). Support groups for HIV positive females including those with HIV positive infants. Paper presented at the Third International Conference on AIDS, Washington, DC.

Watters, J. K. (1987, June). Preventing human immunodeficiency virus contagion among intravenous drug users: The impact of street-based education on risk behavior. Paper presented at the Third International Conference on AIDS, Washington, DC.

Wiebel, W., & Fritz, R. (1987, December). Nature and scope of substance abuse in Chicago and Illinois December 1987. Community Epidemiology Work Group Proceedings (No. II27–35). Washington, DC: U.S. Department of Health and Human Services.

Willoughby, B., Schechter, M. T., Boyko, W. J., Craib, K. J. P., Weaver, M. S., & Douglas, B. (1987, June). Sexual practives and condom use in a cohort of homosexual men: Evidence of differential modification between seropositive and seronegative men. Paper presented at the Third International Conference on AIDS, Washington, DC.

Zackon, F., McAuliffe, W. E., & Chiron, J. M. N. (1985). Addict aftercare (DHHS Publication No. ADM 85–1341). Washington, DC: U.S. Government Printing Office.

•

CHAPTER SEVEN

Pediatric AIDS Research:
Legal, Ethical,
and Policy Influences

JONI N. GRAY

INTRODUCTION

Until recently, little research has been conducted on pediatric acquired immunodeficiency syndrome (AIDS), AIDS-related complex (ARC), and asymptomatic human immunodeficiency virus (HIV) infection. Some of the reasons for this neglect are that there are few pediatric AIDS cases in relation to the total number of AIDS cases (approximately 1%) (Centers for Disease Control [CDC], 1987), children with AIDS were discovered some time after AIDS first appeared in adults, and, as a group, children with AIDS are not organized, and neither are their advocates (Hayes, 1982; Melton, Koocher, & Saks, 1983). As a result, other, larger groups that were at high risk for AIDS (CDC, 1982), those identified earlier (CDC, 1981) and organized for placing pressure on

The writing of this chapter was supported in part by National Research Service Award 5T32 MH 16156–06 from the National Institute of Mental Health (NIMH) to the University of Nebraska—Lincoln. The opinions expressed in this chapter are those of the author and do not necessarily represent the positions of the NIMH.

medical, research, and political bodies (e.g., gay men) (Budiansky, 1983), were studied more quickly and thoroughly.

Presently, however, attention has begun to focus on preventing the "smaller high risk groups" from growing ("Koop Urges," 1987). For instance, people are recognizing that, as HIV infection continues to spread within the heterosexual community, infant pediatric AIDS cases due to perinatal transmission can be expected to rise ("AIDS and Young Children," 1987; Guinan & Hardy, 1987). In addition, although children and adolescents may contract AIDS in ways similar to those in which adults contact the disease (Institute of Medicine, 1986), they are also susceptible to unique modes of transmission (e.g., sexual abuse) ("Gammaglobulin," 1987) and have unique needs for management of their illness, prevention strategies, and clinical support (Gray & Melton, in press). Furthermore, children with AIDS present state authorities with the task of promulgating controversial policies that must balance concerns related to mandatory school attendance, children's right to an education, and public health protection issues (Weiner, 1986). Thus, to control the incidence of pediatric AIDS, meet children's special needs in the best way possible, and develop policies for pediatric AIDS cases, immediate research attention is warranted.

It is my purpose here to present an overview of the legal, ethical, and policy issues affecting pediatric AIDS research. First, some of the factors that may direct or bias the conception and design of that research are identified. Second, I identify potential problems that may arise as research is conducted, including that of confidentiality. Legal and ethical mandates that pertain to research confidentiality are presented, and suggestions for strategies designed to avoid, improve, or solve potential difficulties are made. While I have no pat solutions to offer, I hope that the awareness gained by discussion of these issues will enhance the research process and generate possible solutions to these potential problems. Finally, I consider the researchers' potential effect on pediatric AIDS policies and broader children's policies as their findings are disseminated.

INFLUENCES ON THE CONCEPTION
AND DESIGN OF RESEARCH

The first stage at which pediatric AIDS research may be influenced is that of conception and design.[1] The choice of topics and ideas is generally influenced by prior research, new information, established societal or professional directions, "research pleas" by policymakers, or identified topics by granting agencies. In addition, the design of the research (operationalized definitions, selection criteria, and the formation of the research question) may be influenced by "outside" factors.

Although these forms of influence perhaps seem obvious, they may be overlooked by researchers. Influences on research directions may be positive or negative; either way, undetected influences may skew research in such a way that it is far from "objective" and is much more "selective" than comprehensive. Thus, pediatric AIDS researchers should be aware of influences on their research so that such forces may be examined for bias, detrimental effects, selectivity, and faulty reasoning. Only by being aware of "outside forces" can researchers counteract, adjust for, or at least report such influences.

The Centers for Disease Control

The Centers for Disease Control (CDC) is the primary structural entity that has influenced the conception and design of AIDS research. The CDC was the first entity to recognized formally and define manifestations of AIDS, its prevalence and incidence, the primary groups affected, and suspected "risk factors" involved (Altman, 1986, chap. 3). The CDC's structure and function influence what information it obtains (Flam & Stein, 1986). Researchers often focus on the directions provided by the CDC without fully understanding why or how these

---

1. Although, technically, *pediatric* usually refers to children under 13 years of age, I will use *pediatric AIDS research* to mean research on infants, children, and adolescents up to age 18 or 19 as well as on the adults involved in pediatric cases—e.g., infected mothers that give birth to offspring with HIV infection.

particular directions are discovered. Therefore, a brief description of the CDC and its functions is presented.

The CDC is the federal agency responsible for controlling and preventing disease in the United States. It investigates illness within an epidemiologic framework, epidemology being the study of distributions and determinants of disease in human populations (MacMahon & Pugh, 1970). Epidemiologic studies are designed to describe the many aspects of a disease, discover its cause, and interrupt its progression. The first part of the investigation, termed *descriptive epidemiology,* portrays the occurence of the disease according to group characteristics such as age, sex, race, ethnicity, occuption, and geographic location. In addition, incidence, prevalence, and mortality rates may be included (Flam & Stein, 1986).

An awareness of the CDC's structure and function is important because they influence the type of knowledge that is obtained (or what area of inquiry is overlooked), which in turn influences the direction of research. Researchers should not allow the CDC's findings to dictate their research focus, thereby closing off other possible avenues of discovery.

Furthermore, researchers may want to question their decision to defer the task of defining AIDS, its related manifestations, and its prevalence within groups to others—namely, the CDC—because the CDC's reporting methods sometimes reflect their own purposes more than what would be useful for a particular research project or a "true" picture of the phenomenon. For example, the CDC originally reported the incidence of AIDS within groups in a hierarchical manner; that is, persons with AIDS that belonged to more than one of the identified "risk groups" were placed only in the most prevalent group (e.g., gay men and adolescents who were also intravenous drug users would be counted only in the homosexual risk group) ("Update," 1986a). This practice (which has now been altered to reflect more accurate numbers for intravenous drug use among gay persons) (CDC, 1986) resulted in an exaggeration of the size differences among risk groups, distorting the number of persons in each group that were affected and influencing which groups researchers chose to focus on.

In addition to prevalence-reporting issues, children with AIDS who are targeted for research are usually selected on the basis of the diagnostic interpretations by physicians of the CDC's surveillance definitions for pediatric AIDS. Physicians' diagnoses may vary, however, and the CDC's definition has been criticized for being both under- and over-inclusive (Goedert & Blattner, 1985). These criticisms along with continual refinements in diagnostic procedures (e.g., methods for detecting HIV infection in newborns [Harnish, Hammerberg, Walker, & Rosenthal, 1987; Johnson, Nair, & Alexander, 1987]) have resulted in alterations in the CDC's definitions (CDC, 1985).

Researchers need to be aware of revisions in definitions because research that relies on the CDC's changing definitions and physicians' variable diagnoses may result in distorted results, particularly when data collected during two different definitional periods are compared. Unfortunately, researchers do not use standardized criteria for characterizing the syndrome and its diagnosis either, adding to the difficulty of making comparisons among research findings. Pediatric AIDS researchers should therefore be careful to report what criteria for participant selection were used.

Societal Attitudes and Professional Trends

Society in general and professional trends also may influence researchers in several ways. Although this point may seem more philosophical than practical—and I will not attempt specifically to describe influences that are constantly changing—it is important for pediatric AIDS researchers to be cognizant of their research "context" when conceptualizing and structuring their research projects. Problems can be addressed more creatively if researchers are aware of the influences that shape their thoughts and research. Such an awareness can also prevent researchers and policymakers from unknowingly becoming dogmatically committed to an idea or area and therefore dismissing new ways of examining problems without due consideration. It is particularly important that people conducting pediatric AIDS research be aware of any personal biases or prejudices that could potentially influence their work because strong beliefs concerning abortion, pregnancy outside marriage, promiscuity, and intravenous drug use may unduely bias the manner in which research is designed.

INFLUENCES ON THE CONDUCT OF RESEARCH
Ethical and Legal Impositions

In addition to various degrees of indirect influence from diverse sources on pediatric AIDS research, there are explicit directives from ethical guidelines and legal regulations that primarily affect the "second" stage of research—implementation. The effects of these explicit directives on research conduct are much more tangible and defined than are those of the influences on the early stages of research process previously discussed. Ethical guidelines are promulgated by professional organizations (Gray & Melton, 1985, n. 16), and legal regulations pertaining to the conduct of social science research involving human participants are constructed and sanctioned primarily by the federal government ("Protection of Human Subjects," 1984).

Although many professional organizations have their own standards for ethical conduct, the most detailed code is that of the American Psychological Association (1981; hereafter referred to as the APA Principles); therefore, only the APA code will be discussed. Psychologists are bound by the APA Principles. For nonpsychologists, these principles may serve as guidelines for ethical conduct. The primary legal framework for the protection of human participants in psychosocial research is found in the regulations of the Department of Health and Human Services (DHHS) (Protection of Human Subjects, 1984), which govern all research funded by the DHHS. In general, all research conducted by universities, schools, and health care facilities, and therefore much, if not all, psychosocial research on pediatric AIDS, is covered by the DHHS regulations. In addition, the Office of Science and Technology's proposed common Federal Policy for the Protection of Human Subjects

184

(Federal Policy, 1988) would apply these regulations to 14 additional federal departments and agencies.[2]

The restraints on research embodied in these two codes have developed over the years in response to the necessity of protecting research participants' interests (Gray & Melton, 1985, n. 1). For the most part, research with human participants is conducted for the good of society rather than the individual (*Dow Chem. Co. v. Allen*, 1982; *Andrews v. Eli Lilly & Co.*, 1983; *Richards of Rockford, Inc. v. Pacific Gas & Elec. Co.*, 1976). In order to protect human dignity and welfare, the APA Principles and the DHHS regulations therefore both require minimization of risk to participants (American Psychological Association, 1981, principles 9, 9b, 9g; Protection of Human Subjects, 1984, sec. 46.111(1)) and the weighing of potential risks and benefits (principles 1a, 9, 9a; sec. 46.111(2)), with the aid of outside ethical advice (principle 9a1; secs. 46.107, 46.109), when determining whether a study should be conducted. Researchers are also generally required to receive informed consent from participants (principles 6, 9d; secs. 46.111 (d) (4)–(5), 46.116–7), honor an individual's freedom to decline or to withdraw from participation (principle 9f; secs. 46.111(8), 46.116(8)), and protect participants' privacy and the confidentiality of data (principles 1b, 5, 5b, 5c, 9j; secs. 46.111(a)(6), 46.116(5)). Only the APA code, however, requires that results be reported ethically (preamble and principles 1a, 4): psychologists are obligated to "minimize the possibility that their findings will be misleading . . . especially where their work touches on social policy or might be construed to the detriment of persons in specific age, sex, ethnic, socioeconomic, or other social groups" (principle 1a).

2. Those agencies are the Department of Agriculture, the Department of Energy, the National Aeronautics and Space Administration, the Department of Commerce, the Consumer Product Safety Commission, the Agency for International Development, the Department of Housing and Urban Development, the Department of Justice, the Department of Defense, the Department of Education, the Veterans' Administration, the Environmental Protection Agency, the National Science Foundation, the Department of Health and Human Services, and the Department of Transportation.

The DHHS has additional requirements for research involving children (Additional Protections, 1986). Benefits to children participating in research do not need to be great if the research does not involve more than minimal risk (sec. 46.404). However, if there is a prospect of direct benefit to the child, research involving greater than minimal risk may be conducted (sec. 46.405). In addition, if research involves greater than minimal risk with no direct benefit to individual participants but is likely to yield generalizable knowledge about the child's condition, research with the proper constraints may be performed (sec. 46.406). If research does not fit into one of these three catagories, it will not be approved or supported by the DHHS unless there is an opportunity to understand, prevent, or alleviate a serious problem affecting the health or welfare of children and proper consent and assent is given (sec. 46.407).

An examination of the risks and benefits in a project often reveals conflicting interests among the various parties. For example, a group under study has an interest in the results of the project. However, in socially sensitive research, breaches of confidentiality or careless reporting of findings may harm the participants in the study and the groups they represent, the very people the project was meant to help. Then again, participants' privacy needs may clash with society's need to gather information that may be useful in protecting the public health. Finally, researchers' interests are not always coextensive with those of society (Committee for the Protection of Human Participants in Research, 1985, p. 26).

Obviously, the conflict of interests that exists in pediatric AIDS research is not easily resolved. However, in order to assist researchers in balancing the needs of the various parties involved, a discussion of some of the potential benefits and harms involved in pediatric AIDS research will follow. This discussion serves only to outline the general issues involved, not to provide a comprehensive list of possible conflicts for any particular research project.

Harms and Benefits Involved in Pediatric AIDS Research

Several possible harms are involved for partcipants in pediatric AIDS research. For example, as a result of a research study, children may experience physical discomfort when blood samples are taken; young children may be emotionally upset when separated from their parents; children and adolescents may be disturbed by confronting possible death; and adolescents may experience guilt associated with sexual experiences or drug use. Disclosure of childrens' medical status as a result of research participation, or the mere disclosure of participation in AIDS research, may result in the stigmatization, isolation, exclusion from school, and family rejection of the participants because of others' fear of contracting AIDS and prejudices toward drug use, promiscuity, and homosexuality. These same consequences are likely to occur for the participants' parents and other family members. In addition, parents may be confronted with accusations and/or guilt associated with their own prior sexual behavior or drug use that was responsible for their initial HIV infection, which was then transmitted perinatally to the child.

Although the benefits and harms involved differ among research projects, almost no individual child participant will receive immediate, direct benefit from AIDS research—most children will not survive long enough for any benefit gained through present treatment trials. However, altruistic feelings, knowing that one is "doing the right thing," and the feeling of protecting family members may be enhanced by research participation. In addition, both participants and their parents may be provided with current information, individual or family counseling, and support group participation. Benefits to society and the researcher are more abundant. For instance, a cure or preventive strategy may be developed for curtailing the spread of AIDS among children; the emotional needs of persons with AIDS and those close to such persons may be defined, enabling proper clinical intervention; and researchers may gain prestige and recognition from their research.

The most pervasive potential harms involved in pediatric AIDS research are those associated with the infringement of privacy.[3] Such

3. The assumption is made that minors are "persons" entitled to the same privacy as adults. Although only the term *participant* will be used, when privacy rights of participants are discussed, participants' parents or guardians are to be included when appropriate (e.g., intravenous-drug-using mothers who infected their offspring with HIV during pregnancy may be involved in many of the studies conducted on pediatric AIDS).

harm may result from the intrusive nature of the research or from the maintenance or disclosure of confidential information. Pediatric AIDS research is inherently intrusive because it often requires inquiry into sensitive, personal areas such as sexual and drug practices. In addition, when selection for the study is based on a group characteristic (e.g., intravenous-drug-using parents), mere identification as a potential research participant is intrusive and involves some breach of privacy. Furthermore, when the study focuses on responses to AIDS, the evocation of private thoughts may be accompanied by distress that would not otherwise have occurred (Joseph et al., 1984).

In order to protect privacy, participants should retain as much control over personal information as possible. In keeping with the APA Principles, the Committee for the Protection of Human Participants in Research (1985, p. 26) issued the following guidelines for researach on AIDS:

> In general, researchers should minimize the intrusiveness of studies insofar as possible. Whenever possible, data should be derived from clinical interviews and archives which would already be collected. Under most circumstances, potential participants should be contacted only after they have volunteered directly, or permission for contact has been obtained by an appropriate intermediary who is the source for identification of the participant (e.g., personal physician; the AIDS patient, when the population to be studied includes patients' lovers or acquaintances). When more intrusive procedures appear necessary for the conduct of a study, the researcher is especially obligated to consider and seek advice about the merits of the study in the face of the invasion of privacy (Principles 9 and 9a). The researcher should warn potential participants when the content of an interview or questionnaire may be disturbing (Principles 9d and 9f) and permit them to refrain from participating or to withdraw if they choose (Principle 9g) . . . [C]areful debriefing and follow-up should be undertaken to identify and prevent or alleviate stressful effects of participation (Principles 9g and 9i).

Although these recommendations are helpful in general, they do not address the issues involved with child participants very well. For example, "permitting" participants to refrain or withdraw from research participation may mean little when the participant is 5 years old and does not really understand that he or she has the right not to do what adults tell him or her to do. (Further limitations of these recommendations and additional guidelines for research with child participants are discussed below when the issue of informed consent is raised.)

Researchers also must address the problem of confidentiality. The participant who has produced personal information retains an interest in controlling access to that information. The principle of beneficence requires that researchers make an effort to shield participants from harm that might potentially result from their participation (principle 9g). When the content of the research information collected is sensitive, preservation of confidentiality becomes critical to the protection of participants (*Lora v. Bd. of Education,* 1977, p. 571).

The typical insult to privacy entailed in disclosure of identifiable research data without the consent of the participant is exacerbated in AIDS research by the adverse social, legal, and economic consequences that may result from breaches of confidentiality. There is ample evidence for stigma resulting from the diagnosis itself. Persons with AIDS often must face being shunned by others who have a fear of contracting AIDS or who are unable to deal with people who have a potentially terminal illness. The social isolation that often results when acquaintances know of the diagnosis makes coping with a serious illness more difficult (Nelson, Maxey, & Keith, 1984). Furthermore, because of the irrational nature of the fear of AIDS, some stigma may accrue from mere participation in a study about AIDS, even if one does not actually have the illness.

Disclosure of research data, or simply the fact of participation, can also be harmful because of the stigma to which "risk groups" are already vulnerable. Gay adolescents can be subjected to the same type of discrimination that gay men have experienced for some time (Novick, 1984). Intravenous drug users, who may already be perceived as weak, undisciplined, unproductive members of society that are willing to engage in whatever criminal behavior is necessary to maintain their habit, are very likely to be further stigmatized if it is known that they are the parents of infants with AIDS. Other stigmas involved in cases of pediatric AIDS are those attached to prostitution, teenage or unwed mothers, and promiscuity among heterosexual women in general.

Some of the groups considered to be most at risk for AIDS are also vulnerable to legal sanctions. Gay adolescents face at least the threat of criminal prosecution in the 25 states where homosexual acts are still crimes (*Rights of Gay People*, 1984). Intravenous drug use is illegal throughout the United States, as are the possession and sale of drugs and drug paraphernalia (Novick, 1984).

Thus, if identifying, "private" information about pediatric AIDS research participants is released to legal authorities, school personnel, health care workers, and others, participants may be harmed socially and legally. This potential harm may extend beyond participants with HIV infection, ARC, or AIDS to their families and friends (e.g., social stigma, child abuse information reporting).

Not only the participants and those associated with them but also ultimately society as a whole may be harmed by breaches of confidentiality in research on AIDS. If potential participants perceive a risk of involuntary disclosure of their data, they may be deterred from participating in research, and researchers may be afraid to pursue the study of socially sensitive topics. In the short term, the search for a vaccine and a cure for AIDS would be frustrated. In the long term, the pursuit of socially sensitive knowledge more generally might be hindered, with adverse consequences for human welfare (*Andrews v. Eli Lilly & Co.*, 1983; *Lampshire v. Proctor & Gamble Co.*, 1982).

The simplest answer to the problems of confidentiality, short of failing to conduct research at all, would be to avoid keeping identifiable data (Office for Protection from Research Risks, 1984). However, as a practical matter, deletion of sufficient personal information to prevent "deductive disclosures" of participants' identity may be impossible in many instances (Boruch & Cecil, 1979). Furthermore, even if the identity of participants could be kept disguised, this solution may be undesirable for several reasons, as stated by the Hastings Center task force on AIDS research: "(a) The researcher may need to inform a research subject about a medical condition requiring treatment; (b) the researcher requires linking one set of data with other sets; (c) the researcher requires linking information gathered at different times; or (d) the researcher requires verifying the reliability of the data" (Bayer, Levine, & Murray, 1984, pp. 2–3).

In short, the interests of both society and the participants themselves in confidentiality are mixed. Although failure to protect confidentiality adequately may adversely affect both the pursuit of knowledge about AIDS and the welfare of participants, failure under all circumstances to keep identifiable information also may deter development of knowledge crucial to understanding AIDS. Such de facto prohibition of longitudinal research and combination of data sets would obviously be detrimental to the welfare of society and the participants.

Legally Sanctioned Encroachments on Confidentiality

Thus, although there are often competing interests surrounding privacy issues, it is clear from the preceding discussion that forced disclosure of identifiable data in AIDS research may have substantial costs for participants, researchers, and society. Therefore, it is important to carefully examine ways in which disclosure may be compelled. Such scrutiny may allow investigators to foresee and, when possible, prevent unplanned disclosures (Bayer et al., 1984) and encourage policymakers to strengthen legal protection of the confidentiality of data gathered in research on pediatric AIDS. An examination of the potential risks of compelled disclosures of data also assist researchers in accurately informing potential participants of the limits of confidentiality protection.

Confidence can be breached by the legal system in several ways. Disclosure of records may be mandated by state reporting laws, agency regulations, or federal statutes. Records may also be subject to disclosure through subpoena by the judicial, legislative, or executive branch of government. Finally, a research participant's confidential records may be voluntarily disclosed by the researcher without the participants' consent. The legal system may contribute indirectly to this "voluntary" breach of confidentiality by not providing adequate sanctions against such disclosures.

State Reporting Laws: AIDS: Many states require physicians and hospitals to report various diseases to state and local health departments for surveillance purposes. The CDC has entered into cooperative agreements with many states for AIDS surveillance—serving to relay states' statistics to the CDC. In addition to general state reporting statues, reporting requirements for AIDS have also been enacted.

State reporting requirements for AIDS can be classified into three groups: statutes concerned with CDC-defined AIDS, which is reportable in every state; HIV antibody tests, which are reportable in Arizona, Colorado, Georgia (without names), Idaho, Montana, Nevada, South Carolina, and Wisconsin; and state general provisions, which do not specify HIV antibody reporting but require the reporting of any "case, condition, or carrier state" relating to listed diseases, including AIDS (e.g., Minnesota—Gostin & Curran, 1987b; Matthews & Neslund, 1987).

Although there are strong practical arguments against having researchers report any "case, condition, or carrier state" relating to AIDS, it is conceivable that states could begin to require researchers testing for HIV antibodies to report these findings to state health departments. Such legislation would probably be considered constitutional according to criteria set forth in the case of *Whalen v. Roe* (1977; Gostin & Curran, 1987b).

State Reporting Laws: Abuse and Neglect: In addition to the possibility of researchers being required to report information about HIV-positive participants, pediatric AIDS researchers may find themselves in the position of being required to report child abuse or neglect of participants or by parents of participants to local child abuse and neglect agencies.

All states now have child abuse reporting laws (Wadlington, Whitebread, & Davis, 1983, p. 789). Although statutes vary in their definitions of who must report child abuse, they usually require reporting from health care professionals, teachers, and social workers. If any physician, nurse, medical examiner, or other medical or mental health professional is required to report abuse, as suggested by the Juvenile Justice Standards Project (1977), medical and psychological researchers may indeed be included in states' abuse-reporting legislation. In addition, some states mandate that "any person" is responsible for reporting abuse that they are aware of (DeKraai & Sales, 1984, pp. 314–315).

The chances for abuse or neglect being found in pediatric AIDS research are perhaps particularly high when dealing with the population of intravenous-drug-using parents and their children. Because of the parents' drug addiction, their ability to provide adequate child care may be impaired. Also, any research population of parents that have AIDS may be prone to child neglect because of their illness. Furthermore, as in the entire population, sexual abuse may be discovered among some research participants and/or their families. Obviously, if such abuse or neglect situations arise and researchers are required to report them, their participant population may be reduced—if parents or participants withdraw from the study after they have been reported. Although the infant or child participant may be helped by such reporting, the adult participant or the parents of participants will most likely be surprised and harmed.

The courts have not yet ruled on whether researchers must report abuse and neglect. However, researchers should be aware of their many conflicting responsibilities in such a situation. Pediatric AIDS researchers are required to protect their participants from harm arising out of research (although by protecting adult participants they may be harming child participants, and vice versa). In addition, if researchers knowingly do not file required abuse or neglect reports in order to protect their adult participants, they may be creating liability for themselves (Juvenile Justice Standards Project, 1977). Unfortunately, there is no easy resolution to this dilemma. However, one solution may be for researchers to inform potential participants and their parents or guardians—before they agree to participate in the study—of the possibility that abuse and neglect would be reported by them if they were informed or became aware of such activity.

Agency Regulations and the Freedom of Information Act: In contrast to direct reporting requirements, confidentiality breaches may occur inadvertently through "routine uses" of data or contractual agreements with funding agencies. These types of disclosures are rarely forbidden by the legal system and are not uniformly regulated by internal procedures (Gray & Melton, 1985). Pediatric AIDS researchers conducting publicly funded research may minimize the possibility of unnecessarily broad access to raw data by seeking to have any audits or secondary analyses conducted on the research site, preferably by a private contractor. Such a strategy also reduces the possibility of public access to the data under the federal Freedom of Information Act of 1967 (1982) (Gray & Melton, 1985). It is only when research data come under government control that an agency record is created for purposes of the Freedom of Information Act (*Forsham v. Harris,* 1980). Ergo, the most effective strategy to protect such confidential data is to prevent the creation of any "agency record," so that the raw data are clearly outside the reach of the act (Morris, Sales, & Berman, 1981). Thus, insofar as reports to granting agencies can be limited to summaries and analyses of data and audits can be performed on site by private contractors, researchers can avoid unintended disclosure of confidential information to a myriad of government workers and the public.

Subpoena: Another threat to confidential material is presented by subpoena power. Subpoenas may be issued by the judiciary for use in a pending civil or criminal case, by the legislature, or by administrative agencies for investigatory purposes. The subpoena power represents a unique threat to participants' confidentiality for at least three reasons. First, subpoenas may be issued for reasons that are unforseeable and have little to do with the purpose of research (*In re Grand Jury Subpoena,* 1984). Thus, it is often difficult to provide much usable information to potential participants about risks to confidentiality posed by subpoenas. Second, when, as is the case with most AIDS research, many

194

participants may have engaged in illegal conduct (e.g., teenage intravenous drug use, prostitution, child abuse), information gathered in the course of research may be sought for the purpose of prosecution (Kershaw & Small, 1972). Third, because subpoenaed material may enter the public domain through admission in litigation or a legislative or administrative hearing, there is a risk of wide dissemination of confidential information and, therefore, a great risk of embarrassment and other adverse consequences for participants.

Duty to Warn: Belitsky and Solomon (1987) have stated that, under the concept of duty to warn, "a physician with knowledge of a diagnosis of AIDS who fails to disclose the information to a foreseeable victim could be found liable" (p. 203). Several issues raised by this topic are important for pediatric AIDS researchers. First, what are the legal mandates on which a duty to warn is based? Second, what does a duty to warn mean, and who is a foreseeable victim? Third, if such a duty exists, who does it exist for? Are researchers included in the legal mandate?

The leading case dealing with the duty to warn is *Tarasoff v. The Regents of the University of California.* In this case, the California Supreme Court imposed a duty on psychotherapists to protect third parties from the potentially dangerous acts of their patients. The court held that, when a therapist determines, or should have determined, that a client presents a serious danger of violence to another, he or she incurs an obligation to use reasonable care to protect the intended victim against such danger. Discharge of this duty, the court noted, might include warning the intended victim or calling the police. *Tarasoff* was the first case to impose a duty to warn potential victims of injury that might result from a client's intentional actions. *Tarasoff* is particularly significant in a consideration of AIDS because the transmission of the disease can, in some instances, be viewed as the result of intentional action (Belitsky & Solomon, 1987).

Under *Tarasoff,* the duty of care owed extends only to third parties in foreseeable danger. Thus, there must be a specific threat to a specific individual, not to a statistically probable victim (Gostin, Curran, & Clark, 1987). In some states, the duty to warn third parties is controlled

by statute. However, even in these states, *Tarasoff* represents the domi-
nant trend and has yet to be rejected by the highest court of any state
(Belitsky & Solomon, 1987). Nevertheless, a small number of jurisdic-
tions differ in their interpretation and acceptance of the *Tarasoff* rule.

Some courts do not require that there be an identifiable victim to establish liability (*Lipari v. Sears, Roebuck & Co.,* 1980). In *Lipari,* the
court held that liability is established by the existence of foreseeable
danger to any member of a targeted class of people. Obviously, the im-
plication of this type of reasoning in an AIDS situation is tremendous.
For example, it would seem that a professional covered by the duty to
warn (e.g., a physician, a therapist, or, possibly, a researcher) who knew
of a person with AIDS that did not make any attempt to prevent the
spread of HIV from himself or herself to others and who also knew that
there were several persons in danger of contracting HIV from such a
person would have to contact the health department or the police in order to fulfill that obligation.

Such an action, although breaching confidentiality, would comply
with the finding in *Tarasoff* that a professional will not be liable unless
he or she is able to control the dangerous situation by initiating procedures for criminal or civil confinement or by warning those in a position
to take protective measures. Whether the action was appropriate may
depend on what a reasonable professional would do in the particular
situation. Unfortunately, under this type of reasoning, the law gives
professionals little practical guidance as to their legal responsibilities
for carrying out their duty to warn.

Although the actual steps to be taken are unclear, Gostin and Curran
(1987a) suggest at least a threshold obligation to advise "patients" of
their responsibility to warn close contacts of the infection and to behave
safely. Goston recommends that only when there are strong grounds for
believing that a specific contact is in serious danger from exposure to
HIV and has not been informed should "physicians" notify the contact
of the positive serologic status of the "patient."

Thus, if the duty to warn applied to researchers, they would in general be required to take some type of appropriate action if there were a

known danger to a specific person that could be averted by the research-er's action. However, there are many reasons to suspect that this duty would not apply to pediatric AIDS researchers.

Tarasoff is based on the rationale that the therapist-patient relation-ship is sufficient to place a duty on the therapist for the benefit of other persons. The duty to protect third parties from contracting an infec-tious disease predates *Tarasoff* (*Davis v. Rodman*, 1921). This duty ap-plies to physicians because they also have a special relationship with their patients (*Davis; Hofmann v. Blackmon*, 1970).

Whether researchers have a duty to warn will therefore hinge at least in part on whether a court find that there is a special relationship be-tween a researcher and his or her participants. This finding may vary de-pending on the researcher involved and the research conducted. For instance, a full-time social psychologist conducting a survey study may not be found to have a "special" relationship with his or her partici-pants. However, a practicing physician or psychotherapist who is con-ducting research of an intimate nature—for example, an interview type study where medical questions are answered by the "physician" side of the researcher or issues are discussed in a therapeutic manner by the "psychotherapist" side of the researcher—may be more likely to be judged to be in an "intimate" relationship with his or her participant. In addition to such findings that must be made by a court before they are clear, there are outlined statutory duties that are more directive. None of the state duty-to-warn statutes refer to a duty owed by researchers to third parties in potential danger from research participants.

In addition, most pediatric AIDS research is focused on young chil-dren, who are unlikely to place persons in danger intentionally. In all probability, they are not endangering anyone through irresponsible sexual contact or the sharing of needles in intravenous drug use. It is also unlikely that they are threatening family members by intentional acts of exposure that the family would be unaware of or that school-mates or others would be placed in such danger.

Furthermore, there are strong tendencies in most public policies against disclosure of confidential information to third parties, particularly when there is a great need to protect such information. For instance, several courts have held that the confidentiality of information gathered for purposes of epidemiologic research should be safeguarded (*Farnsworth v. Procter & Gamble Co.*, 1985; *In re District 27 Community School Board v. Board of Education of the City of New York*, 1986), the rationale being that the progress of medical research depends on the availability of individuals willing to participate in studies and that such willingness often hinges on the preservation of confidentiality. This same rationale should apply to psychosocial research on pediatric AIDS.

Thus, there are many factors to consider and many arguments to be made on the issue of a duty to warn for pediatric AIDS researchers. Of course, the ultimate determination, if action is ever brought, will be made by the courts. Until that time, researchers should not be overly concerned about possible legal repercussions for not informing third parties of forseeable danger from their research participants. Researchers should, however, consider the possibility of facing such a situation and what their most ethical response might be. At the least, they should attempt to persuade participants to inform their contacts of potential danger and perhaps alert participants that failure to do so could lead to further actions by the researcher to protect such third parties (if this is what the researcher intends to do).

"Voluntary" Disclosures: The last threat to confidentiality by the legal system is indirect—a researcher's voluntarily disclosing confidential information without participants' consent. While there are few, if any, legal sanctions against such breaches, professional self-regulation pursuant to voluntary codes of ethics may provide protection if researchers have not been legally compelled to disclose their data (Keith-Spiegel & Koocher, 1985). In addition, New York and California have enacted statues dealing with the protection of confidential information in AIDS research that provide penalties for violations of confidentiality (these statutes are discussed in the following sections).

Legal Means of Protecting Confidentiality

Besides providing for or encouraging the disclosure of confidential information, the legal system also protects confidential data in several

ways. Certificates of confidentiality can be issued for a particular research project so that all confidential material involved in that study is
completely protected from forced disclosure. Statutes can be designed
to give all or certain researcher-participant interactions complete or
partial immunity to subpoena and other forms of compelled disclosure
(see Gray and Melton, 1985, in press). The court can use a balancing test
to determine on a case-by-case basis whether particular data should be
recognized as privileged or whether it would be overly burdensome to
require disclosure. Finally, granting agencies and statutes may place
limitations on researchers' voluntary disclosures.

The Public Health Service Act: The Public Health Service Act provides for certificates of confidentiality. These certificates offer one of the
best protections of confidentiality because they guard against all compelled disclosures of identifying information. However, the protection
offered by these certificated is not automatic; rather, it requires a grant
of confidentiality. This Public Health Service Act (sec. 242(a)) permits
the secretary to: "authorize persons engaged in biomedical, behavioral,
clinical, or other research (including research on mental health, including research on the use and effect of alcohol and other psychoactive
drugs), to protect the privacy of individuals who are the subject of such
research by withholding from all persons not connected with the conduct of such research the names or other identifying characteristics of
such individuals. Persons so authorized to protect the privacy of such
individuals may not be compelled in any federal, state, or local civil,
criminal, administrative, legislative, or other proceedings to identify
such individuals."

Note that new language has been added to this section by the Health
Omnibus Programs Extension of 1988 (Health Omnibus, 1988). Title
I, subtitle M, section 163(2) added for inclusion "biomedical, behavioral, clinical . . . research." *Research* is defined broadly as any "systematic study directed toward new or fuller knowledge of the subject
studied" (Protection of Identity, 1987, sec. 2a(2)(c)). This extension is
very important for AIDS pediatric researchers. The majority of their research should be covered by at least one of the listed areas and therefore
be eligible for a certificate of confidentiality.

The act's protection is discretionary, and the new implementing regulations are still under construction; however, there appears to be no reason that a researcher who fits the above definition would not be granted such a certificate. Unfortunately, few researchers have been aware of the possibility of acquiring certificates of confidentiality, and fewer still have gone to the trouble of apply for them (Nelson & Hedrick, 1983). To obtain a certificate before the new implementing regulations are completed (for the prior regulations, see Protection of Identity, 1987), contact the Office for Protection from Research Risks for further information.[4]

The Public Health Service Act also offers another protection with potential importance for pediatric AIDS researchers. Section 308(d) of the act (42 U.S.C.A. sec. 242m(d)) provides: "No information, if an establishment or person supplying the information or described in it is identifiable, obtained in the course of activities undertaken or supported under section 304, 305, 306, 307, or 309 may be used for any purpose other than the purpose for which it was supplied unless such establishment or person has consented (as determined under regulations of the Secretary) to its use for such other purpose."

Section 304 (42 U.S.C.A. sec. 242b(a)(1)) outlines the authority and scope of activities respecting research: "The Secretary, acting through the National Center for Health Services Research and Health Care Technology Assessment and the National Center for Health Statistics, shall conduct and support research, demonstrations, evaluations, and statistical and epidemiological activities for the purpose of improving the effectiveness, efficiency, and quality of health services in the United States." Refer to sections 305 (42 U.S.C.A. 242c), 306 (242k), 307 (242l), and 309 (242n) for further details concerning the agencies' scope of activities. Examine the other provisions in section 308 (242m) for information pertaining to application procedures for grants or contracts offered by these agencies.

As a result or recent structural administrative changes, these protec-

4. The Office for Protection from Research Risks is located at the following address: Building 31, Room 5B59, 9000 Rockville Pike, Bethesda, MD 20892. The phone number is 301–496–7005.

tion provisions extend to CDC activities in some instances. Anyone applying for a grant or contract from the CDC should ascertain their potential for protection under this section.

If the protection offered by section 308(d) applies to your project, be aware that its protection is only as good as you and your granting agency make it. The section's protection rests on the phrase "any purpose other than the purpose for which it was supplied." Thus, identifiable information obtained during a research project may be disclosed without consent for the purpose for which it was obtained. Confidentiality protection therefore extends only to information not included in the project's "purpose description." For example, if I simply declare the purpose of my project to be the generation of knowledge related to intravenous drug use and AIDS, without specifying that such knowledge is not in any way to be used for criminal prosecution, I may be leaving my materials vulnerable to potential acquisition by subpoena.

New York and California AIDS Statutes: Currently, there are at least two state statutes that protect the confidentiality of AIDS research. The New York statute (New York Public Health Law, 1984) provides an absolute privilege against admission of information gathered in AIDS research as evidence in any legal proceeding. This statute also permits the commissioner of public health to give researchers access to the department's records of mandatory reports of AIDS cases. Thus, this statute provides protection against disclosures of confidential information to the legal system while providing for a continuous flow of information to researchers so that research is not curtailed.

The California statute (California Health and Safety Code, 1986) is much more narrow than the New York statute. This statute specifies confidentiality standards only for using the HIV antibody test in AIDS research. These standards include required informed consent with a description of intended disclosures prior to participation and establishing civil and criminal repercussions for violations of confidentiality (Matthews & Neslund, 1987). This statute would apparently protect against the threat of researchers having to report HIV findings to local and state health agencies, at least for research conducted in California.

Judicial Protection of Confidentiality: If a researcher does not have protection for the confidentiality of her or his research data provided by one of the above mentioned statutory provisions and is concerned about protecting sensitive confidential research information, he or she may have to rely on judicial protection of confidentiality. Judicial protection is less desirable than statutory protection because statutes provide clear statements of policy *before* there is an attempt to breach confidentiality. Under judicial protection, the court decides whether order compliance with a subpoena for research information *after* a subpoena or other intrusion is ordered and the researcher has moved to quash the subpoena (an ethical obligation under APA principles 3d and 5).

In deciding whether to enforce a subpoena, the court must examine and weigh many factors pursuant to prevailing procedural rules. The rules of civil and criminal procedure are very similar in their provisions governing discovery. The Federal Rules of Civil Procedure (1986) provide that "parties may obtain discovery regarding any matter, *not privileged,* which is relevant to the subject matter involved in the pending action" (sec. 26(b)(1)). The Federal Rules of Evidence (1986) maintain that for privileges to be recognized they must be constitutionally derived, statutorily created, recognized at common law, or, for civil proceedings, prevailing in state law (sec. 501).

No absolute privilege has been recognized for researcher-participant interactions in statute (aside from New York's AIDS statute) or in any other legal realm (Gray & Melton, 1985). However, when a privileged relationship is not found, an additional argument for the protection of confidentiality from the judiciary can be made. Rule 45(b) of the Federal Rules of Civil Procedure and rule 17(c) of the Federal Rules of Criminal Procedure provide that, although a subpoena can be used to force production of documentary evidence, a court may quash or modify the subpoena if it is unreasonable and ("or" for criminal) oppressive ("Forced Disclosure," 1984). Of particular importance for psychosocial research on pediatric AIDS, discovery may also be limited if justice so demands in order to protect a person from embarrassment (Federal Rules of Civil Procedure, sec. 26(c); Gray & Melton, 1985).

Protections against "Voluntary" Disclosures: Thus far, the ways in which the legal system may compel breaches of confidentiality and protect confidential information have been discussed. In addition to these direct methods, the legal system may exercise control over researchers' abuse of participants' privacy in their studies. Only California (California Health and Safety Code, 1986) has specifically established statutory civil and criminal repercussions for violations of confidentiality in AIDS research. However, AIDS researchers may be liable for civil sanctions for disclosure of confidential information without participants' consent under general legal tort, contract, and/or misrepresentation bases (Gray & Melton, 1985; Teitelbaum, 1983).

However, given that persons with AIDS are seldom in a position to initiate legal action against researchers and the after-the-fact nature of such action, they are not the most desirable or effective means for protecting against "voluntary" disclosures of confidential information by researchers. In addition, because these legal means are not uniformly effective, they are seldom enacted. Instead, the regulation of researchers' behavior is primarily through administrative mechanisms.

Proposals for psychosocial research on pediatric AIDS almost invariably involve more than minimal risk to participants (Bayer et al., 1984) and should therefore be accorded full institutional review board examination before research implementation. This examination should serve to ensure that ethical standards pertaining to participants' privacy will be upheld. Unfortunately, review of the adequacy of protections built into a research design does not guarantee that all researchers will in fact exercise proper ethical management of the data. Therefore, researchers who willfully breach confidentiality should be subject to administrative sanctions, perhaps including termination of their research grant, a mandatory refund of grant monies, suspension of pending future grants, the attachment of a record of the incident to any application for future grants, or termination of eligibility for any grant awards (Greenstein, 1984).

Informed Consent

Unfortunately, none of the legal means for protecting privacy provides absolute protection against forced or "voluntary" disclosure of confidential information for the majority of pediatric AIDS research. Compounding this fact is the severity of potential harm that may be caused by the disclosure of confidential information, the lack of significant benefits for participants, and the vulnerability of child participants. Because of these factors, when confidential information is to be collected and retained by researchers, participants or their parents or guardians should be fully informed of the associated risks, including those from confidentiality breaches, and to whom and when data may be disclosed. In addition, participants or their parents or guardians should give their informed, competent, voluntary consent to data retention and disclosure when they agree to participate in the research.

There are, of course, countervailing pressures that work against such complete honesty. For instance, if all possible harms were discussed in detail, few people would be willing to participate. A second consideration is that, if the consent form is constructed in such a way that no promise or expectation of privacy is created for participants, a researcher's case for maintaining confidentiality might be weakened (Gray & Melton, 1985) and participants therefore placed at greater risk of harm. On the other hand, promises of confidentiality that are not based on any legal right may not be recognized and may result in liability to the researchers for voluntary breaches of such promises. The question to be resolved, then, is how all these concerns can be balanced in an informed consent form while complying with legal and ethical requirements for informed consent (Informed Consent Requirements, 1984).

For research that requires informed consent, consent must be obtained under circumstances that provide the participant sufficient opportunity to consider whether to participate and that minimize the possibility of coercion or undue influence and in language that the participant or guardian can understand (45 C.F.R. sec. 16.116, 1984). Attending to these requirements is particularly important when conducting research with children who have AIDS. Children who are at a developmental stage that includes an ability to understand and give informed consent must be made to understand that they have the ability to decline participation even if their parents want them to be in the research. The factors relevant for consideration in a decision whether to participate must be clearly and simply presented so that the participants can make a truly informed decision. In addition, all communication with the participant must be appropriate for his or her developmental level and ability to understand. It should not be assumed that children or adults with AIDS are at comprehension levels "normal" for their age group. Developmental and cognitive regressions are common in persons with AIDS and must be taken into consideration when informed consent is being elicited.

The basic requirement for informed consent is the presentation of whatever information may be relevant to a particular participant's decision whether to participate (APA principle 9d; 45 C.F.R. sec. 46.116). Thus, the researcher must outline why the study is being conducted, including the potential benefit to society or participants, what the research procedure will be, what risks may be involved, and any other factors relevant to the participant's decision of whether participation is worthy of his or her investment of time and assumption of risk. (This section applies primarily to adult participants, parents, or guardians. Special informed consent requirements for children are discussed in the following section.)

Specifically, federal regulations require the following. (1) There must be a statement that the study involves research, an explanation of the purposes of the research and the expected duration of the subject's participation, a description of the procedures to be followed, and identification of any procedures that are experimental. (2) There must be a description of any reasonably foreseeable risks or discomforts to the subject (45 C.F.R. sec. 46.116(a)(1)). (3) There must be a description of any benefits to the subject or to others that may reasonably be expected from the research (secs. 46.116(a)(2)–(3)). (4) There must be disclosure of appropriate alternative procedures or courses of treatment, if any, that might be advantageous to the subject (sec. 46.116(a)(4)). (5) There must be a statement describing the extent, if any, to which confidentiality of records identifying the subject will be maintained (sec. 46.116(a)(5)). (6) For research involving more than minimal risk, there must be an explanation as to whether compensation or medical treatment is available if injury occurs and, if so, what they consist of or where further information may be obtained (sec. 46.116(a)(6)). (7) There should be an explanation of whom to contact for answers to pertinent questions about the research and research subjects' rights and whom to contact in the event of a research-related injury to the subject (sec. 46.116(a)(7)). (8) There should be a statement that participation is voluntary, that refusal to participate will involve no penalty of loss of benefits to which participants are otherwise entitled, and that the participants may discontinue participation at any time without penalty or loss of benefits to which they are otherwise entitled (sec. 46.116(a)(8)).

In accordance with the fifth requirement, pediatric AIDS researchers should do their best to be candid about potential breaches of confidentiality while still stressing that every measure possible will be taken to protect confidentiality (Bayer et al., 1984; Gray & Melton, 1985). Unfortunately, some researchers have only rarely concerned themselves with confidentiality issues that may arise after the study is completed. Such a disregard for potential breaches of confidentiality has serious ramifications in AIDS research, where disclosures can be devastating to the participants.

It is clear that under current law absolute guarantees of confidentiality cannot be made. Participants should be informed whether information will be retained after the research is completed, for how long, in what form, and with what safeguards, if any. Perhaps most important, all reasonably foreseeable breaches of confidentiality should be explained to participants. (For a discussion of the likelihood of disclosures of confidential data through the legal threats described previously, see Gray & Melton, 1985.)

The potential disclosure of data falls into four categories. First, there are disclosures that involve minimal risk to participants' privacy and may occur without consent or further notice. For example, unidentified, summarized information may be published. Second, disclosures may occur that do involve significant threats to privacy but do not require participants' consent. In instances such as subpoenas, participants should be notified of the impending disclosure if their identities remain known to the researcher so that they themselves may attempt to take protective action (although, realistically, there is not much that child participants could do on their own against such disclosures). Third are disclosures to which consent is given by virtue of agreeing to participate in the study. For example, if the researcher makes clear an intention to share data with public health authorities, third parties under a duty to warn, and so on, participants may decide whether to participate in the study under such a condition. Care should be taken, however, not to make potential disclosures so broad that participants cannot make an informed decision. A fourth type of disclosure is one that will occur only with the participant's consent but for which consent is not now being given. In such a circumstance, participants obviously must be contacted again. Therefore, they must have already given their informed consent to the maintenance of identifying information and future intrusions by the researcher. Researchers' detailed descriptions of reasonably forseeable potential confidentiality disclosures will at least give participants forewarning of possible harms resulting from disclosures, even though they may not be able to be avoided. Thus, forewarned, research participants (or their guardians) can decide for themselves whether they wish to participate in the research and risk the potential breaches of confidentiality.

In addition to alerting participants of possible confidentiality disclosures, it is very important in pediatric AIDS research, pursuant to the sixth and seventh requirements, to inform potential participants about remedies that will be available if participants are harmed as a result of their involvement in research. In particular, participants should be notified of any mental health services that will be provided by the researchers in case of distress resulting from the study. Furthermore, in order to increase benefits received for participating in the research, participants should be alerted to other sources of help, including assistance for medical concerns related to AIDS, substance abuse, and so forth, whether or not the assistance needed resulted from participation in the study. Researches should request funding for such activities from their granting agency.

Counseling and assistance are also likely to be needed in pediatric AIDS research. For instance, if a child is tested for HIV and the results are positive, a researcher must expect to provide, or arrange for, extensive support while such information is being disclosed and after such disclosure is made. Another example of a possible future research-generated problem stems from a child's involvement in treatment research in which some participants receive the treatment drug, others receive a placebo, and the study is conducted in a blind fashion so that the participants and their parents are unaware of who is receiving the treatment drug and who is receiving the placebo. In this situation, the parents, and perhaps the child, are likely to experience anxiety since they are hoping to have the child receive the treatment drug and may in fact be involved in such research only in order to receive treatment.

Furthermore, although such a consideration is not mandated, the emotional needs of researchers and their assistants should be anticipated. The death of any participant is hard to confront, but it is perhaps particularly difficult when the participant is an infant or a child.

In addition to what factors should be included in the consent form, researchers also need to consider how such informed consent is obtained and from whom consent is obtained.

Procedures for Obtaining Informed Consent: Pediatric AIDS researchers should be aware that written forms are not necessarily the optimal means of providing information (particularly for children) and recording consent. Obviously, written forms provide a largely indisputable record of the consent and therefore provide some protection to the researcher. However, there are two countervailing considerations.

First, participants often do not comprehend or attend carefully to written forms (Lidz et al., 1984). In view of the significance of the decision to be made, the researcher bears a special obligation to ensure that consent is truly informed. If written forms are used, special attention should be given to the forms' readability, including a consideration of participants' level of reading comprehension (Elwork, Sales, & Alfini, 1982; Grunder, 1978). The written forms should be supplemented by oral discussion (Roth et al., 1982), and consideration should be given to the use of two-part consent forms, which include questions at the end to ensure that potential participants understand the information that has been disclosed.

Second, consent forms themselves may represent a threat to privacy. If identifying information is removed from research data, the forms may represent the only identifiable record of participation. If the forms are then disclosed, participants may be individually vulnerable to subpoena or other inquiry about private behavior that may be inferred from the nature of the study. When consent forms do represent a demonstrable threat to privacy, federal regulations permit consent without such documentation (45 C.F.R. sec. 46.117(c)(1) (1984)).

Who Consents: A number of problems are involved in obtaining informed consent for participation in pediatric AIDS research. In addition to providing confidential procedures and structuring a consent form in such a way that all relevant information is presented to participants in an understandable manner, further problems are raised when participants are minors. In particular, researchers must determine from whom consent should be obtained and how this determination should be made.

In the Code of Federal Regulations, there are additional provisions outlined for protection of children involved as participants in research ("Additional Protections," 1986). *Children* are defined as "persons who have not attained the legal age for consent to treatments or procedures involved in the research, under the applicable law of the jurisdiction in which the research will be conducted" (sec. 46.412(a)).

Researchers must be able to distinguish between persons who have a legal right to consent to research participation, and "children" who are subject to federal Code provisions, that, in general, require parental or guardian permission for participation (45 C.F.R. sec. 46408[b]). [The exception to required parental or guardian permission for children's participation in research is contained in section 46.408(c) of the Code. This section provides that for research involving conditions or participants for which parental or guardian permission is not a reasonable requirement for their protection, requirements for parental permission may be waived by the IRB if other appropriate mechanisms for the participants' protection is substituted.) The Code's definition of children leaves the determination of child status to "the applicable law of the jurisdiction in which the research will be conducted" (i.e., state law). General state "age of majority" standards usually center around 18 years of age (Wadlington, 1983); however, particular majority standards vary across states. Furthermore, individual states may not provide a clear standard for legal age of consent for research purposes. The Code does not appear to leave age of consent for research to state's general "age of majority," instead it refers to the "legal age for consent to treatments or procedures involved in the research." A state may have different consent age standards for various treatments and procedures, none of which, or more than one of which, may apply to a given research project.

Beyond discovering what applicable state consent standards are (as difficult as that may be) further exploration needs to be made concerning what these standards should be. Presently, there is no coherent agreement among scholars concerning this question. Keith-Speigel (1983), sent a consent survery sample to authorities in child development areas asking them to specify an age, generally speaking, at which minors are as capable as adults of meaningfully consenting to participate in a study that would be relatively easy to describe fully to potential participants. Their answers ranged from 2 to 17, with a mean age of 11.

In addition to legal age for consent or "permission" determinations, researchers must ascertain, for identified children, when to obtain the child's assent to research participation. Assent is defined by the Code of Federal Regulations as "a child's affirmative agreement to participate in research. Mere failure to object should not, absent affirmative agreement, be construed as assent" (sec. 464-2)b)). According to the Code, the acting institutional review board "shall determine that adequate provisions are made for soliciting the assent of the children, when in the judgment of the (board) the childrern are capable of providing assent" (sec. 46408)a)).

Thus, these Code provisions suggest that perhaps what is needed is not a set age but rather a method for assessing a minor's capacity to assent from a developmental perspective, assuming she or he is given sound, developmentally appropriate information (Keith-Speigel, 1983). In 1977, the National Commission for the Protection of Human Subjects of Biomedical and Behavioral Science Research issued a report entitled "Research Involving Children." Although this report represents one of the most thorough and definitive considerations of issues surrounding competency to consent and throughout the document there is concern with minor participants' wishes, the report is silent on procedures for assessing competence (Keith-Speigel, 1983).

The DHHS requirements for assent ("Additional Protections," 1986, sec. 46.408(a)) state: "In determining whether children are capable of assenting, the [institutional review board] shall take into account the ages, maturity, and psychological state of the children involved. This judgment may be made for all children to be involved in research under a particular protocol, or for each child, as the [board] deems appropriate." Tapp and Melton (1983) believe that this focus is mistaken. Instead of asking whether a child is competent to assent, one should ask whether the child could be taught to exercise competent decision making. However, whether this type of obligation should be ethically required of researchers is yet to be decided.

In addition, at least legally, the minor participant's assent is not always required. According to the DHHS requirements (sec. 46.408(a)), "If the [institutional review board] determines that the capability of some or all of the children is so limited that they cannot reasonably be consulted or that the intervention or procedure involved in the research holds out a prospect of direct benefit that is important to the health or well-being of the children and is available only in the context of the research, the assent of the children is not a necessary condition for proceeding with the research."

When assent is not received from a child participant, the importance of "proxy consent" is augmented. In all but a few rare exceptions (sec. 46.408(c)), parents or legal guardians must give their permission for children to participate in research (sec. 46.408(b)). The ability of parents or guardians to give consent for their children's participation in research is perhaps one of the most controversial issues relative to research participation by minors.

The policy behind the DHHS provisions for this type of situation is similar to its policy for additional protections with research involving fetuses and pregnant women—which may also be at issue in pediatric AIDS research ("Additional Protections," 1975). That is, if there is minimal risk involved in the research or if there is a potential for great benefit to the child or fetus, the parents may give their consent for participation in absence of assent by the participant.

In addition, greater potential harms or decreased potential benefits involved in research may require the permission of both parents (if living and entitled to custody) rather than only the consent of one parent (sec. 46.408(b)). Obtaining permission for research participation for children that are wards of the state may be even more difficult (sec. 46.409). With the increased incidence of foster care for children with AIDS, research permission requirements from state agencies may hamper research conducted with this participant group.

Children who are wards of the state or any other agency, institution, or entity can be included in research (at least research conducted or supported by the DHHS) only if such research is "(1) related to their status as wards; or (2) conducted in schools, camps, hospitals, institutions, or similar settings in which the majority of children involved as subjects are not wards" (sec. 46.409(a)). If researchers include child participants who are wards of the state and their participation requires any type of travel arrangements or other inconveniences for the persons immediately responsible for them (e.g., foster parents), researchers should also seek assent from these persons, although this is not required by regulation.

In addition to these complexities, even if the aforementioned consent problems are resolved for an individual case, problems may arise in ongoing research when legal guardianship changes or when a child's (or an adult's) mental ability declines as a result of the progression of AIDS, leaving the individual incompetent to utilize her or his right to terminate participation in research. For example, if the legal guardian of a child with AIDS has consented to research that includes ongoing testing for 6 months but then loses guardianship during this period, must the new guardian also give her or his permission? Must assent from participants be obtained more than once during a longitudinal study in case the person at some time during the research becomes incapable of consenting to such research?

Unfortunately, commentary on such issues is scarce. However, the resolution of almost all the issues raised thus far depends on individual decisions for each research project, not on uniform solutions. Thus, when researchers are fully informed about the issues involved, they may at least anticipate, plan for, and, it is hoped, successfully deal with these problems before, during, and after their occurrence. This chapter will have served its purpose if it has increased researchers' knowledge about potential problems encountered in research and alerted policymakers to those problem areas in need of legal rectification.

THE POTENTIAL EFFECT OF PEDIATRIC AIDS RESEARCH ON LEGAL AND POLICY ISSUES

While pediatric AIDS research is influenced by other disciplines, it in turn has the opportunity to have an effect beyond related research concerns. For example, research methods may work to prevent legal or other attempts to force disclosure of confidential research information. In addition, research findings can influence legal, social, political, and medical policy on AIDS. Pediatric AIDS researchers can instigate policy construction and change in areas other than AIDS, including broader policy forums for infants, children, and adolescents on such topics as child-care strategies for hospitalized infants and children, competency to consent guidelines for research (Melton, 1987; Melton et al., 1983), and more explicit sex education programs.

Methodological Protection of Confidential Information

One way that pediatric AIDS researchers can prevent legal encroachments on research confidentiality is to "mask" confidential information

213

or not retain identifying information. If feasible, researchers should not collect any identifying information from their participants. If strict anonymity can be arranged, researchers would have no identifying information about their participants or confidential information solicited from them that could be linked to them directly or through deductive disclosures. With such an arrangement, researchers could in effect put a halt to the disclosure of confidential information solicited by subpoenas or Freedom of Information Act requests.

In addition, if researchers limit their reports to granting agencies to summaries of analyzed data, and audits are performed on site by private contractors, researchers would avoid unintended disclosure of confidential information to a myriad of government workers, through routine uses, and the public through Freedom of Information Act requests, and they would prevent the use of research data as a registry for public health enforcement purposes (Boruch, 1984; Morris et al., 1981).

Moreover, there are several established methodological strategies available to assist researchers in protecting the confidentiality of research data. Identifiers can be linked to coded systems and kept separate so that only the researchers have access to the data. Strategies such as the randomized response method (Boruch & Cecil, 1979, 1983) can be implemented. Other methodological strategies individually devised or suggested specifically for AIDS research can also be attempted (Gray & Melton, in press). Finally, researchers can be protective of their participants' confidentiality when reporting their results.

Reporting Results

Several issues are involved in the reporting of pediatric AIDS research results. Not only should researchers scrutinize their reports for possible obvious or deductive disclosures that would compromise participants' confidentiality, but they also need to decide at what stage results should be disclosed (e.g., preliminary or final) and in what manner results should be released. Acquired immunodeficiency syndrome has been the subject of extraordinarily rapid review for grants and publication, with announcement of findings prior to publication (Batchelor, 1984;

Brandt, 1983). The wisdom of such premature releases has been questioned on the grounds that misleading impressions may be given by preliminary, incompletely analyzed data that can erroneously lead society as a whole, particular groups, or policymakers into panic or complacency (Matherne, 1984).

In accordance with these objections, the Committee for the Protection of Human Participants in Research (1985) emphasized the need for caution in deciding whether to release results voluntarily prior to conclusion of a study and peer review:

> In the midst of these pressures [for premature disclosure of results], it its important that researchers not lose sight of the social sensitivity of the topic. At minimum, no service is done by reporting data which have been inadequately analyzed or are based on a sample too small or skewed to reach reliable conclusions. Mistaken reports, even if well intended, may result in unwise public policy, undue public alarm (or undue complacency), and stigma for affected groups. When preliminary data suggest ways of reducing risk, there must be a determination of whether the potential benefits of the possibly valid warning are outweighed by the harm which may result from reports which may ultimately be found to be erroneous. In a matter of great moment, there may be an imperative to facilitate research and its dissemination, but such an obligation is not furthered by abandonment of the principles of scientific investigation and communication. [p. 26, col. 5]

Even if normal schedules for publications and release of results are followed, the problem of how to report results remains. Because of the significance that is likely to be attached to new findings about AIDS, researchers bear a special obligation to identify the limitations of the research, to discuss alternative interpretations of findings, and to retain control of the dissemination of the results insofar as possible in order to minimize misleading reports (APA principles 1a, 1c). An example of the risks involved in failure to exercise such caution came when investigators first reported AIDS in children (Oleske et al., 1983). With a boost from an editorial in the *Journal of the American Medical Association,* the researchers erroneously concluded that AIDS could be communicated simply through close contact, with the result of creating undue anxiety and increasing pressure to segregate "risk groups" (Fauci, 1983). Pediatric AIDS researchers have a responsibility to avoid such erroneous conclusions and an obligation to attempt to ensure that the results of their research are used in the service of human welfare (APA Principles, preamble, principle 9).

Potential Policy Implications of Pediatric AIDS Research

Beyond assuring that research results are portrayed accurately, pediatric AIDS researchers should become involved in events that take place after they have released their results, such as attempting to ensure that their results are not inaccurately reported by others or used for inappropriate reasons (APA principle 1a). Furthermore, they should consider what role they may play in the use of their data for public policy-making and legal constructions. The APA has taken a lead in promoting psychologists' involvement in these processes.

The Task Force on Psychology and Public Policy was charged by the APA Board of Social and Ethical Responsibility for Psychology with examining ways to increase the involvement, awareness, knowledge, and education of psychologists in the public policy process, especially when the public interest is of primary concern (Task Force on Psychology and Public Policy, 1986). The task force recognized that "the myth of 'value-free' psychologists pursuing 'truths' about human behavior is no longer a functional ideology for our profession" (p. 914). Although this statement refers only to psychologists, it is equally applicable to all social scientists.

The task force public policy explained that a broader perspective is essential in our increasingly specialized and politicized society. They recognized that social scientists' efforts to "promote the public interest have been hampered by out-moded conceptions of what 'proper' activities for (social scientists) are" (Task Force on Psychology and Public Policy, 1986, p. 914). The task force takes the position that there is a false distinction between basic and applied research that must be broken down so that all researchers think of the policy implications of their work. Pediatric AIDS researchers in particular must consider the ramifications their research may have on policy decisions. Indeed, researchers cannot avoid being involved in the political, legal, and policy decisions regarding AIDS. The only question is whether researchers will be active, aware participants in these processes or simply live in others' footnotes.

In the area of psychology and law, Melton (1987) notes that "studies of legal authorities' use of social science knowledge (e.g., Hafemeister & Melton, in press) show that such use is substantially more likely when researchers make systematic efforts to diffuse their work into the legal system" (p. 488). Melton points out that explicit attempts to apply psychological science to legal assumptions can be seen as part of a larger movement to increase the ecological validity of research (Bronfenbrenner, 1979) and to fulfill the profession's social responsibility (American Psychological Association, 1981). Pediatric AIDS researchers can fulfill their social responsibilities in several ways in various areas and at separate, although not always distinct, levels of policy formation.

Levels of Policy Formation: Hayes (1982) discusses three levels of decision making in the policy framework. The first level is termed the *high* level and involves political issues. Is there a problem that is a legitimate object for government action? At this level, research may bring to light high-level issues, but it rarely settles them (e.g., documentation of the AIDS phenomenon). The next level is termed the *middle* level and involves choices about the means to achieve the goals of the high level. Research plays an important role at the middle level. For instance, the high-level goal for AIDS is to stop its spread and find a cure and vaccine with which to eradicate it. By the discovery of HIV and the ability to test for HIV antibodies, researchers provided a means for curtailing its spread. The *low* level involves the implementation of the means chosen at the middle level to accomplish the goals determined at the high level. "It is a technical contest over how best to implement an agreed-on approach to a problem" (Hayes, 1982, p. 63). At this level an issue might be whether to administer the ELISA test once or twice or to use the Western Blot test for detecting HIV antibodies also.

Roles for Researchers: How researchers choose to interact with policy decisions depends on the viewpoint they take of their proper professional and personal roles. Reynolds (1979) discusses four "identities" researchers may claim for integrating their professional and personal selves. The first is the "autonomous investigator." These researchers have the single-minded pursuit of knowledge as their goal and care little about practical applications of their work. This identity would be difficult for most pediatric AIDS researchers to live with. It would mean that they do not assume any responsibility for or interest in how their research affects those under study (outside the research context), the groups represented by participants, or broad social policy in general.

The next identity Reynolds describes is the "applied scientist." These researchers generally act in an advisory capacity, the final decisions regarding application resting with nonresearchers. Pediatric AIDS researchers can be effective in this role. For example, they can advise policymakers about the feasibility and desirability of urging HIV antibody testing for mothers-to-be and those applying for marriage licenses. However, short of incorporating such testing into their research projects, the widespread implementation of such testing rests with nonresearcher policymakers.

Pediatric AIDS researchers can also be effective in the last two roles described by Reynolds—the "societal mentor" and the "social activist." The "societal mentor" is more emotionally involved in the role than the applied scientist is but does not need to actually conduct research. The "societal mentor," when encountering a condition or activity in society that is inconsistent with her or his values, responds by way of a social commentary or critical essay. In this capacity, a pediatric AIDS researcher might decry the decision not to allow children with AIDS to attend regular classes or point out the lack of compassion shown for infants and children who are being raised by hospital personnel because the parents have abandoned them and not enough foster parents are willing to care to infants and children with AIDS.

Finally, as a "social activist," a pediatric AIDS researcher could attempt to change directly the mechanisms, processes, structures, or institutions of society. The social activists are distinct from the social mentors in that social mentors generally restrict themselves to persuasive arguments, whereas social activists emphasize changing specific programs, procedures, or even occupants of societal positions. Pediatric AIDS researchers as social activists might speak out and attempt to change the composition of a federally appointed task force on AIDS if they feel that it does not represent important points of view.

The number and variety of policy and legal decisions pediatric AIDS researchers can become involved in is limited only by their imagination and initiative. They should do all they can to keep current with policy and legal decisions that are being discussed, anticipate areas in need of policy, and report research data and commentary in places that are likely to reach policymakers and legal authorities. Melton (1987) reports the recommendations of the Society for Research in Child Development study group (Melton, in press) for bringing psychology into the legal system: report research where it is accessible to users; use informal networks to diffuse information; use professional organizations; look for opportunities to apply research; and meet legal professionals (or policymakers) on their own terms.

Future Directions/Recommendations
In addition to striving to have an effect on legal and policy decisions related to AIDS, pediatric AIDS researchers also have an opportunity to affect broader policy issues. Broad policies for children have been receiving increased attention (Hayes, 1982; Melton et al., 1983; Steiner, 1976). Most notably, policies for research with children could be furthered by the work of pediatric AIDS researchers.

There are many broad policy areas that pediatric AIDS researchers could become involved in. For example, an understanding of women's and infants' health issues raised by AIDS could contribute to general policies concerning family planning, pregnancy testing, prenatal clinics, and abortion (Benjamin, 1987). Work with hemophiliac children could add to the general hemophiliac research literature (Williams, 1987). The clarification of child abuse and neglect issues, including policies and practices for protective services, dependency petitions, and foster care, could be furthered by solutions discovered by pediatric AIDS researchers in response to their encounters with these problems during the conduct of their research (McIntosh, 1987). Minority issues could be considered in the light of the disparity in representation of minority children with AIDS that live in the marginal society of poverty, minimal education, and drug abuse (Villarreal, 1987). Home or alternative care arrangements for appropriate and cost-efficient care for infants and children with AIDS could set precedents for future medical care of infants and children (Barrick, 1987). Policies surrounding sex and drug awareness education, support services for teenage mothers, and counseling services for gay adolescents could be influenced by recommendations promulgated by pediatric AIDS researchers (Quackenbush, 1987). The list of topics is almost endless.

In summary, various stages in the research process are influenced or coerced by different disciplines such as law, ethics, and policy. In turn, pediatric AIDS research and researchers have the potential to have an effect on legal mechanisms and policy decisions related to AIDS and broader issues involving children. However, whether this effect is large or small, organized or chaotic, planned or happenstance, depends on the researchers involved.

REFERENCES

Additional protections for children involved as subjects in research. (1986). 45 C.F.R. § § 46.401–409.

Additional protections pertaining to research, development, and related activities involving fetuses, pregnant women, and human in vitro fertilization. (1975). 45 C.F.R. § § 46.201–211.

AIDS and young children: Emerging issues. (1987, February 21). In *Hearing sum-*

mary before the U.S. House of Representatives by the Select Committee on Children, Youth, and Families. Washington, DC: U.S. Government Printing Office.

Altman, D. (1986). *AIDS in the mind of America*. Garden City, NY: Anchor/Doubleday.

American Psychological Association. (1981). Ethical principles of psychologists. *American Psychologist, 36*, 633–638.

Andrews v. Eli Lilly & Co. 97 F.R.D. 494 (N.D.Ill. 1983).

Barrick, W. (1987, February 21). AIDS and young children: Emerging issues [Testimony]. In *Hearing summary before the U.S. House of Representatives by the Select Committee on Children, Youth, and Families*. Washington, DC: U.S. Government Printing Office.

Batchelor, W. F. (1984). AIDS: A public health and psychological emergency. *American Psychologist, 39*, 1279–1284.

Bayer, R., Levine, C., & Murray, T. H. (1984, November/December). Guidelines for confidentiality in research on AIDS. *Institutional Review Board*, pp. 1–3.

Belistsky, R., & Solomon, R. A. (1987). Doctors and patients: responsibilities in a confidential relationship. In H. L. Dalton, S. Burris, & the Yale AIDS Law Project (Eds.), *AIDS and the law: A guide for the public* (pp. 201–209). New Haven, CT: Yale University Press.

Benjamin, R. (1987, February 21). AIDS and young children: Emerging issues [Testimony]. In *Hearing summary before the U.S. House of Representatives by the Select Committee on Children, Youth, and Families*. Washington, DC: U.S. Government Printing Office.

Boruch, R. F. (1982). Methods for resolving privacy problems in social research. In T. Beauchamp, R. Faden, R. Wallace, & L. Walters (Eds.), *Ethical issues in social science research* (pp. 292–314). Baltimore: Johns Hopkins University Press.

Boruch, R. F. (1984). Should private agencies maintain federal research data. *Institutional Review Board, 6*(6), 8–9.

Boruch, R. F., & Cecil, J. S. (1979). *Assuring the confidentiality of social research data*. Philadelphia: University of Pennsylvania Press.

Boruch, R. F., & Cecil, J. S. (1983). *Solutions to ethical and legal problems in social research*. New York: Academic Press.

Brandt, E. (1983). The public health service's number one priority. *Public Health Reports, 98*, 306–307.

Bronfenbrenner, U. (1979). *The ecology of human development: Experiments by nature and design*. Cambridge, MA: Harvard University Press.

Budiansky, S. (1983). Confidential matters. *Nature, 304,* 478.

California Health and Safety Code. § § 199.30–40 (West Supp. 1986).

Centers for Disease Control. (1981). Kaposi's sarcoma and pneumocystic pneumonia among homosexual men—New York City and California. *Morbidity and Mortality Weekly Report, 30,* 305–308.

Centers for Disease Control. (1982). Update on acquired immune deficiency syndrome (AIDS)—United States. *Morbidity and Mortality Weekly Report, 31,* 507–514.

Centers for Disease Control. (1985). Revision of the case definition of acquired immunodeficiency syndrome for national reporting—United States. *Morbidity and Mortality Weekly Report, 34,* 373–376.

Centers for Disease Control. (1986). Update: Acquired immunodeficiency syndrome—United States. *Morbidity and Mortality Weekly Report, 35,* 17–21.

Centers for Disease Control. (1987). Update: Acquired immunodeficiency syndrome—United States. *Journal of the American Medical Association, 257,* 433–441.

Committee for the Protection of Human Participants in Research. (1985, July). Ethical issues in research on AIDS. *APA Monitor,* p. 26.

Davis v. Rodman. 227 S. W. 612 (Ark. 1921).

DeKraai, M. B., & Sales, B. D. (1984). Confidential communications of psychotherapists. *Psychotherapy, 21,* 293–318.

Dow Chem. Co. v. Allen. 672 F. 2d 1262 (7th Cir. 1982).

Elwork, A., Sales, B. D., & Alfini, J. (1982). *Writing understandable jury instructions.* Charlottesville, VA: Michie.

Farnsworth v. Procter & Gamble Co. 758 F.2d 1545 (11th Cir. 1985).

Fauci, A. S. (1983). The acquired immune deficiency syndrome: The ever-broadening clinical spectrum. *Journal of the American Medical Association, 249,* 2375–2376.

Federal policy for the protection of human subjects; Notice and proposed rules. (1988, November 10). *Federal Register, 53*(218), 45659–45682.

Federal Rules of Civil Procedure. 28 U.S.C.A. §§ 26(b)(1), 45(b) (1986). St. Paul, MN: West.

Federal Rules of Criminal Procedure. 18 U.S.C.A. § 17 (c) (1986). St. Paul, MN: West.

Federal Rules of Evidence. 28 U.S.C.A. § 501 (1986). St. Paul, MN: West.

Flam, R., & Stein, Z. (1986). Behavior, infection, and immune response: An epidemiological approach. In D. A. Feldman & T. M. Johnson (Eds.), *The social dimensions of* AIDS: *Method and theory* (pp. 61–75). New York: Praeger.

Forced disclosure of academic research. (1984). *Vanderbilt Law Review, 37*, 585–620.

Forsham v. Harris. 45 U.S. 169 (1980).

Freedom of Information Act of 1967 5 U.S.C. § 552 (198 2).

Gammaglobulin being used to treat pediatric AIDS cases. (1987, March 15). *AIDS Record, 7*(1), 6.

Goedert, J. J., & Blattner, W. A. (1985). The epidemiology of AIDS and related conditions. In V. T. DeVita, Jr., S. Hellman, & S. A. Rosenberg (Eds.), *AIDS: Etiology, diagnosis, treatment, and prevention* (pp. 1–30). Philadelphia: Lippincott.

Gostin, L., & Curran, W. J. (1987a). AIDS screening, confidentiality, and the duty to warn. *American Journal of Public Health, 77*, 361–365.

Gostin, L., & Curran, W. J. (1987b). Legal control measures for AIDS: Reporting requirements, surveillance, quarantine, and regulation of public meeting places. *American Journal of Public Health, 77*, 214–218.

Gostin, L. O., Curran, W. J., & Clark, M. E. (1987). The case against compulsory casefinding in controlling AIDS—testing, screening and reporting. *American Journal of Law and Medicine, 12*(1), 7–53.

Gray, J. N., & Melton, G. B. (1985). The law and ethics of psychosocial research on AIDS. *Nebraska Law Review, 64*, 637–688.

Gray, J. N. & Melton, G. B. (in press). *Psychosocial research on AIDS: Legal, ethical and methodological implications.* Baltimore: John Hopkins University Press.

Greenstein, R. L. (1984). Federal contractors and grantees: What are your First Amendment rights? *Jurimetrics, 24*, 197–209.

Grunder, T. M. (1978). Two formulas for determining the readability of subject consent forms. *American Psychologist, 33*, 773–775.

Guinan, M., & Hardy, A. (1987). Epidemiology of AIDS in women in the United States, 1981–86 J. *ournal of the American Medical Association, 257*, 2039–2042.

Hafemeister, T. L., & Melton, G. B. (in press). The impact of social science research on the judiciary. In G. B. Melton (Ed.), *Reforming the law: Impact of child development research.* New York: Guilford.

Harnish, D. G., Hammerberg, O., Walker, I. R., & Rosenthal, K. L. (1987). Early detection of HIV infection in a newborn. *New England Journal of Medicine, 316*, 272–273.

Hayes, C. D. (Ed.). (1982). *Making policies for children: A study of the federal process.* Washington, DC: National Academy Press.

Health Omnibus Programs Extension of 1988. Publ. No. 100–607 (1988). *U.S. Code, Congressional and Administrative News, 9.* St. Paul, MN: West.

Hofmann v. Blackmon. 241 So.2d 752 (Fla App. 1970).

Informed Consent Requirements. 45 C.F.R. § 46.116 (1984).

In re District 27 Community School Board v. Board of Education of the City of New York. 130 Misc.2d 398, 502 N.R.S.2d 325 (Sup. Ct. 1986).

In re Grand Jury Subpoena. 750 F.2d 223 (2d Cir. 1984).

Institute of Medicine. National Academy of Sciences. (1986). *Confronting AIDS: Directions for public health, health care, and research.* Washington, DC: National Academy Press.

Johnson, J. P., Nair, P., & Alexander, S. (1987). Early diagnosis of HIV infection in the neonate. *New England Journal of Medicine, 316,* 273–274.

Joseph, J., Emmons, C., Kessles, R., Wortman, C., O'Brien, K., Hocker, W., & Schaefer, C. (1984). Coping with the threat of AIDS: An approach to psychosocial assessment. *American Psychologist, 39,* 1297–1302.

Juvenile Justice Standards Project. (1977). *Standards relating to abuse and neglect.* Cambridge, MA: Ballinger.

Keith-Spiegel, P. (1983). Children and consent to participate in research. In G. B. Melton, G. P. Koocher, & M. J. Saks (Eds.), *Children's competence to consent* (pp. 179–211). New York: Plenum.

Keith-Spiegel, P., & Koocher, G. P. (1985). *Ethics in psychology: Professional standards and cases.* Hillsdale, NJ: Erlbaum.

Kershaw, D. N., & Small, J. C. (1972). Data confidentiality and privacy: Lessons from the New Jersey negative income tax experiment. *Public Policy, 20,* 257–280.

Koop urges AIDS test before getting pregnant. (1987, March 25). *New York Times,* p. B4.

Lampshire v. Proctor & Gamble Co. 94 F.R.D. 58 (N.D.Ga. 1982).

Lidz, C., Meisel, A., Zerubavel, E., Carter, M., Sestak, R., & Roth, L. (1984). *Informed consent: A study of decisionmaking in psychiatry.* New York: Guilford Press.

Laparia v. Sears, Roebuck & Co. 497 F. Supp. 185 (1980).

Lora v. Bd. of Education. 74 F.R.D. 565 (E.D.N.Y. 1977).

McIntosh, J. (1987, February 21). AIDS and young children: Emerging issues [Testimony]. In *Hearing summary before the U.S. House of Representatives by the Select*

Committee on Children, Youth, and Families. Washington, DC: U.S. Government Printing Office.

MacMahon, B., & Pugh, T. F. (1970). *Epidemiology—principles and methods.* Boston: Little, Brown.

Matherene, J. G. (1984). Forced disclosure of academic research. *Vanderbilt Law Review, 37,* 585.

Matthews, G. W., & Neslund, V. S. (1987). The initial impact of AIDS on public health law in the United States—1986 *Journal of the American Medical Association, 2 7,* 344–352.

Melton, G. B. (1987). Bringing psychology to the legal system: Opportunities, obstacles, and efficacy. *American Psychologist, 42,* 488–495.

Melton, G. B. (in press). Judicial notice of "facts" about child development. In G. B. Melton (Ed.), *Reforming the law: Impact of child development research.* New York: Guilford.

Melton, G. B., Koocher, G. P., & Saks, M. J. (Eds.). (1983). *Children's competence to consent.* New York: Plenum.

Morris, R. A., Sales, B. D., & Berman, J. J. (1981). Research and the Freedom of Information Act. *American Psychologist, 36,* 819–826.

Nelson, R. L., & Hedrick, T. E. (1983). The statutory protection of confidential research data: Synthesis and evaluation. In R. F. Bourch & J. Cecil (Eds.), *Solutions to ethical and legal problems in social research* (pp. 213–236). New York: Academic Press.

Nelson, W. J., Maxey, L., & Keith, S. (1984). Are we abandoning the AIDS patient? *Registered Nurse, 47*(7), 18–19.

New York Public Health Law. §§ 2775–2779 (McKinney Cum. Supp. 1984).

Novick, A. (1984, July). *Memo on ethical aspects of AIDS research.* Unpublished manuscript.

Office for Protection from Research Risks. National Institute of Health. (1984, December 26). *Guidance for institutional review boards for AIDS studies.* Bethesda, MD: Office for Protection from Research Risks, National Institute of Health.

Oleske, J., Minnefor, A., Cooper, R., Jr., Thomas, K., de la Cruz, A., Ahdich, H., Guerrero, I., Joshi, V. V., & Desposit, F. (1983). Immune deficiency in children. *Journal of the American Medical Association, 249,* 2345–2349.

Protection of Human Subjects. 45 C.F.R. pt. 46 (1984).

Protection of identity—research subjects. 42 C.F.R. pt. 2a (1987).

Public Health Service Act. 42 U.S.C. § 242 (1982).

Quackenbush, M. (1987, February 21). AIDS and young children: Emerging issues [Testimony]. In *Hearing summary before the U.S. House of Representatives by the Select Committee on Children, Youth, and Familes*. Washington, DC: U.S. Government Printing Office.

Reynolds, P. D. (1979). *Ethical dilemmas and social science research*. San Francisco: Jossey-Bass.

Richards of Rockford, Inc. v. Pacific Gas & Elec. Co. 71 F.R.D. 388 (N.D.Cal. 1976).

Rights of gay people: The revised edition of the basic ACLU guide to a gay person's rights. (1984). Carbondale, IL: Southern Illinois University Press.

Roth, L. H., Lidz, C. W., Meisel, A., Soloff, P. H., Kaufman, K., Spiker, D. G., & Foster, F. G. (1982). Competency to decide about treatment or research: An overview of some empirical data. *International Journal of Law and Psychiatry, 5*, 29–49.

Steiner, G. Y. (1976). *The children's cause*. Washington, DC: Brookings.

Tapp, J. L., & Melton, G. B. (1983). Preparing children for decision making. In G. B. Melton, G. P. Koocher, & M. J. Saks (Eds.), *Children's competence to consent* (pp. 215–234). New York: Plenum.

Tarasoff v. The Regents of the University of California. 551 P.2d 340 (1976).

Task Force on Psychology and Public Policy. (1986). Psychology and public policy. *American Psychologist, 41*, 914–921.

Teitelbaum, L. E. (1983). Spurious, tractable and intractable legal problems: A positivist approach to law and social science research. In R. F. Boruch & J. S. Cecil (Eds.), *Solutions to ethical and legal problems in social research* (pp. 11–47). New York: Academic Press.

Update: Acquired immunodeficiency syndrome—United States. (1986a). *Journal of the American Medical Association, 255*, 593–598.

U.S. Department of Health, Education and Welfare. (1973, November 16). Protection of human subjects: Policies and procedure. *Federal Register, 38*, 31737–31749.

Villarreal, S. F. (1987, February 21). AIDS and young children: Emerging issues [Testimony]. In *Hearing summary before the U.S. House of Representatives by the Select Committee on Children, Youth, and Families*. Washington, DC: U.S. Government Printing Office.

Wadlington, W. J. (1983). Consent to medical care for minors. In G. B. Melton, G. P. Koocher, & M. J. Saks (Eds.), *Children's competence to consent* (pp. 57–74). New York: Plenum.

Wadlington, W. J., Whitebread, C. H., & Davis, S. M. (1983). *Children in the legal system*. New York: Foundation Press.

Weiner, R. (1986). *AIDS: Impact on the schools*. Arlington, VA: Education Research Group.

Whalen v. Roe. 429 U.S. 589 (1977).

Williams, J. R. (1987, February 21). AIDS and young children: Emerging issues [Testimony]. In *Hearing summary before the U.S. House of Representatives by the Select Committee on Children, Youth, and Families*. Washington, DC: U.S. Government Printing Office.

•

American Psychological Association Policy on AIDS Education

This official policy was adopted by the Council of Representatives of the American Psychological Association in February 1988.

WHEREAS the epidemic of the acquired immunodeficiency syndrome (AIDS) currently threatens the physical health, mental health, and civil liberties of many persons in American society, and

WHEREAS, in 1986, the APA adopted a comprehensive resolution outlining its strong commitment to public education regarding AIDS and its prevention as well as education to combat irrational public fears of AIDS and its transmission, and

WHEREAS empirical research has demonstrated that, in addition to imparting knowledge, educational programs designed to effect behavioral change should address topics of decision making, risk assessment, attitude change, group norms, and other social and psychological processes, and

WHEREAS an important strategy for such education should be to provide children and adolescents of all cultural and socioeconomic groups with information about AIDS that is gender relevant, culturally sensitive, and appropriate to their level of intellectual, emotional, and social development, and

WHEREAS the U.S. surgeon general, Dr. C. Everett Koop, has asserted that "education concerning AIDS must start at the lowest grade possible as a part of any health and hygiene program," and

WHEREAS effective AIDS education for all age groups must address the behaviors through which AIDS can be transmitted, including but not limited to sexual behavior and sharing of intravenous needles and paraphernalia, and must do so as accurately and explicitly as possible while remaining appropriate to the age and developmental level of the members of the targeted audiences as well as their culture and language.

THEREFORE, be it resolved that the APA supports the *Surgeon General's Report on Acquired Immune Deficiency Syndrome* (1986).

BE IT FURTHER RESOLVED that the APA urges that information about AIDS, its transmission, and its prevention be incorporated into elementary and secondary school curricula in conjunction with educational programs concerning sexuality, drug use, health, and family issues and that such education be provided at the earliest grade possible and in a manner appropriate to the child's level of intellectual, emotional, and social development. Priority should be given to culturally and linguistically appropriate prevention and education efforts targeted at black, Hispanic, and Native American youths. The development of such curricula and programs should be accomplished with all deliberate speed by local boards of education, working closely with parents.

BE IT FURTHER RESOLVED that the APA recognizes the importance in AIDS prevention of providing clear and accurate information about sexual behaviors and sharing of needles and syringes and that the APA deplores attempts by governmental or other institutions to restrict the effectiveness of community-based AIDS-prevention organizations.

BE IT FURTHER RESOLVED that the APA urges increased funding

from government and private sources for basic and applied research and evaluation relevant to AIDS education and risk reduction.

BE IT FURTHER RESOLVED that APA urges its members to provide their expertise to develop, implement, and evaluate AIDS education and risk-reduction programs.

The Contributors

Dale D. Chitwood is research associate professor at the University of Miami School of Medicine, Department of Oncology, Division of Cancer Control. He has conducted research on drug abuse for the past 15 years and since 1985 has been involved in the research of AIDS and IV drug abuse. He currently is principal investigator of an NIDA-funded grant studying the epidemiology of HIV among IV drug users and is co–principal investigator of an NIDA-funded community demonstration project to lower risk behaviors among IV drug users.

Sally E. Dodds is the executive director of Health Crisis Network, Inc., the largest AIDS-service organization in Florida. She is also assistant clinical professor in the Department of Psychiatry at the University of Miami School of Medicine. She serves on the advisory boards of the National Institute of Mental Health Biopsychosocial Research Center on AIDS and the Veteran's Administration Medical Center AIDS Program. Her publications include articles on AIDS care and prevention.

Joni N. Gray is an advanced J.D./Ph.D. student in law and social psychology at the University of Nebraska–Lincoln. She has served on the APA Division 37 Task Force on Pediatric AIDS since 1986 and has authored articles and presentations on the legal and ethical dimensions of psychosocial research on AIDS. She is the author, with G. B. Melton, of *Psychosocial Research on AIDS: Legal, Ethical and Methodological Implications* (in press).

Heather C. Huszti is completing a postdoctoral fellowship in hematology-oncology/pediatric psychology in the Department of Pediatrics and the Department of Psychiatry and Behavioral Sciences at the University of Oklahoma Health Sciences Center. She has conducted and evaluated AIDS prevention programs both in the public schools for adolescents and at the hospital for high-risk adolescents and adults. She is a consultant to state and local health departments in the development of prevention programs.

Marcy Kaplan is the project manager of the Los Angeles Pediatric AIDS Network, an OMCH Pediatric HIV Demonstration Project that began in August 1988 and provides hospital-based clinical social-work intervention and case management for children with HIV and their families at several hospitals in Los Angeles County. She was formerly the social worker and program coordinator of the Pediatric AIDS Program at Childrens Hospital Los Angeles.

Marsha B. Liss is professor of psychology and human development and the coordinator of the M. A. Developmental Lifespan Program at the California State University, San Bernardino. Her work focuses on social development, applications of developmental psychology, social policy development, and psychology and law. Her publications include articles and chapters on children's play, institutionalization of children, and child-care workers.

Patrick J. Mason is assistant professor in the Department of Pediatrics at the University of Oklahoma Health Sciences Center. He serves on the Oklahoma Bureau of Maternal and Child Health Hemophilia Program's HIV Prevention Planning Committee as well as on several other committees and task forces on AIDS. His publications include articles on the psychosocial aspects of pediatric AIDS.

Brian E. Novick is assistant clinical professor of pediatrics in the Division of Allergy and Immunology at the Albert Einstein College of Medicine. He has been involved in the care and treatment of HIV-infected children and their families since 1982. His publications include articles on the medical aspects of pediatric AIDS. He serves on the New York City AIDS Task Force and is a consultant nationwide on issues relating to HIV infection in children.

Roberta A. Olson is associate professor of clinical psychology in the Department of Psychiatry and Behavioral Sciences at the University of Oklahoma Health Sciences Center. She has been involved in consultation and psychotherapy with chronically and terminally ill children and their families and served on the APA Division 37 Task Force on Pediatric AIDS. Her publications include articles on pediatric psychological aspects of AIDS and care programs.

Jeffrey M. Seibert, formerly research associate professor of pediatrics and psychology at the University of Miami is on the staff of the Center for Attitudinal Healing in Tiburon, California. He chaired the APA's Division on Child, Youth and Family Services Task Force on Pediatric AIDS from 1986 to 1988. His publications include articles on the psychosocial aspects of pediatric AIDS.

Anita Septimus is coordinator and supervisor of the Comprehensive Family AIDS Program at the Albert Einstein College of Medicine. She has contributed chapters on psychosocial aspects of caring for children with AIDS and their families to several books. She serves on the advisory boards of the New York Community Trust Funds AIDS Project and the Sunburst National AIDS Project, California, and is a member of the New York Governor's Task Force on Women and AIDS.

Helen Viviand is the coordinator of the Employee Assistance Program for the Dade County, Florida, schools. She has been involved in policy issues associated with employees with AIDS and children with AIDS in the Dade County schools. She also directs support groups for

Dade County teachers and staff who work with children who have AIDS as well as for Dade County employees with AIDS. She is a member of the Dade County Task Force on AIDS.

Marilyn Volker is the director of educational services at Health Crisis Network of Miami, Florida. She is certified as a sex educator with the American Association of Sex Educators, Counselors, and Therapists. She is an associate professor in the Department of Family Medicine at the University of Miami School of Medicine.

Index